Food Culture in
Spain

Food Culture in
Spain

F. XAVIER MEDINA

Food Culture around the World
Ken Albala, Series Editor

GREENWOOD PRESS
Westport, Connecticut · London

Library of Congress Cataloging-in-Publication Data

Medina, F. Xavier.
    Food culture in Spain / F. Xavier Medina.
        p. cm. — (Food culture around the world, ISSN 1545–2638)
    Includes bibliographical references and index.
    ISBN 0–313–32819–6 (alk. paper)
    1. Cookery, Spanish. 2. Food habits—Spain. I. Title. II. Series.
    TX723.5.S7M43 2005
    394.1'0946—dc22   2004019695

British Library Cataloguing in Publication Data is available.

Library of Congress Catalog Card Number: 2004019695
ISBN: 0–313–32819–6
ISSN: 1545–2638

First published in 2005

Greenwood Press, 88 Post Road West, Westport, CT 06881
An imprint of Greenwood Publishing Group, Inc.
www.greenwood.com

Printed in the United States of America

∞™

The paper used in this book complies with the
Permanent Paper Standard issued by the National
Information Standards Organization (Z39.48–1984).

10   9   8   7   6   5   4   3   2   1

The publisher has done its best to make sure the instructions and/or recipes in this book
are correct. However, users should apply judgment and experience when preparing recipes,
especially parents and teachers working with young people. The publisher accepts no responsibility for the outcome of any recipe included in this volume.

Contents

Series Foreword

The appearance of the Food Culture around the World series marks a definitive stage in the maturation of Food Studies as a discipline to reach a wider audience of students, general readers, and foodies alike. In comprehensive interdisciplinary reference volumes, each on the food culture of a country or region for which information is most in demand, a remarkable team of experts from around the world offers a deeper understanding and appreciation of the role of food in shaping human culture for a whole new generation. I am honored to have been associated with this project as series editor.

Each volume follows a series format, with a timeline of food-related dates and narrative chapters entitled Introduction, Historical Overview, Major Foods and Ingredients, Cooking, Typical Meals, Eating Out, Special Occasions, and Diet and Health. Each also includes a glossary, resource guide, bibliography, and illustrations.

Finding or growing food has of course been the major preoccupation of our species throughout history, but how various peoples around the world learn to exploit their natural resources, come to esteem or shun specific foods and develop unique cuisines reveals much more about what it is to be human. There is perhaps no better way to understand a culture, its values, preoccupations, and fears, than by examining its attitudes toward food. Food provides the daily sustenance around which families and communities bond. It provides the material basis for rituals through which people celebrate the passage of life stages and their connection to divinity. Food preferences also serve to separate individuals and groups from each other, and as one of the most powerful factors in the construction of identity, we physically, emotionally and spiritually become what we eat.

By studying the foodways of people different from ourselves we also grow to understand and tolerate the rich diversity of practices around the world. What seems strange or frightening among other people becomes perfectly rational when set in context. It is my hope that readers will gain from these volumes not only an aesthetic appreciation for the glories of the many culinary traditions described, but also ultimately a more profound respect for the peoples who devised them. Whether it is eating New Year's dumplings in China, folding tamales with friends in Mexico or going out to a famous Michelin-starred restaurant in France, understanding these food traditions helps us to understand the people themselves.

As globalization proceeds apace in the twenty-first century it is also more important than ever to preserve unique local and regional traditions. In many cases these books describe ways of eating that have already begun to disappear or have been seriously transformed by modernity. To know how and why these losses occur today also enables us to decide what traditions, whether from our own heritage or that of others, we wish to keep alive. These books are thus not only about the food and culture of peoples around the world, but also about ourselves and who we hope to be.

Ken Albala
University of the Pacific

Introduction

This book offers an overview of Spanish food and eating habits, taking into account Spain's long and complex history, along with its distinctive social, cultural, linguistic, geographic, political, and economic characteristics. From the perspective of non-European students and general readers, the history, culture, and eating practices of Spaniards may be unknown. Information on Spain may be lacking, stereotyped, or unreliable. Today it is common, for example, to find food resources and recipes devoted to Spanish cooking on the Internet. Yet, most of them are biased or confuse Spanish elements with others belonging to different cuisines, such as the Latin American and southern European ones.

This book will discuss foodstuffs, culinary methods and practices, lifestyles, space, sociability, and commensality in an attempt to consider the Spanish food culture today in context.

SPAIN WITHIN THE EURO-MEDITERRANEAN CONTEXT

Spain is a country in southwestern Europe and it occupies most of the Iberian Peninsula. It borders Portugal to the east, France to the north, and Morocco to the south. It boasts a wide variety of landscapes: a large central plain, some of the most important mountain ranges of Europe, and nearly 5,000 miles of coast. It is washed by the Mediterranean and the Cantabrian Seas and by the Atlantic Ocean, and it also includes two archipelagoes: the Balearic and the Canary Islands. Modern Spain has an impressive heritage and is the result of the combination of various cultures and nationalities throughout a long historical process. Spain lies at the crossroads between Europe and North Africa; thus it has always been a land of passage, a cultural, racial, linguistic, and of course gastronomic melting pot (Indo-Europeans, Phoenicians, Carthaginians, Greeks, Romans, Germans, Arabs, etc.). In addition, Spain has maintained a close relationship with other nations (Italy, France, Portugal, Hispanic America, the Philippines, Morocco, and equatorial Africa), which has helped to shape today's eating practices in Spain and, through Spain, in Europe. Spain's role in introducing products from the Americas into the rest of Europe during the sixteenth century was pivotal.

CUISINES WITH STRONG PERSONALITIES AND GOOD PRODUCTS

Gastronomy in Spain has always been of major importance. Cuisine in Spain is regional. Most Spanish cuisines have evolved around strong regional identities and representative elements that have changed through the centuries and have developed to such an extent that nowadays some chefs, representative of the new Spanish cuisine (such as the Basque and the Catalan ones), are among the most important cooks in the international gastronomic panorama. Another important aspect to take into account is the quality of Spanish products. Spain was an agricultural country until the mid-twentieth century: the mild climate and the quality of the soil have facilitated the production of widely appreciated foods that are highly competitive on the international market. The Spanish food industry made a good start at the end of the nineteenth and beginning of the twentieth century; however, it would not fare well in the following decades due to various historical events, particularly the Spanish civil war. Only in the second half of the twentieth century would food-related activities become established, and only at the cost of a strong dependence on foreign multinational companies.

LIFESTYLE

There is more to eating than the ingestion of foodstuffs; it is not only a biological function, but it has strong social and cultural components that must be highlighted when considering food culture in Spain. All the more so, if one considers that this is a country where eating is conceived of as a social act, as an activity that must be shared with others.

Spaniards highly value eating with their family, friends, and colleagues. Sharing food fosters social relationships and it is not uncommon for meetings to be articulated (or ended) around a dining table. It is unusual to see a person eating alone in a restaurant or drinking alone in a bar (unless she or he is forced by specific circumstances). As a matter of fact, such situations are avoided, which shows how socially important meals are in Spain (and in Mediterranean areas in general). In Spain, "eating alone is like not eating at all." Another feature of the Spanish society that is worth highlighting in this respect is that people like eating and drinking out. The climate, with its mild temperatures, is typical of a southern European country, but it is never extreme, and it allows outdoor celebrations and meals almost all year long (except, perhaps, in the harshest winter months). Eating out includes popular feasts, communal meals, or simple visits to restaurants, establishments with outdoor tables, bars, cafés, and so forth.

FOOD CULTURE IN SPAIN

The various chapters of this book describe Spanish food culture. The first chapter examines how food practices in the Iberian Peninsula have changed over the centuries, how different cuisines have been created through the abandonment or incorporation of various products and dishes, and how they have evolved up to the present.

The second chapter is devoted to the various foodstuffs and their role within Spanish cuisines. The third chapter deals with the various cooking methods, equipment, and utensils, as well as with who cooks, in what situations, and where. The fourth chapter, "Typical Meals," discusses aspects such as meals times and lifestyles; the second part includes a survey of the different Spanish regional cuisines, each with its own personality, products, specialties, influences, and climate.

The fifth chapter is about eating out. As previously observed, eating and drinking out is a very frequent social activity in Spain, and this chapter considers the history and typology of establishments (restaurants, bars, cafés, taverns, etc.) and spaces where these activities are carried out.

Seasonal festivities and the celebrations of events related to the individual's life cycle are highly ritualized occasions in which food also plays an outstanding role. These aspects are dealt with in the sixth chapter, which is a survey of the main festivities held through the year, as well as of the main events that mark a person's life (birth, wedding, death). Last, the seventh chapter discusses the most significant aspects of the Spanish diet and health, reflecting on the future of the Spanish eating regimen. Although the Spanish diet has always been synonymous with the Mediterranean diet, it is now undergoing some transformations.

Hopefully, the reader will find this book a useful guide to the various elements that make up Spanish food culture: tastes, aromas, textures, as well as company and conversation.

Timeline

300,000 B.C.	Middle Paleolithic. Fire is discovered and used in Iberia.
25,000–15,000 B.C.	Late Paleolithic. Cave paintings (Altamira) of hunting scenes.
7000–5000 B.C.	Transition to the Neolithic. First records of agricultural activities, animal stabling, ceramic making, and food storage. Cave paintings (Mediterranean area) of human scenes, hunting scenes, and honey and plants collection.
5000 B.C.	Ancient remains of beer in western Europe (Cova Sant Sadurni, Barcelona).
Circa 1100 B.C.	The Phoenicians arrive in Iberia and found Cadiz, the most ancient city in the west of Europe. They develop trade in this area and start cultivating olive trees. They establish fish-salting plants in their colonies in the south of the peninsula.
1000 B.C.	Indo-European invasion of the peninsula. New agricultural techniques, introduction of new foods (e.g., lentils, cabbage, millet); introduction of iron and improvement of bronze techniques.
700 B.C.	The first Greek settlers reach the Catalan coast (Roses, Empúries). They increase viticulture and almond crops, introduce wine production as well as certain kinds of table utensils and earthenware. The Carthaginians, from North Africa, arrive in Ibiza and later on in the Mediterranean costal regions.

500 B.C.	Agriculture becomes more important than shepherding.
218–197 B.C.	Rome conquers the Iberian Peninsula.
200 B.C.–400 A.D.	Roman Age: Establishment of rural housing (*villae*), specialization and increase in grain, grapes, olive crops, and so forth. Exploitation of salt mines (food storage); intensive trade relationships in the Mediterranean area. Exportation of wheat, wine, and oil from Baetica and Tarraconensis regions to Rome and other colonies. Introduction of new products such as apricots, melons, and lemons.
100 A.D.	Christianity is introduced into Roman Spain; subsequent emphasis on ritual food (bread and wine).
411–415	Hispania (Latin term for the Iberian Peninsula) is invaded by Germanic peoples. Visigoths arrive.
568–586	First attempt at unification of the peninsula made by an independent kingdom. The Roman age in Hispania is over.
587	Visigothic kings convert to Catholicism.
711	Muslim troops cross the Strait of Gibraltar and invade the Iberian Peninsula. Beginning of the Arabian rule and of the age of the emirate.
718	Christian Reconquest (*Reconquista*) starts in the northern territories.
758	Beginning of the Caliphate of Cordoba, the most magnificent age of Muslim Spain (Al-Andalus). Beginning of water culture in the east of the peninsula, irrigation farming, development of rice crops, and so forth.
800s	Musician Ziryab arrives at the Court of Cordoba and introduces the refinements of the Near East: table manners, serving order of food, and new products, such as asparagus.
1009–1090	Dismantling of the Caliphate. Independent Muslim kingdoms (*taifas*). Christian Reconquest advances toward the south.
1200s–1400s	Christian kingdoms progressively gain more territories and definitively expel Muslims with the reconquest of the last Andalus kingdom, Granada, in 1492.

1300s–1600s	Basque whalers fish in the north of Europe; introduction of cod and consolidation of its consumption in the Iberian Peninsula. In the seventeenth century the French expel the Basques from the fishing area of Newfoundland (Canada).
1324	Appearance of *Sent Soví*, the most important Catalan cookbook, the most ancient cookbook in Spain, and one of the oldest in Europe.
1400s–1500s	Specialized cultivation of sugar cane in the Canary Islands.
1400s–1700s	Importation and spreading of products from the Americas: potatoes, tomatoes, peppers, turkey, chocolate, and so forth. At the same time, European foods (wine, oil, grains, etc.) and plants (except olive trees) are introduced and acclimatized in the Americas.
1492	Two worlds meet when Christopher Columbus's expedition reaches the Antilles (West Indies). First contact with American products. Beginning of the Castilian conquest of the new continent. Conquest of Grenada, the last Muslim kingdom in the Iberian Peninsula. The Jews are expelled from Spain.
Early 1500s	The Iberian Peninsula experiences famine, due to a long drought and bad crops.
1512	The kingdom of Navarre joins the Castilian Crown. Almost all the peninsula—except Portugal—comes under the rule of one monarch.
1518–1520	Appearance of *Llibre de Coch* in Catalonia, cookbook by Ruperto de Nola that was published also in the Castilian language in Toledo in 1525.
1521	Hernán Cortés conquers the Aztec Empire (Mexico). Products, such as cocoa, are sent to Spain.
1561	Under King Philip II, Madrid is proclaimed, for the first time, capital and official residence of the Spanish Court.
1580–1668	The Portuguese Empire takes part of the Spanish Crown under Philip II, increasing the Spanish commerce of food and spices to Portuguese territories in Africa and Asia.
1599–1611	Publication of important cookbooks: *Libro del arte de cozina*, by Diego Granado (1599); *Libro de arte de cozina*, by

	Domingo Hernández de Maceras, in Salamanca (1607); *Arte de Cozina, Pastelería y Vizcochería y Conservería*, by Martínez Montiño (1611).
1700s–1800s	Beginning and consolidation of the influence of French cuisine in Spain.
1714–1717	Bourbon dynasty. The boundaries between Spanish kingdoms disappear, and so do taxes and tolls.
1716–1780	Spanish painter Luis Meléndez perfects still life, depicting Spanish food of his time, including some products from the Americas, such as tomatoes and chocolate.
1755	The Botanic Garden is created in Madrid. It will serve as laboratory for the introduction of American plants into Spain and Europe.
1766	Publication of the book: *Arte Cisoria, o Tratado del Arte de Cortar del Cuchillo* (On the art of cutting food), by the Marquis of Villena.
1800s	The first big covered markets are built in Spain. The most remarkable ones are those of Barcelona. Spreading of taverns, inns *(fondas)*, first cafés, and restaurants.
1808–1814	Independence War against Napoleon's French Empire.
1810–1824	Spain loses most of its colonies in the Americas.
1848	Opening of the first railway in Spain (Barcelona-Mataró). Revolution of food transportation, especially for fresh products.
1872	*Cava*, or sparkling wine champenoise style, is introduced in Catalonia, in the county of Penedès.
1898	Spanish-American War and definitive loss of the last Spanish overseas territories: Cuba, Puerto Rico, the Philippines, and the Pacific islands.
Late 1800s	Urban development and first migratory movements of importance in Spain. Industrial revolution in Catalonia and the Basque and Cantabrian areas. Consolidation of the Spanish food industry. Beginning of tourism and catering.
Early 1900s	Folklore and reclamation of traditional recipe books of Spanish regions. Publication of numerous cookbooks,

such *as La cocina española antigua,* by Emilia Pardo Bazán (1914), and *La Cocina Completa,* by the Marchioness of Parabere (1933).

1914–1917	First World War. Spain remains neutral.
1923–1929	Fascist dictatorship under Primo de Rivera.
1931–1939	Second Spanish Republic.
1933	Law for the creation of the designation of origin of Spanish wine.
1936–1939	Spanish civil war.
1939–1945	Second World War. Spain remains neutral.
1939–1975	Military dictatorship of General Francisco Franco. Postwar period of food scarcity during the 1940s and 1950s.
1946–1951	International political and economic isolation of Spain.
1953	Commercial and political deal of Franco's regime with the United States. End of the isolation.
1955	Spain enters the United Nations.
1960–1980	Industrial development policies in Spain. Great international tourist promotion of the country. Mass interior migrations from the rural areas to the city, especially to industrial centers (Catalonia, Basque Country, Madrid). Creation, in the big cities, of a great number of restaurants and establishments that specialize in different Spanish gastronomies.
1970	The designations of origin is extended to other products besides wine. Creation of the National Institute for the Designation of Origin (INDO), controlled by the Spanish Ministry of Agriculture.
1970–1980	Birth and consolidation of the movements known as "New Basque Cuisine" (due to renowned cooks, such as Juan María Arzak and Pedro Subijana), and some time later, of the "New Catalan Cuisine" represented by Ferran Adrià and Santi Santamaria.
1973	The French company Carrefour opens the first Spanish hypermarket near Barcelona.
1975	Burger King opens the first fast-food restaurant in Spain, in Madrid.

1975–1978	Period of democratic transition in Spain.
1978	The new Spanish democratic Constitution is approved and the present "State of Autonomic Regions" is established.
1980s on	Worldwide "food fears" with various cases of dioxin contamination of chicken, beef, pork, and fish; mad cow disease; and so forth.
1984–1994	Spanish television broadcasts the first cooking program "Con las manos en la masa" ("With one's hand in the dough"), which is a big success all over Spain.
1985 on	A large number of "ethnic" restaurants are opened in various Spanish cities (mainly Barcelona and Madrid), coinciding with the boom of foreign immigration. From 1995 on, the number of such restaurants will multiply.
1986	Spain and Portugal enter the European Community. Spain enters the Free European Market (which affects the agricultural sector and food exportation). Progressive legal convergence with the European Union for the regulation of agricultural and food-related activities.
1986	The first Spanish fast-food chain-franchise is opened in Barcelona. It is the bocadillería (sandwich bar) Bocatta and it is characterized by a "local" food philosophy.
1990 on	Health warning about the change in Spanish eating practices. Promotion of the Mediterranean diet as the healthiest food model.
1990 on	International success of Spanish high cuisine. Spanish chefs are in the spotlight.
1991	In Barcelona the second Spanish fast-food sandwich-franchise—Pans & Company—is opened.
1994 on	Popularity and exportation (in the form of franchises) of Basque gastronomy and pintxos (small portions of various foods, similar to tapas). The Basque-Catalan chains Lizarrán, and later on Sagardi, will spread all over Spain.
1995 on	Basque chef Karlos Argiñano popularizes gastronomy and has the most viewers for his TV-cooking program.
1998	The European agricultural policies of Farm Commissioner Franz Fischler lead to a reduction of olive oil pro-

duction in southern European countries. Olive oil crisis in Spain and opposition to EU agrarian policies.

2000 on   Mad cow crisis (*bovine spongiform encephalopathy*, BSE). Appearance of the first mad cow in Spain toward the end of 2000. As of October 2004, 465 cases have been reported in Spain.

2004   For the first time a Spanish chef, Catalan Ferran Adrià, is recognized as the top chef by the *New York Times* and *Le Monde* (Paris).

1

Historical Overview

FOOD IN THE PREHISTORIC AGE

In prehistoric times, the Iberian Peninsula was a vast, natural space with a wide variety of climates. It stretched from the Mediterranean Sea to the Atlantic Ocean and encompassed the inner Meseta (plateau) and the important mountainous areas, which provided abundant game and a variety of wild fruits, plants, and roots.

Settlements along the terraces of some rivers (Tajo and Guadalquivir) and on the Atlantic Ocean date from the early Paleolithic era, a period in which those animals that had adapted to warmer climates started giving way to other species that were fitter for cold temperatures, such as woolly rhinoceros, mammoths, and so forth. Such animals were difficult to hunt and were only occasionally eaten. Smaller animals, such as rabbits, birds, insects (worms and ants), reptiles (snakes and lizards), as well as shellfish and other easy prey of coastal and river areas, were more common as a food source. The diet was based mainly on wild fruits, plants, eggs, and honey. As fire was not mastered until the Middle Paleolithic era (about 300,000 years ago), food was ingested without being previously processed.

In most of the peninsula (the Castilian Meseta, Mediterranean, and Cantabrian areas) there are traces of Mousterian and Cro-magnon industry that date from the Middle Paleolithic era. During this period, game consumption increased and cooking practices developed due to the mastering of fire. The archaeological remains found in various peninsular digs show that in this period the most hunted animals were goats, horses, boars, deer, roe, rabbits, and birds. Elephants, oxen, lynx, bears, and wolves were less frequently captured and some of them were more valued for their furs than for the meat they provided.

Evidence of the late Paleolithic era can be found in two areas: the Cantabrian and the Mediterranean. Food consumption did not vary much in this period; deer, horses, and bovines were the chief prey. These and other animals are abundantly represented in what is regarded as the most important artistic work of the Paleolithic era: the Franco-Cantabrian cave paintings of Altamira, located in the Cantabrian Cordillera. Other hunting and harvesting scenes can be found in the remarkable cave paintings of the Levant, which belong to the Neolithic period.

The scarce remains of fish and fishing-related tools suggest that this food was not common in the diet of prehistoric Iberian people. Fish remains found in archaeological sites were always fresh-water species.

Some archaeological digs, for example, Isturitz in the Basque Country or Atapuerca in Burgos, also attested to cannibalistic practices in this and in later stages (between 6,000 and 4,000 years ago). Outside the peninsula, traces of human bones that had been broken to extract the marrow were found in French and German sites dating from the Neolithic period.

However, vegetables, fruits, and roots, which have seldom left archaeological traces, were still the main food source. Remains of pine seeds, hazelnuts, acorns, walnuts, and endemic wild fruits such as blackberries, raspberries, strawberries, pears, plums, and olives have been found.

Evidence of the stabling of animals (goats, sheep, pigs, and bovines) as well as agricultural practices, ceramic making, and food storage (jugs, silos, etc.), date from a later period, between 7000 and 5000 B.C. The onset of the Neolithic period brought along greater independence from the environment and, above all, the possibility to settle permanently and to abandon, to a large extent, seasonal nomadism. The new production mode of such settlements was based on agriculture and livestock farming and it brought about the division of labor.

Among the grains cultivated from this time on were various kinds of wheat, rye, and oats (millet, which had been already known in Europe around 3000 B.C., made its appearance in the Iberian peninsula two thousand years later). Other cultivations included pulses (broad beans and peas), carob pods, dried fruits, fresh fruits (pears, apples, olives, wild grapes, figs), wild fruits, vegetables, roots, mushrooms, and snails. Vines were native to Mediterranean areas, but their cultivation did not become established in the Iberian Peninsula until the sixth century B.C., when the

Greeks imported them to their Iberian colonies and the Romans subsequently intensified the crops.

Evidence shows that the Canary Islands, the Atlantic Archipelago that lies opposite the northern coast of Africa, were not settled by the peoples of northeast Africa until the late Neolithic period. The resulting culture was called *guanche* and was specific to the Isle of Tenerife.

There, the diet mainly consisted of vegetables, seeds, fruits, wild fruits, and grains (chiefly wheat and rye). Grain flour was called *gofio* and it remains the main staple. They also ate animal products (milk and some varieties of cheese, and goat, boar, lamb, pigeon, and even dog meat). In coastal areas, shellfish and fish, such as the thick-lipped gray mullet, complemented the diet.

Apparently, the different parts of the peninsula first shared similar characteristics during the Eneolithic period, or Copper Age. The culture known as the "Bell-shaped vase" civilization, which owes its name to the shape of the ceramic pieces discovered, extended to most of the territory. Small game, such as rabbits, partridges, and other birds, as well as large game, such as deer and boars, were still an important source of food. Fish consumption increased and most species came from rivers (trout, eels, barbels, etc.) although sea shellfish were also collected. However, as a sedentary lifestyle increased and agriculture developed with the onset of the Eneolithic, or Copper Age, in the south of Portugal, eastern Andalucia, and Valencia, livestock farming became increasingly important. As a consequence, there was a rise in meat consumption (goat, pork, sheep, ox, etc.) to such an extent that, in Roman times, pigs became the most eaten animals. There are also records of sophisticated products, such as beer, dating from this period.

THE IBERIAN AGE

Around the year 1000 B.C., Indo-European tribes crossed the Pyrenees to settle in the Iberian Peninsula. They brought with them influential cultural elements, such as the dialects from which the Iberian and Celtiberian languages would later develop. They also introduced new foods, such as millet, lentils, and cabbage, as well as new agricultural techniques related to grain farming, storage methods, domesticated animals, and iron and advanced bronze techniques.

All these novelties would flourish and improve during the Iberian Bronze Age, between the sixth and second centuries B.C. At this time, the Phoenicians, Carthaginians, and Greeks founded their first colonies along the present-day Spanish Mediterranean coast. This was the Iberians' first contact with more culturally developed civilizations.

The Phoenicians built Gadir (present-day Cadiz, the most ancient city in the West) and other settlements along the Andalucian coastline between the seventh and fifth centuries B.C., whereas the Carthaginians settled on the Isle of Ibiza.

The Greeks founded the colonies of Roses (Rhodes) and Ampurias (Emporion) on the northern coastline of present-day Catalonia in the fifth century B.C., immediately after the foundation of Massalia (Marseille, 600 B.C.). The life of local Iberian tribes was deeply affected by the presence of such cultures. The Phoenicians, important traders who, from their trading post of Gadir, exported food as far away as Athens, contributed to the development of a thriving Tartesian civilization. The Greeks influenced the production and storage systems of those tribes who lived near the Catalan coastline: as a consequence, from the fourth century B.C. onward, grain production was expanded and silos were built to facilitate trade with the Carthaginians and with the Greek colonies of Ampurias and Roses. The latter re-exported Iberian products, such as grains and honey, to other colonies or to Athens itself.

The Greek influence on agriculture was prominent: important products, such as wine, were introduced in the peninsula, as well as new crops, such as almond trees and grapes, whose wild varieties had been known since the Paleolithic era. Olive trees had also been known from ancient times, together with the oil-extracting technique, but only in the southern half of the peninsula and in the Mediterranean area. Greek cuisine, likewise, included typically Mediterranean elements, such as olive oil, grains and bread, wine, fish, and various meats, including poultry and rabbit.

Grains (mainly wheat, although barley and millet were also cultivated) were eaten in the form of bread, porridge, or soup. The consumption of domestic meat varieties (lamb, goat, pork, etc.) increased, whereas game progressively lost importance, although it still carried weight in the Iberians' diet (especially rabbits and deer). Meat was eaten roasted and, most often, boiled.

In coastal areas the Iberians also collected mollusks and already practiced some fishing.

Evidence shows that in the sixth century B.C., herding predominated over agriculture in some hamlets, but a hundred years later, this situation had been reversed. Such a change was crucial to the development of production as well as to the creation and development of settlements.

In the second half of the third century B.C., the Carthaginian imperialist campaigns, with the ensuing occupation of the south of the Peninsula, the foundation of Cartagena, and Hannibal's offensive against Rome in 219 B.C., triggered the Roman assault and the occupation and Romanization of the whole peninsula.

THE ROMAN AGE

The Romans entered the Iberian Peninsula from Greek colonies such as Ampurias, which served as the landing base for the first Roman expedition (218 B.C.). By the end of the second century B.C., after stifling the resistance of indigenous tribes and annihilating the Carthaginian offensive, the Romans definitively settled in the peninsula. Their expansion was relatively fast (Numancia, the last outstanding Iberian redoubt, was taken in the year 133 B.C.) and the degree of Romanization was high, except in some of the mountainous territories of the Basque-Cantabric cornice.

One of the first cities founded in Spain by the Romans was Itálica, situated five and half miles north of contemporary Seville and established in 206 B.C., and it blossomed rapidly as a military headquarters and a cultural center. At its peak, in the second and third centuries A.D., Itálica supported a population of several thousand. Both Roman Emperors Trajan and Hadrian were born there. Hadrian eventually bestowed imperial largesse on the city during his reign in the second century A.D., adding marble temples and important buildings. Itálica's amphitheater seated 25,000 spectators and was the third largest in the Roman Empire. Unlike other cities, nothing was built on top of Itálica in post-Roman times. Itálica is, therefore, beautifully preserved as a Roman city.

The Roman occupation brought deep changes in the social, political, and economic life of the peninsula. Urban life was affected by the building of a network of Roman roads and bridges that improved communications. Likewise, agriculture and productive methods advanced, and the occupied territory was turned into Roman Hispania.

Around the end of the first century B.C. rural houses (villae), appeared. These were agricultural centers of production that extended and intensified crops, especially grains (the most appreciated ones were wheat and oats coming from Bética in eastern Andalucia), but also vines and olive trees.

The province of Bética, and to a lesser extent that of Tarragona, were important oil suppliers to Rome. The importance of such centers in this respect is somehow endorsed by the popular belief that the famous Mount

Testaccio in Rome was built in one hundred years by piling up the fragments of oil amphoras coming from the Bética province. Testimonies on the use of olive oil for frying, making sauces, and cooking vegetables and cakes can be found in the work of authors such as Horace, Juvenal, and Columella, the latter definitely Spanish, from Gades (the modern Cádiz).

Wine production was also widely extended at this time. While the Iberians had been in contact with Greece, their wine consumption had been scarce, partly due to the fact that special jugs and craters were needed for storage. For this reason, in most Iberian settlements beer had been the most popular drink. During the Roman age (from the first century B.C. onward), grape crops and wine production and consumption expanded considerably. Hispanic wines were highly appreciated for their quality and they were widely exported to Rome and Italy as well as to the colonies (especially to the near Galia).

The Latin author Martial, for example, praised the wine produced in the province of Tarragona, comparing it to the best wines of Italy. Wine was not consumed pure, as it is nowadays, but rather drunk hot or mixed with pine resin, dried fruits, aromatic herbs, honey, spices, or simply with water.

Food preservation was also boosted during the Roman age due to a more intensive use of the existing salting plants, particularly on the Mediterranean coastline. As a consequence, fish (especially tuna and mackerel) could be salted and thus preserved longer, and the fishery trade benefited from this preserving method.

It is worth mentioning, in this respect, the fish-based sauce called *garum*, a favorite of Roman gastronomy, which had previously belonged in the Greek cuisine. *Garum* was a liquid seasoning made from fermenting fish in saltwater. *Garum* produced in the area of Cartago Nova (present-day Cartagena, in the region of Murcia) was particularly appreciated in Rome. It had a strong taste and could be mixed with wine, oil, vinegar, or just water. Another, cheaper, variety was the *hallex*, a sort of half-rotten *garum*.

Salt also had other possible applications to food preserving. The various preparations of pork, salted and air-dried in drying plants, for example, were highly utilized. The ham from Ceretania, today's Cerdenya, in the north of Catalonia, which had already been praised by the poet Martial in the first century B.C., was a favorite, and the pigs bred in this area were considered to be of great quality. They fed on acorns and other wild fruits, just as they do nowadays in certain areas of Spain, such as Extremadura or the province of Salamanca.

Records of Roman stews can be found in the Roman Apicius's *De re coquinaria,* which includes numerous recipes of all kinds: lamb, kid, and chicken stews, popular pulse and vegetable preparations, fish in various sauces, and poultry (including cranes and peacocks).

Figs were certainly a favorite of both Romans and Greeks. They were left to dry in the sun and packed for exportation to Rome and Greece. Pears, pomegranates, and cherries from Lusitania, and Mediterranean grapes and raisins were also renowned, as well as the sweet olives that came from the areas of Emérita and Lusitania, which were dried in the sun and whose taste was even richer than that of raisins.

Among the novelties introduced from the East in Roman times were peaches, apricots, melons, and lemons. The latter were imported from Persia.

But for a few exceptions and despite the quality and fame of many of its products (wine, oil, *garum,* sausages, fruits, etc.) the Roman Hispanic cuisine seems to have been rather simple and detached from the culinary lavishness of the capital of the empire in Rome.

THE VISIGOTHIC KINGDOM

In the third century A.D., the Empire's deep crisis affected the Hispanic provinces, which were already undergoing a process of Christianization. The invasions of Germanic peoples (Suevi, Alani, and Vandals), which started in the year 408, put an end to the Roman rule in the Iberian Peninsula. The Visigoths, a Germanic tribe that was allied with Rome and was becoming increasingly Romanized, defeated the invaders and ended up settling permanently in the peninsula. When the Roman Empire disappeared in 476, the Visigoths began to create their own kingdoms in Galia and, later on, in Hispania. They eventually founded a Visigothic kingdom, which by the fifth century would already encompass most of the Iberian Peninsula, and established its capital in Toledo.

The arrival of the Visigoths in Hispania did not bring a serious break from the Roman food tradition, although there was a loss in variety and richness, both as far as products and recipes were concerned.

Both the *Liber ludiciorum,* a Visigothic legal compendium, and the *Chronicles of Saint Isidore of Seville* make numerous references to food during the Visigothic age.

The products consumed were basically the same as in the previous age, grains being the staple food. Records show that various kinds of bread were made: leavened and unleavened, dark, soft, and so forth. Livestock were raised in large numbers and the most valued meats were pork, sheep, beef, poultry, and game. Fish was less valued, although both sea- and fresh-water species were eaten (salmon, to mention one).

The Visigoths learned from the Roman tradition how to cultivate lentils, broad beans, chickpeas, peas, lettuce, leeks, chard, squash, and radish, and how to use the Hispanic olive oil, a novelty in their Germanic diet, which was previously characterized by the use of animal fats. The most eaten fruits were apples, pomegranates, dates, peaches, pears, plums, grapes, figs, dried fruits, and nuts such as hazelnuts, almonds, chestnuts, walnuts, and acorns. Spices, which were brought from the East, were also highly valued, especially pepper, but also cinnamon, ginger, aromatic herbs, and saffron. The latter was already cultivated in the peninsula at that time and is still today an expensive crop that is grown using traditional techniques.

The Visigoths were fond of wine, produced in its different varieties: young, white, red, sweet, mixed with honey, herbs, and spices, or cooked. They also made apple cider and various kinds of beer. The favorite beer, called *celia*, was made from fermented wheat germ and later diluted and fermented again together with mild wine. Other alcoholic and alcohol-free drinks were made from honey (*hydromel*, *oxymeli*, *melicratum*, etc.).

FOOD IN ANDALUSIAN SPAIN

After the death of King Vitiza in 710, the Visigothic monarchy (which was not hereditary but elective) underwent an important succession crisis.

The Muslim Berbers of northern Africa, which were under the rule of the Caliph of Damascus, took advantage of this political weakness and entered Hispania in the year 711. Their expansion was fast and they occupied almost the entire Iberian Peninsula, except the Visigothic strongholds in northern Asturias and Cantabria and in the Basque mountains. They crossed over the Pyrenees and went on up to the French town of Poitiers, where they were eventually stopped. From this moment on, the Christians of the north started the reconquest of the peninsula, creating different Hispanic kingdoms and counties (Asturias, León, Galicia, Portugal, Castille, Navarra, Aragon, and the Catalan counties) and, little by little, they recovered the lost territories. The Emirate of Cordoba became independent in 756 and turned into an independent Caliphate in 929. The dismembering of the Caliphate of Cordoba into small kingdoms, called *taifas*, from 1031 on facilitated the Christian Reconquest. Yet, the reconquest was rather slow, and the Muslims stayed in the Iberian Peninsula for over seven centuries, leaving a deep cultural legacy, especially in the south. Their influence on food practices, cooking, and cultivation techniques was also noteworthy and is still seen in many of the current food-related words belonging to Romance Spanish languages, such as Castilian, Catalan, and Galician.

However, Andalusi cooking is not as well known today as it could be wished for, though its legacy is present in many of the basic Spanish dishes, above all in the southern and eastern regions.

Grains, chiefly wheat, but also millet, barley, oats, rye, and grain sorghum were the base of Andalusian cooking. Besides the locally cultivated wheat, there are records of continuous importation of African wheat dating from the ninth century. The staple ingredient for flour was wheat, although millet, sorghum, starch, broad beans, and chickpeas were also used for making porridge and paps, bread (leavened or unleavened), cakes, and pastry (sponge cakes, buns, doughnuts, fritters, and puff pastry). Wheat semolina also played an important role in some dishes.

In the ninth century, Abou-I-Hassan, known as Ziryab (a musician arrived from Damascus, who imported all the refinements of that court), made his quasi-mythical appearance at the Court of Cordoba. Besides introducing asparagus, he brought a sort of revolution in the practices and manners of the Cordobese court. Music, attire, and food underwent radical changes as he introduced the refinements, table etiquette, and equipment of Eastern cooking. These included the order that courses had to be served, which was the following: cold starters, meat and poultry, hors d'oeuvres, pastas and couscous, soups, and then pies, cakes, and other sweet desserts. Before Ziryab's arrival all the courses were served at once, without order, and people chose according to their own taste. This was also the way food was eaten in the Christian West and it would remain unchanged for most of the Middle Ages.

The extensive cultivations of olive trees were almost exclusively devoted to the making of olive oil. Excess produce was destined for exportation.

Broad beans, chickpeas, lentils, and lupines were the pulse varieties that stood out, and vegetables such as lettuce, chard, artichokes, spinach, cucumbers, onions, garlic, eggplants, turnips, leeks, celery, and squash were also intensively cultivated in Al-Andalus (Arabic for Andalusia). Many contemporary words—not only of plants and vegetables—in Spanish have an Arabic origin, such as *alcachofas* (artichokes), *berenjenas* (eggplants; *alberginies* in Catalan), *aceite* (oil), *alubias* (beans), and so forth.

Fruits were considered like sweets to be eaten on special festivities and occasions and were not regarded as nutritious foodstuffs. The most eaten fruits were apricots, peaches, lemons, watermelons, figs, pomegranates, *membrillos* (quinces), grapes, apples, and dried fruits and nuts, such as raisins, almonds, acorns, palm hearts, and dates (it was thanks to the Muslims that the date palm became acclimated in the peninsula: the largest palm grove in Europe can be found today in the town of Elche, in eastern Spain). Although rice was not imported by the Arabs and had already been known in previous ages, rice farming was improved in this period due to their advancement in water technology, which made extensive irrigation farming possible in eastern Spain.

Milk and dairy products, such as cheese, were largely emphasized in Andalusian cooking, and they were basic in many popular recipes, such as fresh cheese fritters.

Meat, however, seems to have been a relatively scarce food. It was considered a luxury and was not always affordable for the less wealthy population. The most widely eaten meats were poultry (chickens, hens, pigeons, ducks), quail chickens, cranes, rabbit, ram, and lamb (the latter was common during important festivities, like that of Aid-el-kbir). Just as Christians did with pigs, these peoples used almost every part of rams: their tallow, their meat (which was roasted, dried, salted, and preserved in the form of jerky and sausages), their entrails, and their heads, which were baked in an earthen oven. The animals were slaughtered according to the rules of the Koran, the Islamic holy book: facing Mecca, the site of pilgrimages, their throats were slit with one deep slash performed by the hand of a purified person who had been socially accepted for this task. The animal was left to bleed afterward.

Lamb and *Membrillo* (Quince) Stew

Ingredients
- lean lamb meat
- garlic clove
- pepper to taste
- pinch of saffron
- olive oil
- salt
- onion
- *membrillo* (quince)
- pinch of cinnamon

- some sugar
- handful of currants

Preparation

Salt the meat and then fry it in olive oil until it is browned. Cover it with water and add the garlic clove and onion, cleaned and whole (to prevent them from melting), the pepper, the salt, saffron to taste, and the currants. Cook on low heat for approximately 20 minutes. Meanwhile, cut the *membrillo* (quince) into four wedges without separating them completely and boil for a few minutes in a little water. When it is ready, sprinkle with cinnamon, sugar, and a touch of pepper. Serve the meat on a dish with bits of *membrillo*.

Andalusian cooking was always open to the influence of other cuisines, such as the ones of the Christian North and, in turn, it influenced them. The result was the creation of tasty dishes that melded both traditions, such as the *puchero* or *olla* (meaning "hotpot" and "stew," but today almost exclusively referring to food) in all its peninsular varieties: Andalusian and Castilian stews, including the ones made in Madrid and Valencia, and the Catalan *escudella i carn d'olla* (stew with meat), which are related to Arabic dishes such as couscous. Another example of the encounter of the two traditions is the nougat from Alicante, a typical Arabic dessert made from honey and almonds, which, through the centuries, ended up becoming the dessert of the Christian festivity par excellence: Christmas.

Partly in keeping with the tradition that had developed on the Mediterranean coastline (Malaga and Almuñecar, for example) since the Phoenician period, bluefish was largely eaten both fresh (sardines) and salted or preserved in the form of dried and salted tuna (*mojama*), tuna roe, or albacore tuna in spiced marinade.

In the Iberian Peninsula, due to the use of Eastern spices, these preparations became progressively milder until they acquired a delicate taste. The most used aromatic herbs were fennel, basil, coriander, caraway, mint, and rosemary, as well as local spices, such as saffron, which is largely cultivated in the south and the east of the peninsula, and also pepper and cinnamon.

Grape crops were still important in Al-Andalus. Grapes were eaten fresh, whereas sweet, cooked must was used for making *sapa*, a boiled-down syrup that, like honey, was used as sweetener.

Despite the Koranic prohibition of alcohol otherwise observed in Muslim Andalusian cooking, wine production was continued, and the drink kept being consumed, commercialized, and even praised by many poets.

Marketplaces played an important role in the purchase of food, as still happens today in many Arabic towns and villages. They were very popular, and almost all the necessary foodstuffs could be acquired there, including the "illicit" ones like wine, because it was consumed both by Jews and Mozarabic Christians (Christians living in the Iberian Muslim area).

Jewish communities had been present in the Iberian Peninsula from Roman times. These Hispanic communities were called "Sephardic" (from Hebraic "Sepharad": Spain). As for the Muslims, pork meat—but not wine—was a prohibited food, and olive oil was very common in the Sephardic cuisine. From the Middle Ages on, pork became an important cultural marker, because it was a food eaten uniquely by Christians. Christians were divided into two different groups: *old* Christians (who actually ate pork), and *new* Christians (that is, Muslims and Jews who had converted to Christianity and avoided consuming pork despite their conversion).

THE MIDDLE AGES

The Emirate and, subsequently, the Caliphate of Cordoba and the Muslim kingdoms reached their apogee and then entered a phase of decline and military retreat as the Christian kingdoms of the north progressively gained ground and became more solidly established. The Christians' military strength increased as they recovered the southern territories of the peninsula.

Various kingdoms were slowly created through matrimonial alliances and warfare policies and they became increasingly powerful: the independent county of Castille became a kingdom in 1035 and absorbed other territories (León and Galicia), whereas Portugal became independent in the twelfth century, keeping out of the orbit. The kingdom of Navarra would not be annexed until well into the sixteenth century. In the northeast, the Catalan counties, which had become independent from the French Empire, joined the kingdom of Aragon, a strong state that would further expand into the Mediterranean (to the Balearic Islands, Languedoc, Provence, Corsica, Sardinia, southern Italy, and even Athens and Neopatria in Greece).

During the Late Middle Ages, a remarkable phenomenon took place in the Christian area: the population grew along with the expansion to the south and agricultural exploitations increased. Markets consolidated and so did the interaction between the urban and rural world and the international relationships. However, during the Middle Ages the growing population did not always rely on steady food supplies and had to face various periods of crisis and scarcity. These were aggravated by a feudal structure that was based on an ever-growing gap between high and low social strata.

The sources of food supply varied enormously from city to country because city dwellers relied on the market, whereas rural inhabitants tended to be self-sufficient, when possible, and bought from the markets only what could not be produced or obtained by their own means.

Vegetables and grains (chief ingredients of popular dishes such as vegetable hodge-podge and stews), together with bread were the main staples of the masses, who did not enjoy much variety of foods. Meat became a prerogative of privileged classes and thus, a sign of distinction and power. Although the broadening of international commerce facilitated the importation of wheat crops from other areas, supplies failed during the frequent periods of scarcity. At this time the *Sent Soví,* the most important Catalan cookbook appeared—the oldest cookbook in Spain, and one of the oldest and most important in Europe.

The bubonic plague, in the year 1348, exacerbated the already difficult situation and caused a heavy demographic loss. The subsequent loss of workers resulted, on one hand, in a fall in agricultural production, and on the other, in a moderate rise in livestock farming, although the animals in question were the least expensive (goat, sheep, pigs) and in general, quantities were not abundant.

Lamb was reserved for important occasions and, among birds, poultry were more frequently eaten than wild species.

Meat was most often boiled with spices and herbs, to make it softer and to improve its taste. The lack of fresh meat was compensated by the masses with the consumption of pulses and vegetables (onion, cabbage, lentils, broad beans, etc.) and especially of bread. Nuts were also eaten. Pine nuts, hazelnuts, and above all almonds, were used for various culinary applications. Vegetables, such as squash, turnips, chard, cucumbers, and borage were less frequently used. Wild aromatic herbs such as thyme, rosemary, sage, bay leaf, and fennel were the main seasoning ingredients. Honey was the sweetener par excellence, and it was used on special occasions to prepare cakes and pastries.

Menjar Blanc (White Dish)

Ingredients
- 1/2 cup of rice flour
- almond milk (2 tbs. of ground almonds blended in a 1/2 cup of hot water)

- 3 tbs. sugar
- 1 tbs. rosewater
- cinnamon

Preparation

Blend the rice flour with cold water to a smooth, thin paste. Gradually, add almond milk to rice flour mixture, stirring constantly. Slowly, bring to a boil over moderate heat, stirring frequently. Add the sugar and cook for about 12 minutes. Stir in rosewater and remove from heat. Pour into a serving bowl or mold. Serve with cinnamon sprinkled on top.

Local wine was a euphoriant and mostly unrefined. It was widely drunk, although watered-down vinegar was also a refreshing drink then. In this period, uncommon nutritious and therapeutic qualities were attributed to wine (and to meat, too); it was given to patients in hospitals and it was used for making medicines.

Fruit was still considered a superfluous and luxury foodstuff. It was scarcely eaten by lower classes and the elite did not eat it in abundance, either.

The diet of this period also included cheese, eggs, and fish (often salted, for preserving). With the exception of sardines and tuna, fish was expensive and there was not much variety, not even in sea towns. Fish was, in any case, less popular than meat, as it was believed to be of inferior quality. It was mainly associated with religious penitence and ecclesiastical imposition, rather than with gastronomic enjoyment.

During the recurrent periods of scarcity the diet of less privileged classes dramatically changed and included less habitual foods, such as wild fruits and seeds, roots, bracken, sweet sorghum (usually reserved for animals), and even bark and the ground shell of dried fruits.

As for game, it progressively lost importance as the Middle Ages approached their end.

THE ARRIVAL OF FOOD FROM THE AMERICAS

The end of the Middle Ages and the onset of the Renaissance thought characteristic of the modern age coincided, in Spain, with various significant events.

The Canary Islands, which from the fourteenth century onward had been visited in succession by the Genoese, the Catalan-Aragonese of Mallorca, the Portuguese, and the Normans, definitively came under Castilian sovereignty by the end of the fifteenth century. The reconquest was also completed in 1492, as the last Muslim kingdom of the Iberian Peninsula, Granada, was conquered. The "Expulsion" of the Spanish Jews (Sephardi) from the Iberian Peninsula, and the beginning of the Sephardi Diaspora also occurred in 1492. The Sephardi people took their language and their kitchen around the world.

Probably, the most significant event as far as food is concerned was the encounter between two worlds as, also in 1492, the expeditions financed by the Crown of Castille reached the Antilles and the American continents. The consequence was a worldwide food revolution in which the European passion for spices played an important role.

Other momentous political changes in the sixteenth century would take place on one hand, when the Castilian and Catalan-Aragonese Crowns, the French County, Flanders, and the Low Countries became part of the German Empire under the rule of Emperor Charles I, who started the Habsburg dynasty. On the other, when the Aragonese-Catalan domain extended to Italy the reciprocal food influences were remarkable.

Eventually, when the kingdom of Navarra joined the Castilian Crown in 1512, almost all the peninsula came under the rule of one monarch except Portugal, which was part of the empire only from 1580 to 1668. All these territories kept, however, their internal autonomy, currency, borders, and tolls. A definitive political union under a centralized state would not exist until well into the eighteenth century, when the Bourbon dynasty came to the throne.

The arrival of food from the Americas represented a turning point in European food history. Spain, which became the metropolis of an increasing number of conquered territories, was the venue by which the new foodstuffs were introduced. The acceptance and use of food varied according to time and place, though. For example, vegetables, such as peppers, were widely and quickly accepted, whereas it took years before tomatoes were introduced in the culinary and food practices of Spain and Europe at large.

The arrival of food from the Americas in Spain, and hence in Europe, coincided with the exportation of European foodstuffs to the Americas. Among the exported foods were Mediterranean wheat and vines, which acclimatized in the new Western lands. As for olive trees, they adapted to the New World at first but were subsequently prohibited by the metropolis, a situation that would not change until the nineteenth century. This cross-trade significantly affected the European Hispano-American population, who did not always accommodate their taste to local food and practices and continued to consume imported Spanish food. The latter became an ethnic marker that separated original Spaniards from native Americans. Highly caloric foodstuffs, such as potatoes and maize, were only partially incorporated in the diets of the Europeans, except in those of the less privileged classes who, having no access to imported items, had to adapt to local food.

European products were imported not only into the New World, but also into the recently colonized Canary Islands. Bread, for example, was imported from the peninsula in 1478, together with grain crops such as wheat, and vinegar, pulses, and sugar. Around the year 1500, the first cows made their appearance on the islands, followed by wool sheep and poultry, some fruit-bearing trees, and vegetables (e.g., eggplant, cucumbers, cabbage, squash, turnips, melons, lettuce, onions, and broad beans).

From the fifteenth and sixteenth centuries onward, the islands turned into a major center for the production of high quality sugar cane. This crop moved from the Mediterranean to the Portuguese Atlantic Islands (mainly Madeira) and over to the Canary Islands. New World products progressively found their place within the Spanish food system. In most cases this happened thanks mostly to the lower classes who, in times of crisis, were less reluctant to try and introduce new foodstuffs in their diet. Thus, some vegetables, such as potatoes and beans, became the staple subsistence food and joined or replaced the existing traditional products and the local recipes and culinary lore. Potatoes, for example, and to a lesser extent beans, were easily incorporated in the various stews that were typical of Spanish cuisine, replacing other ingredients, such as chestnuts, eggplants, and even chickpeas. The introduction of products such as potatoes was not easy, though, and no precise date is associated to the beginning of its urban consumption, although it is known that, at first, potatoes were used by the poorest people and in barracks, prisons, hospitals, and poorhouses.

If foodstuffs such as tomatoes, peppers, and potatoes came to be considered as "local" products, it was due to their fulfillment of certain necessary expectations: first, their good acclimatization; second, their easy integration into the local food culture and recipes; and last, but not least, their sensory qualities (taste, color, and texture). To become part of the food practices of a society, a food of this kind must easily adapt to the ecosystem. Yet, it must also necessarily offer a certain degree of economic and nutritional advantages and, above all, it is essential for it to fit into the imaginary and the representational system of the society in question. As far as the Spanish case is concerned, some products integrated more or less easily, whereas others, such as maize, were not really incorporated into Spanish culture and food habits, as they were, for example, in France and northern Italy.

The differences between the upper and the lower classes were even greater in this period, known in Spain as "the golden age." On one hand, the overseas enterprises in general and the favorable political situation of the empire in Europe brought good economic times for the monarchy, the nobles, and the trading bourgeoisie alike. Such wealth is proved by the unprecedented abundance of food and the development of an exquisite courtly cuisine. Meat (poultry and wild birds, big and small game, pork and sausage, veal and ram, the latter particularly appreciated) was abundant and so were sweet desserts and fruits, whereas there was less variety of fish (mainly trout, but also tuna, eel, and barbel) and of vegetables, which were mostly eaten as an accompaniment to meat dishes. Whenever possible, the diet was highly caloric and the most valued foods were meat and sweets.

Around 1518 to 1520, in Catalonia and in the Catalan language, the Rupert of Nola's cookbook *Llibre de Coch*, appeared. It was published later in the Castilian language. In the following decades, other elaborate books on cuisine appeared. Later, *El libro del arte de cozina* (*Book of the Art of Cuisine*; Salamanca, 1607) and the well-known *El Arte de Cozina, Pastelería y Vizcochería y Conservería* (*The Art of Cuisine, Baking, Patisserie, and Conserving*; 1611) by Francisco Martínez Montiño, were published.

On the other hand, the less privileged classes suffered more directly from social problems, wars, and famine, and their options when it came to obtaining food were far fewer than those of the more powerful social strata. In their diet, the most important foods were bread and soups with various ingredients (vegetables, herbs, bread, bones, offal), whereas meat was scarce and, if eaten at all, it belonged to lesser quality animals (goats, pigs, poultry) and usually consisted of the less valued parts of these. In coastal areas there was more fish (sardines, especially those fished in Galicia, and tuna), although it was not eaten in abundance, together with vegetables and herbs, eggs, cheese and cottage cheese, olives, milk, fruit, and local wine.

The richest banquets took place on festive occasions and celebrations during which meat was more abundant (cooked on a skewer, for example). The main animals eaten were young bulls, pigs, small game (rabbits and hares, partridges, etc.), and poultry such as chickens, hens, ganders, and turkeys, which had been introduced from the Americas. Another festive food was the so-called *olla podrida* (literally, "rotten pot"), a typical stew with a wide variety of ingredients. The *olla podrida* may be considered to have been, during the golden age, the national dish par excellence in the Iberian Peninsula. Today it exists in various permutations in the various regional stews (Madrid, Andalucian, and Catalan *escudella*). All these foods were accompanied by local wine.

As mentioned, wine consumption was mostly local because the high transportation fares prevented it from being traded on a large scale. The most distinguished wines under the Crown came from Andalucia (Jerez, Cazalla, Constantina, etc.), La Mancha (Toledo and Ciudad Real), Madrid (which supplied the Court with renowned wines, such as San Martín de Valdeiglesias, Pinto, or Valdemoro), Castilla la Vieja, León, Extremadura, and the Canary Islands, which provided excellent malmseys.

The wines from Catalonia and the Levant, as well as those from Aragon (Cariñena and Calatayud, for example), were particularly renowned in the Catalan-Aragonese territories. Other wine-based popular drinks were the *hipocrás* (made from mature wine, sugar, cinnamon, ambar, and musk), the *carraspada* (watered-down wine cooked with honey and spices), and a similar preparation called *aloja*. Other types of alcoholic drinks were various eau-de-vie and aromatic waters made from anise, cinnamon, orange flower, and lemon, as well as sorbets. In the Levant, people also drank *horchata de chufa* or tigernut milk (made from the juice of the *cyperus esculentus sativus* tuber), a sweet drink typical of the area of Valencia. Beer began to be brewed in the sixteenth century, when Emperor Charles I, and later on his son Philip II, invited German brewers to move to the peninsula. Yet beer consumption did not consolidate until the seventeenth century and the drink would not become popular until the end of the nineteenth century.

Among the foods imported from the New World, chocolate was a unique case, because it was immediately accepted. It was introduced in the Iberian Peninsula in 1520, and its consumption quickly increased, especially among the wealthier strata of the population, as soon as sugar began to be added to its preparation. The indigenous use of chocolate was quite different, as cocoa was mixed with spicy and bitter ingredients.

Such was its popularity that, as early as at the beginning of the seventeenth century, there were already mills devoted to its making. In the eighteenth century, when chocolate became more solidly established in the rest of Europe, especially in Italy and France, this sweetened preparation became known as "Spanish chocolate."

THE EIGHTEENTH AND NINETEENTH CENTURIES

The Spanish kingdoms underwent a severe crisis in the seventeenth century. The population decreased and the labor force along with it. In addition, as a consequence of the expulsion of the Morisco people—the Muslim population who had converted to Christianity—in 1609, the agricultural crisis was aggravated. Trade with the New World also suffered from an internal crisis in the same period, due to the increasing commercial intervention of other countries. This, together with monetary inflation, created a rather difficult economic situation. To make things worse, there was no unity in the foreign policies of the various kingdoms, which enjoyed considerable internal and external autonomy despite being united under one crown.

The whole century was characterized by a succession of domestic revolutions. In 1640, Catalonia revolted against Spain and placed itself under the protection of Louis XIII of France, but the revolt was quelled in the 1650s. As a consequence, the north of Catalonia (Roussillon and Cerdagne) was lost and the borders between the two countries shifted upward to the Pyrenees. At the same time, Portugal obtained its independence. The Habsburg dynasty ended and paved the way for a restless eighteenth century, marked by the War of the Spanish Succession. Eventually, after years of internal fighting, the French Bourbon dynasty gained access to the throne (1701–1714). Their victory meant the end of the Habsburg dynasty and, for the first time, the beginning of a centralized regime at the Court of King Philip V in Madrid. Consequently, Spain entered within the French area of influence and underwent institutional and jurisdictional restructuring, becoming what could be called a proper "Spanish State." Yet this was achieved with considerable losses, such as those of Gibraltar and the Isle of Menorca, which passed into British hands (Menorca only temporarily, whereas Gibraltar is still today under British rule), a change that brought along severe internal impoverishment and malaise. The apogee of this century, politically and culturally speaking, corresponded to the "enlightened" monarchy of Charles III (1759–1788).

As can be appreciated, this historical moment was pregnant with transformations, which were also reflected in the food. On one hand, the access to the throne on the part of the Bourbon dynasty brought a distinctive French influence on courtesan food habits, as well as on a small part of the bourgeoisie. On the other, the rest of Spanish society still clung to traditional dishes and practices.

In the sixteenth century, culinary influences had traveled from the Iberian Peninsula toward France. Among the foods introduced from Spain were sugar and eau-de-vie, both already used by Spanish people during the Middle Ages, as well as New World products such as tomatoes, peppers, potatoes, maize, and chocolate, which became progressively popular in France, together with other exciting infusions such as tea and coffee.

In the eighteenth century this tendency was reversed and France became the country that represented the culinary norm: the simplification and refinement of stews—the base of today's cuisine—the variety of the ingredients, and the harmony of the dishes became, from this time on, the most significant trend.

In the eighteenth century there was a certain continuity as far as the abundance of meat is concerned, although poultry consumption increased to the detriment of other meats. Fish was hardly eaten (mainly when Lent made it mandatory), whereas sweet desserts were abundant. Popular cuisine was still based on the stew "pot" (with hen and few other meats), soup, pork, and sausage and, when possible, some vegetables, and a little fruit and fish in coastal areas (salted cod played an important role, especially during Lent). In the Cantabrian area, apple cider became an important drink. Most of the products coming from the New World started to definitively integrate in the different Spanish cuisines. Peppers had been accepted relatively easily in the seventeenth century, but other foods, such as tomatoes and potatoes, were steadily incorporated in the diet only from the eighteenth century onward.

The Spanish painter Luis Meléndez (born in Naples in 1716) perfected the still life genre in this era. In his paintings, he reflected the Spanish food of his time, frequently including some New World products, such as tomatoes and chocolate.

Peix amb Suc (Fish in Sauce)

Ingredients
- 4 large slices of dusky sea perch (or 8 small ones)
- 2 tomatoes
- 1 onion
- 4 garlic cloves
- parsley
- salt to taste
- olive oil

- flour for coating fish
- a potful of stock (made from the fish head)

Preparation

Peel and dice the onion, and sauté together with garlic cloves, chopped up tomatoes, and some finely chopped parsley in the oil. In the meantime, prepare some stock by boiling the fish head with a little salt. Once the onion, garlic, and tomatoes are ready, cover them with the stock and leave on the burner to thicken. Season and flour the fish slices, place them in an earthen casserole, and coat with the sauce, which had been previously sieved. Let it cook on the stove top, in the earthen casserole, on medium heat for about 15 minutes and serve.

The population explosions that took place in the nineteenth century and in the first decades of the twentieth century in Western Europe were bound to the process of modernization. This phenomenon acquired extraordinary dimensions and was accompanied by a notable decrease in mortality rates and a rise in birth rates. In this sense, the nineteenth century may be considered the century of urban development, industrial projection, migrations, and the beginning of tourism, hotels, and catering.

The nineteenth century, just as the last, started and ended with a crisis and a war. The dynastic crisis in 1808 paved the way for the Napoleonic invasion and the access to the throne of José I Bonaparte, who reigned until the definitive expulsion of the French in 1813, and the return of the Bourbon Fernando VII.

The need for modernization in a country that was anchored in the old regime resulted in a clash between reformation initiatives and absolutist monarchy. The domestic social and economic crisis was aggravated by the loss of the American colonies in 1828 and it eventually led to a progressive liberalization and the beginning of an innovative industrial revolution in the northern regions of the peninsula (especially in Catalonia, with the development of textile industries, and in the Basque Country with the rise of heavy industry). Progressists, democrats, and liberals overthrew Queen Isabel II in 1868. Subsequently, there was a short period of rule under King Amadeo I of Savoia, followed by the First Spanish Republic, which lasted from 1873 to 1874. Afterward, Alfonso XII restored the Bourbon dynasty. His reign was characterized by great social unrest and by the definitive loss, in 1898, of the remaining Spanish colonies of Cuba, Puerto Rico, the Philippines, and the islands of the Pacific, as a consequence of the war against the United States.

The nineteenth century was characterized by urban growth and the increase of the industrial proletariat, especially in the most industrialized areas of the peninsula (Catalonia, the Basque Country, and the Cantabrian Cornice). Production centered on textiles (Catalonia), the metal industry (Basque Country), and mining (Asturias, Cantabria, and other areas). The food industry (flour, biscuits, alcohol, chocolate, sausage, etc.) followed at some distance, although it became increasingly strong through the century and grew to be considerably important in the last decade.

At the end of the eighteenth century, the country had already received European immigrants: namely French and Italians who had immigrated to Catalonia and had left their mark in cooking, as many of them were renowned caterers. From the end of the nineteenth century onward, a new migratory phenomenon began and would continue and increase in the twentieth century: people started to move from the poorest and most rural areas of the peninsula toward the industrialized regions. With immigration, cities such as Barcelona, Bilbao, and Madrid experienced an unprecedented growth.

The deep gap between the gastronomic and technological refinements of the bourgeoisie and the impoverishment of the lower classes still existed, but at the same time the growing cities became centers of cultural expansion and the ideal milieu for multicultural bonds.

It was the case, for example, of Barcelona, a city that became increasingly cosmopolitan and whose cuisine boasted, apart from the traditional Catalan dishes, of inland Valencian, French, and Italian influences. Catalan cooking is, perhaps, the regional Spanish cuisine that has created its own tradition, incorporating and adapting Italian pasta dishes.

Such tradition spread from the typical inns (fondas) and, above all, from the Italian-style restaurants of nineteenth century middle-class Barcelona, fond of cannelloni and opera. Certainly, cannelloni were a typical dish of family meetings. Special pasta recipes already existed in Catalonia in the nineteenth century, but pasta was more commonly eaten by laborers and craftsmen.

The daily diet of laborers included few meat proteins (some lesser valued parts of pork meat, such as bacon), vegetables (cabbage, beans, onions, tomatoes, peppers, potatoes, and maize flour), typical peninsular soups and stews, salted fish such as herring, bread, and some wine.

The nineteenth century was also characterized by large, covered markets, which could be found in all peninsular cities in general, although Barcelona was outstanding in this respect, with the Sant Antoni, Born, and Boquería markets, among others.

As for haute cuisine, Spain was under the direct influence of France. Most of the cookbooks printed in this period were influenced by French cuisine or were direct translations from French. Thus, there was a considerable contrast between the most affluent and the lowest classes in terms of food consumption, and indeed more records have been left on the elite.

As the century advanced, however, the folkloric boom led to the appreciation of popular, mainly rural, culture and within this, gastronomy obviously played an important role. At this time were born some of the most outstanding Iberian dishes, for example, the Catalan *pa amb tomàquet* (bread slices rubbed with tomato, with or without garlic, and dressed with olive oil and salt), the international *paella* (Catalan word meaning

La Boquería market in Barcelona, one of the most important markets in Europe.

Paella cooking in a large pan, North Catalonia.

frying pan and referring to the large pan where the rice was cooked), and *arròs en paella* (rice in *paella*) eaten by Valencian peasants and laborers.

Paella (Rice in *Paella*)

Ingredients
- rice (*paella* rice, arborio, or short-grain) (handful per serving plus some extra ones *or* 1 cup will serve 3–4 people)
- 3 garlic cloves
- 1 chopped onion
- 1 chopped tomato
- 1 lb. pork loin ribs
- 1 small rabbit or chicken cut up
- 1/2 cup peas
- 1/2 cup chopped green beans

- 1 pinch saffron threads
- 1 tsp. salt or to taste
- olive oil
- water (enough to double the quantity of the rice)

Preparation

Sauté the meat (ribs, rabbit, and/or chicken) in a *paella* (typical metal pan, round, flat, and with two handles) with some oil. When the meat is browned, add the chopped onion, peas, beans, whole garlic cloves, and, last the chopped tomato. Add the water to the mixture and bring to a boil. Add the rice and put on high heat. After a few minutes, add the saffron. The rice must cook on medium heat for about 20 minutes uncovered until all the water has been absorbed. Once ready, cover the *paella* with a cotton cloth, let it sit for 5 minutes and then serve.

Note

This recipe follows the traditional Valencian preparation. Different kinds of *paella* may be made using other ingredients: fish, shellfish, snails, meat, vegetables, or even "mix *paella*," the most popular with tourists, which blends in one recipe all the other kinds (meat, vegetables, fish, and shellfish).

As mentioned, the nineteenth century also witnessed the definitive popularization of those foods that were introduced in the diet in the eighteenth century, such as tomatoes. Yet, in non-Mediterranean regions in the north of Spain, some common products were integrated into the food system much later. Rice, for instance, was not customarily used there until the end of the nineteenth century and some vegetables, such as carrots, eggplants, and zucchini, were eaten only well into the twentieth century. The following foods could be found in a Spanish popular market of the nineteenth century: pulses and vegetables (chickpeas, beans, lentils, peas, tender green beans and broad beans, squash, artichokes, spinach, asparagus, tomatoes, peppers, potatoes, sweet potatoes, onions, garlic), fruit (also used as vegetables and as ingredients in sauces: pears, apples, peaches, bitter oranges and lemons, pomegranates, *membrillos*—quinces), dried fruits and nuts (raisins and prunes, pine seeds, almonds, walnuts), various kinds of meat (pork, poultry and lamb were, respectively, the most popular, the most expensive, and the most appreciated ones), fish (fresh fish such as anglerfish, hake, conger, grouper, sturgeon, and barbel, as well as salted fish, especially cod, but also herring, anchovies, tuna, and others that can be still found today), dairy products such as cheese, various herbs and spices, wines and spirits, and even animal species that are nowadays protected, such as the turtle.

A TURBULENT TWENTIETH CENTURY

The nineteenth century finished with the end of the first Spanish Republic, the restoration of the monarchy under King Alfonso XII and, already in 1898, the final crisis following the Spanish-American War and the loss of the American, Asian, and Pacific colonies. During the twentieth century, the labor movements (socialism, anarchism, and, later on, communism) and nationalist movements (chiefly the Catalan, but also the Galician and Andalucian ones) developed up to the end of the Spanish Civil War and became stronger. The colonial policies of the new century focused on Equatorial Guinea and especially on Morocco. Here the Berbers' revolts triggered a military intervention that brought serious social and political consequences.

The industrializing process and urban development continued, and so did the large domestic migratory movements to Barcelona, Madrid, Bilbao, and other large cities. Europe fought from 1914 to 1917 in World War I, while Spain remained neutral. In 1923, following the example of contemporary Italian fascism, a fascist-like dictatorship was established in Spain. Its downfall in 1930 led, some time later, to the fall of the Monarchy of Alfonso XII and the establishment of the second Spanish Republic. The Republic was founded on democratic and progressive principles and it introduced a new constitution and universal suffrage, as well as Statutes of Autonomy for Catalonia, the Basque Country, and, later on, Galicia.

The climax of fascism in Europe and the domestic weakness of the Republic contributed to the outbreak of the Spanish Civil War (1936–1939), the most painful event in twentieth-century Spain. The war ended with the victory of the national faction, led by General Francisco Franco, and with the establishment of a new dictatorship that would last 40 years, until his death in 1975. The period after the war was rather hard. It coincided with World War II, during which Spain was again neutral, and it was marked by hunger, economic difficulties, and heavy migrations from the south of the peninsula (Andalucia, Extremadura, Murcia, La Mancha) toward the more industrialized and prosperous regions of the north (Catalonia and Basque Country), the center (Madrid), Western Europe, and South America.

Between the 1950s and the 1960s the north of the peninsula reached its apogee in terms of development and industrialization, and tourism became one of the most important economic sectors of the country.

After the death of Franco, Spain became a democracy again, and the monarchy was restored with a new constitution under King Juan Carlos I (1978).

From this point on, Spain underwent an overall process of territorial restructuring and state decentralization; Catalonia, the Basque Country,
and Galicia recovered their autonomy, and at the same time 14 other autonomous regions were created.[1]

In 1986, Spain and Portugal entered the European Economic Community. Spain experienced unprecedented economic growth and became one
of the engines of the current European Union.

All these social and political events were directly reflected in the Spanish food trajectory. French influence in the culinary field, especially in
haute cuisine, was still strong, although folkloric and ethnographic initiatives that had already existed in the previous century were enhanced in
order to recover the popular old recipes of the various Spanish regions.
The cookbook of Countess de Pardo Bazán (1913) is an example of this
trend.

The differences between the high and low classes and between rural
and urban milieu still existed during this period.

The outbreak of the Spanish Civil War had gravely affected the Spanish social framework. A large portion of society suffered from hunger, especially the lower strata of the population, as scarcity and rationing
became the norm during the war years. Food shortage also extended to the
postwar period and under the dictatorial regime, the country found itself
politically and socially isolated from the rest of Europe and the world at
large. The fascist ultranationalism defended the "Spanish essence" in all
fields, including the culinary one, and promoted a unifying "typification"
of Spanish cooking, excluding any foreign influence or new tendencies
that might arise in Europe.

At the popular level, however, and without considering the remarkable
scarcity during the Civil War and the postwar periods, there was continuity
as to the kind of foods eaten: wheat and its by-products (especially bread),
vegetables, olive oil and lard, pork by-products and sausage, some meat,
herbs (parsley, garlic, onion), and so forth. Cooking methods also remained
unaltered. Food was boiled, stewed, and fried to prepare the traditional
dishes: soups, stews, hotpots, *migas* (popular dish with the main ingredient
of breadcrumbs), and porridge. The typical menu of the urban middle and
lower labor classes might be as follows: vegetables, pulses, fruit and salads,
some meat (broiled, grilled, in the form of sausage, or as an ingredient for
stews), sardines and cod, olive oil, abundant bread, and eggs. The quantity
and quality of meat proportionally increased with family income.

As far as daily food routines are concerned, in the first half of the twentieth century the main meal was eaten in the evening and it usually con-

sisted of a stew, but in the second half of the century practices changed, due to various reasons: electricity spread to both urban and rural areas, cars became the main transportation means for the family unit, working hours were regularized and reduced, electric household equipment (television, among others), and food technology (freezers and microwaves) reached every home, and women were incorporated into the labor market. All these factors considerably altered eating times, commensality, and type of foods, the main change being a shift of the main meal to lunchtime. Spaniards started to go to bed later and to eat out more frequently, especially at lunchtime, as a consequence of their working schedule and their distance from work. As the living standard increased, evening meals in restaurants became more common too. Even so, those who eat out usually do so choosing *traditional menus* (which include a main course, second course, dessert, and coffee), instead of consuming snacks and sandwiches, as is common in northern European countries. The time devoted by Spanish workers to lunch break (usually between 1:30 and 2:30) is also usually longer than that of their northern counterparts.

Most products are available all year round due to various factors, such as safety and hygiene regulations, food preservation technologies, independence of agriculture from local cultivations and seasons, effective and large-scale distribution, and generalized reduction in price of certain foods. The drawback of such development is that some products have lost variety, quality, and taste. Prepared and precooked foods have found their way into the domestic world, adapting to the new social needs and to people's timetables. Consumption of commercial cakes and pastries has also increased considerably.

From the official data provided by the Ministry of Agriculture, Fisheries, and Food, it can be deduced that the Spanish food system has maintained its Mediterranean character despite the fact that in the last decade of the twentieth century, the consumption of pulses, but especially that of bread and potatoes, has decreased remarkably. Meat and dairy consumption, in contrast, has increased and, to a certain extent, these foods have contributed to homogenizing the Spanish contemporary food system with that of the rest of the Western European countries. In terms of consumption, Spain is halfway between France and Italy: on one hand, Spaniards consume less wheat flour than Italians, the figures in this respect being similar to French ones. On the other hand, the consumption figures relative to olive oil and vegetable fats are more similar to those of Italians, and greater than those of the French.

Fresh and dried fruits, vegetables, and wine are also consumed in large quantities. More specifically, the consumption of vegetables, except potatoes, and of fresh fruit and eggs has notably increased since the 1970s. Fish consumption, despite a slight, variable fall, is rising again. In the last years, wine consumption, except for that of better quality, has fallen slightly, especially among younger generations, whereas there has been an increase in the consumption of other alcoholic drinks, such as beer.

NOTE

1. The other autonomous regions are Andalucia, Aragon, Asturias, Baleares Islands, Canary Islands, Cantabria, Castilla León, Castilla La Mancha, Extremadura, La Rioja, Madrid, Murcia, Navarra, Valencia, and the two autonomous cities of Ceuta and Melilla.

2

Major Foods and Ingredients

Spain imports and exports various food products. Certain foods reflect the agriculture, consumption, and food lore of diverse Spanish regions and cuisines. The following entries provide a brief, and inevitably incomplete, panorama of such foods. Whenever possible, their origin, preparation, importance, social function, and other details have been provided.

GRAINS AND BREAD

In the south of Spain the cultivation of grains possibly dates back earlier than 4000 B.C. Grains, especially wheat, have been a staple in Spain and the Mediterranean, as well as in most parts of Europe. Wheat was and still is the most important grain, followed by other minor grains such as oats, barley, and rye.

Pasta

Pasta consumption in Spain is approximately 11.25 lbs./person/year. In Spain, the conception of "pasta" is dried pasta and not really fresh pasta (a dough made with flour, water, and egg, prepared for immediate consumption and mainly homemade). It was not until the nineteenth century—and particularly during the twentieth century—that pasta became part of the Spanish gastronomy in a regular way, once again due to the Mediterranean influence and the very important rapport between Catalonia and Italy. As mentioned, Catalan cuisine is, perhaps, the only Hispanic cuisine that has created its own tradition, changing and adapting Italian pasta preparations, creating recipes of cannelloni and pasta that are genuine local innovations (cannelloni recipes, for example, are very important in Catalan cuisine, especially during the most important celebrations of the year, such as Christmas, for example).

Pasta also became a common food in other areas of eastern Spain. In Valencia, for example, *fideuá* (developed very recently, in the late twentieth century) is based on pasta (small noodles, in this case), but follows the procedure of *paella*. The use of noodles as a main element in soups and stews has become, in the last century, quite common throughout the country.

Rice

Rice consumption in Spain is relatively high: 15 pounds per person per year, and many dishes in Spanish gastronomy are based on rice. In Spain, rice crops extended from the eastern areas to the rest of the peninsula. Growing in still water, but not very far from the coast, Spanish rice—like that commonly used for *paella*—grows in enormous fields that stretch out for miles. Certain strains of this short-grained rice grow in Spain, and they have a unique capacity to absorb broth while remaining firm. The Valencia region produces a large part of the rice cultivated in Spain, and it is one of the only rice-growing regions in Europe to have a designation of origin (D.O.), but other areas are also important (and also with a protected D.O.): the Ebro Delta, in Catalonia, or the area around the city of Calasparra, in the region of Murcia, are two good examples. The Valencian way of cooking rice has spread to the whole country, to the extent that a local dish such as *paella* has come to be considered the Spanish "national" dish.

Wheat and Bread

Wheat became one of the three elements making up the famous "Mediterranean trilogy" (along with wine and olive oil). Historically and up to today, wheat has been an essential and protected crop and is produced both for domestic consumption and export.

Bread is made from various kinds of grains, although, at least in southern Europe, wheat flour is the major ingredient. Traditionally, bread has been the population's principal food; indeed, it was a staple for Christians, especially for Catholics, who were predominant in Spain. To them, symbolically speaking, bread, together with wine, represents the body of Jesus,

Different kinds of bread.

therefore its importance goes beyond mere food facts; in other words, bread has become a product with an outstanding ideological content.

Bread has always been a staple in the European food system. Etymologically speaking, most European food is only that which "goes with bread," the latter being the essential element of every meal.[1] Historically, the most popular bread has always been white bread, although among the lower social classes bread has been made from different kinds of flours: from combinations from different available grains (rye, buckwheat, oats) to those made from various foods such as acorns and beans.

Bread consumption in Spain is approximately 145 pounds per person per year. Bread is typically bought in the *panaderías* (bread stores). In Spain, there are many different and popular forms of bread: round (with a Catalan name: *pan de payés*, from Catalan *Pa de pagès*, or bread of peasant), the very typical long loaf (with different sizes—normally, in urban contexts, 1/4 kg or 1/2 kg—and different names in the different parts of Spain), rustic loaves, and so forth. There are also many local forms and specialties, some mixing different ingredients: olive oil, herbs, spices, cheeses, and sausages (e.g., Majorcan *sobrasada*). Other popular breads include the French baguettes—very similar to traditional loaves—or Italian *ciabatta*.

Bread is also an important ingredient in traditional Spanish cuisines. Many dishes, such as *gazpacho*, many soups and salads, and especially *migas*, a popular dish whose main ingredient is breadcrumbs, are eaten in various Spanish regions.

In restaurants, no bread and butter plate is normally provided. Bread is set directly on the table. Sometimes bread is also served or used as a popular kind of appetizer, with olive oil and salt.

PULSES

Beans

Although there were already some species of beans in Europe, from the sixteenth century onward, after the contact with the Americas, various new species were imported through Spain. The use of these pulses, from the so-called green and tender beans to dried beans, easily spread throughout the whole territory. Nowadays, some of the most popular regional Spanish recipes use different kinds of beans as the main ingredient: in Asturian *fabada* (a typical dish made with white beans), Catalan *mongetes* with *butifarra* (dried beans with local sausage), beans Rioja style (also known as *pochas*, with *chorizo*), and various hot or cold *empedrados* (literally "stoned").

Symbolically associated with the dead, fava beans were mostly eaten by the lowest classes. They are difficult to digest and cause flatulence. During times of scarcity, they replaced wheat in the making of flour. Favas are included in several popular Spanish recipes ("favas Catalan style" is a particularly renowned one).

Chickpeas

Chickpeas have been cultivated since ancient times. They were characteristic of the diet of humble people and their use became widespread in the various Spanish cuisines. They are the basic ingredient of diverse soups and stews and are eaten dried or boiled, sometimes in the form of purée, as a main dish or as a side dish. Chickpeas are one of the main ingredients of the popular stews in almost all Spain.

Lentils

Lentils are among the most ancient cultivated plants and a rich source of protein and iron. Lentils are the base of several Spanish dishes (such as *lentejas con chorizo*—lentils with *chorizo*) or are used as stuffing. There are lentil salads and tasty lentils with cream. Their consumption, together with that of other pulses, is widespread.

Peas

The cultivation of this Mediterranean plant is very ancient and, throughout history, peas have been eaten by both the rich and poor. In Spain few local strains remain. Instead, mainly European or American strains are cultivated.

VEGETABLES

Artichokes

Artichokes have an Arabic name in Spanish: *alcachofas*. They belong to the family of thistle, and are considered as a healthful food. Artichokes are common in Spanish gastronomies, and they are eaten boiled, baked, in salads, fried in batter, or in a vinegar or oil marinade.

Asparagus

Asparagus was held in high esteem in Al-Andalus. Today, asparagus is commonly used in Spain and has managed to find its place in many Spanish cuisines. Those cultivated in the north of the peninsula (especially in Navarra) are particularly famous. Although asparagus appears in some areas in March, it is best when picked in April or May. A proverb states: "*Espárragos de abril, para mi, los de mayo, para mi amo, y los de junio para ninguno*" (*o "para mi burro*") ("April asparaguses for me, May asparaguses for my master, and June asparaguses for no-one" or "for my donkey"). Asparagus (green or wild asparagus) is eaten both fresh and cooked, especially in omelettes, and boiled asparagus preserves are common all over Spain.

Carrots and Turnips

The Arabs imported carrots into the Iberian Peninsula during the Middle Ages. Little by little, they were introduced into the various cuisines and spread from the Mediterranean area to the Atlantic and northern peninsular regions. Carrots are common ingredients in *cocidos* (stews), soups, creams, and in salads. Turnips are not as widely used as carrots.

Cucumbers

Cucumbers originated in Asia and from there they were introduced into the Mediterranean area. Their freshness made them a common food during hot summers. Cucumbers are related to melons (which, later on, acquired the status of fruit) and they are eaten both fresh, in salads, and as ingredients of traditional peninsular dishes, such as the popular *gazpacho andaluz*.

Eggplants

Eggplants were introduced by the Arabs both into Spain and the south of Italy. In Spain, eggplants were not popular because physicians considered them quite unhealthy. There are, however, a wide variety of eggplant dishes (hot or cold, grilled, fried, in salads) in all Spanish cuisines, which still retain (or are variants of) the culinary tradition of the Al-Andalus origin.

Lettuce and Endive

Lettuce and endive are herbaceous plants grown on irrigated land and are mainly eaten raw, especially in salads. They are considered a fresh and light food and are believed to have sedative properties. They are an essential element of a number of salads and side dishes in Spain. Although the United States is the biggest producer of lettuce, in Europe the main producers and consumers are Spain, Italy, and France.

Mushrooms

Although they are neither vegetables nor herbs, mushrooms are very common in Spanish cuisines. Most of them appear at the end of summer, but their quantity and variety increase at the onset of autumn, a wet, but not yet cold, period. All the peninsular territory boasts a wide variety of mushrooms, some of which (such as the *amanita muscaria*) are highly toxic. Mushrooms are collected directly from their wild habitat and are the ingredients of numerous stews, but they are also eaten alone, especially braised, during popular festivals. Among the most renowned mushrooms are champignons, boletus, delicious lactarius, and French mushrooms. Some varieties are also used for curdling cheese and making other dairy products, such as *cuajada* (milk curd), a typical dessert of the north of the Peninsula.

Baskets with different kinds of mushrooms.

Onions and Garlic

Onions and garlic are very popular all over Spain. They were usually associated with the poorest classes, and since ancient times, they have been renowned for their therapeutic qualities and considered to have several medical applications (as a kind of "natural antibiotic"). As for their culinary applications, they are many and widespread: onions are eaten raw, in salads, candied, in vinegar or oil, in soups, fried, boiled, baked, and so forth.

Garlic, like onion, is thought to have many therapeutic properties. As a food it is used in many Spanish dishes and sauces, from the very well known *allioli* or *ajoaceite* ("garlic oil") to the most diverse stews, fried dishes, and soups. Fried in oil, garlic confers to many dishes a very special flavor and aroma appreciated by almost all of Spain.

Fried Eggs with Garlic

A very easy and tasty popular recipe.

Ingredients
- 2 eggs
- 1 cup olive oil

- 3 garlic cloves
- salt to taste

Preparation

Heat the olive oil in a large skillet. Add the garlic cloves and cook until brown (but never black or "burned") and remove. Fry the eggs as usual, and serve with the fried garlic cloves.

Peppers

Peppers came from the Americas and were introduced into Europe through Spain in the sixteenth century. There are some typical varieties of peppers in Spain (such as the *pimientos de Padrón* in Galicia, or the *Pimientos del Piquillo de Lodosa* in Navarre, for example) and they are commonly eaten either raw, in salads, fried, roasted, in stews, or stir-fried. The current varieties in Spain are the result of the adaptation and evolution of this plant to the Mediterranean and European regions. Thus, although they are related to chili peppers, they are seldom hot.

Potatoes

Potatoes are tubers of Peruvian origin. Baked, fried, pureed, as an accompaniment to other foods, or as a main dish, potatoes are an essential and widely eaten foodstuff in Spain. Many popular dishes, such as tasty fried potatoes and fried eggs (fried always in olive oil), or boiled potatoes and other vegetables, and potato stews, are eaten frequently in Spanish homes (both at lunch and dinner time).

Pumpkins and Zucchini

Pumpkins and zucchini are native to the New World, but similar species of gourds had been cultivated in Spain since ancient times. They have been used for human consumption, livestock feed, and ornamentation. Pumpkin and zucchini can be boiled, stewed, made into soup, or more recently, prepared as creams. One of the most appreciated uses is in a cake called *cabello de angel* ("angel's hair"), which is made from candied pumpkin pulp, an important ingredient in sweets and desserts such as *Ensaïmada* (a soft sweet bread), from Mallorca.

Spinach

The Spanish word *espinacas* stems from the Arabic *ispinah*; the Arabs, in fact, imported this plant from Persia. This vegetable, which became familiar through its consumption during Lent, when people abstained from eating meat, is considered a healthful and inexpensive food. Many recipes with spinach are renowned in Spanish cuisines, such as "spinach Catalan way" (with pine nuts and dried raisins), with béchamel sauce, stuffed, and so forth.

Tomatoes

Some European cuisines, such as the Spanish and the Italian ones, could not be understood without considering the influence of tomatoes. However, whereas certain foodstuffs, such as peppers, were easily accepted and soon became popular, only well into the eighteenth century were tomatoes definitively introduced into the culinary methods and habits of Spain, and of Europe in general. Tomatoes are the ingredients of diverse dishes and stews all over the Spanish territory: from *gazpacho*, whose essential ingredient is tomato, to the Catalan *pa amb tomàquet* (bread with tomato) and the numberless tomato-based sauces, stews, soups, salads, and garnishes.

Gazpacho Andaluz

Ingredients
- 2 lb. tomatoes
- 1 green pepper
- 3 garlic cloves
- 1 cucumber
- 1/2 onion
- 1/2 cup olive oil
- 1/4 cup vinegar
- 1 cup breadcrumbs
- salt to taste

Preparation
Wash, peel, and finely chop the tomatoes. Wash the pepper, remove core and seeds, and chop it. Peel and chop the onion and the garlic cloves. Mix all the vegetables in a bowl and add the breadcrumbs, previously soaked in 1 teaspoon water. Dress with oil, vinegar, and salt to taste. Process the ingredients in a blender and sieve the resulting purée. Serve chilled.

Observations
The quantity and the ingredients may vary according to taste. If a more liquidy *gazpacho* is preferred, cold water may be added while blending the ingredients.

Garnish with finely chopped vegetables (pepper, onion, tomato, cucumber, etc.).

Pà amb Tomàquet (Bread with Tomato, from Catalonia)

Ingredients
- 4 slices of bread (1 per person, from one large, round loaf of bread, Spanish or European-style crusty bread such as baguette or *ciabatta*)
- 2–3 tomatoes
- 1–2 garlic cloves
- olive oil
- salt to taste

Preparation
Grill or toast bread slices. Rub grilled bread with garlic halves, then rub tomato halves into bread—really mash them on there—the goal is to soak the bread slices with this tomato juice. Discard tomatoes, and drizzle bread with good olive oil to taste, then sprinkle with some salt. Later, you can top with your favorite complements: ham, cheese, *chorizo*, and so forth.

HERBS

Anise

Anise is a popular aromatic herb and is widely used to flavor cakes and herbal teas. It is considered digestive and is the main ingredient and name of a traditional Spanish liquor.

Aromatic Herbs (Thyme, Rosemary, Oregano, Basil, Chamomile, Mint, Peppermint)

A wide variety of aromatic herbs are commonly used for cooking. The most popular ones are oregano, thyme, rosemary, basil, dill (especially suitable for fish dishes), chamomile, and mint, but other herbs such as marjoram, chervil, sage, and fennel are also used. These herbs have added flavoring and seasoning to stews, salads, and other dishes along the centuries, and they have been used for making sauces, teas (which were generally considered therapeutic, digestive, and disinfectant), as well as liquors.

Cumin

This herb grows profusely in the Spanish mountains. It is used for its pharmaceutical properties and as a flavoring in numerous stews. Due to its abundant spontaneous growth, cumin used to be considered of scarce economic value—this herb appears in some popular Spanish expressions to convey the idea of something that has very low value.[2]

Parsley

Parsley is one of the most commonly used herbs in all Spanish cuisines. It is employed as an essential garnish and as an element of various sauces (e.g., "green sauce") to go with meat and fish (according to a popular saying, parsley "can be found in all sauces"). Parsley is usually obtained for free from butchers, greengrocers, and fishmongers.

SPICES AND SEASONINGS

Cinnamon

Cinnamon was popular in ancient times as an aphrodisiac. It is commonly used in Spanish gastronomy, mainly for the flavoring of desserts such as the popular *arroz con leche* ("rice with milk"), *leche frita* (fried milk), *leche merengada* (milk with cinnamon and sugar), and ice cream. It is also used for flavoring some stews. Cinnamon's intense aroma and unique flavor are particularly appreciated.

Cloves

Cloves are currently used as intense flavoring for various aromatic dishes and stews. Its scent and flavor are hard, penetrating, and sweet. Therapeutic virtues are attributed to cloves, particularly for toothaches.

Honey

Records show that honey was used in Spain since the Neolithic period in order to preserve fruits and other foods. Subsequently, it started to be used for sweetening the first curd preparations. In ancient times, honey was considered the sweetener par excellence and it was so until sugar became predominant. The use of honey in the flavoring of cakes and as a sweetening agent is still widespread, although it is not as common as sugar. Honey is commonly used in many popular desserts, such as *bienmesabe* (made with honey and ground almonds) and the typical Christmas dessert: *turrón*. The production of honey is also important in many Spanish regions, such as Extremadura, Andalusia, and Catalonia, and should be natural and aromatic (from herbs such as thyme or rosemary, or from flowers).

Mustard

Mustard sauce is used in Spain mainly as a dressing for red meats and, lately, for fast food or frankfurters (sausages). It wasn't really popular in Spain before the second half of the twentieth century.

Pepper

Pepper is one of the most highly valued spices in the world and was considered to have medicinal properties. Whereas most European languages have inherited the name of this spice from the Greek *peperi* and the Latin *piper*, the Spanish term stems from the Latin *pigmentum*, which also gave origin to the word *pimiento*, which refers to the vegetable (green or red peppers).

Pimentón (Paprika)

Also from the Latin *pigmentum* stems *pimentón*, the local Spanish specialties of red paprika, sweet or hot (very different also from other products such as the traditional Hungarian bland paprika), are highly valued spices in many Spanish cuisines. *Pimentón de la Vera* (designation of origin), from the Valle de la Vera (Vera Valley) in Cáceres (Extremadura), is particularly renowned.

The capsicum peppers used to produce the sweet *pimentón* are carefully hand-harvested in September to October and sent to warehouses where they are slow-smoked for 15 days. The whole peppers become drenched with the smoke of smoldering oak logs, adding intense flavor while preserving their natural blood-red color. For the hot smoked paprika, several peppers are milled together to make a decidedly piquant—not hot, but tangy—aroma and flavor.

Pimentón is an ingredient in many typical products, preparations, and dishes in all the Spanish cuisines, from the typical *chorizo* or the renowned *sobrasada* from the Balearic Islands, to other important dishes from the south, or from Castile (such as *callos* or tripe), or from the north (such as the Basque *marmitako*—see recipe in this chapter).

Saffron

Saffron is one of the most used natural colorings and the most expensive one, too. The Arabs systematized its cultivation in Spain, which is currently the world's leading producer and exporter. The process whereby this spice is obtained (the stigmas are removed from the blossoms and dried) is carefully and entirely done by hand. Its high price is, in fact, a direct consequence of this labor-intensive process, usually carried out by women in the countryside. Traditionally, saffron has been chiefly used as natural coloring (in dishes such as *paella*, for example), although it has also been considered to have healing properties.

Salt

Throughout history, salt has been a crucial element for food preservation and a qualitative improvement in the food system. In Spain there are various salt mines, especially along the Mediterranean coast: The most popular ones are those of Torrevieja (Alicante), Cardona (Barcelona), Torrelavega (Cantabria), Puerto de Santa María (Cadiz), and also in the Balearic Islands, Navarre, Murcia, and Oriental Andalusia. Fish, which had been a product for immediate consumption, became a trade item and it became possible to preserve it for long periods. In Spain, the best example of this kind of product is the "omnipresent" codfish, traditionally preserved in salt. Other important traditional foods that have been preserved are, among fish, anchovies, *mojama* (tuna dried and salted), and herring; among pork the best example is ham, dried in a windy room after being salted.

Sugar

The cultivation of the sugar cane, which was imported from Asia at first, was introduced by the Castilians and the Portuguese into their Atlantic islands (the Canary Islands and Madeira), and later on into the Caribbean and Brazil. It subsequently replaced honey as a sweetener for cakes, chocolate, coffee, and teas. Sugar is mainly available white (refined: as granulated, superfine, and powdered sugar) and brown (unrefined). Granulated white sugar is commonly used for baking, preserving, and table use (brown sugar is also offered on the table as an alternative to white sugar). Superfine sugar is used especially in baking, and powdered sugar is used for frostings and decorating desserts. Artificial saccharine or sweeteners and sugar substitutes are also available and are becoming more common in homes and particularly in bars and restaurants.

Vanilla

Vanilla, which is native to Mexico, Central America, and the Caribbean area, started to be extensively cultivated and used from the nineteenth century onward. Vanilla is now popular and profusely used (ice creams, cakes, etc.). Many products are actually industrially flavored with artificial vanilla aroma, rather than natural vanilla.

Vinegar

Vinegar, which is sour, fermented wine, is mainly used as a dressing in Spain for salads, pickles, and sauces, and as an ingredient for the maceration of diverse foods (vegetables, olives, fish, etc.). Spain is one of the largest wine producers and consequently, the production of vinegar is also very important. Wine vinegars from Jerez are particularly aromatic and internationally renowned. Cider vinegar is made in the north of Spain.

FRUITS

Apples

Apple crops were improved thanks to Greco-Roman agriculture. Apples are mainly cultivated in the north of the Iberian Peninsula, in the area stretching from Catalonia to Asturias and Galicia. They are commonly eaten as a dessert (fresh or cooked), or used as an ingredient for certain desserts and cakes. Cider, a popular drink of low alcoholic content, is made from the juice of the apple. Grated apples are popularly believed to be a good remedy against constipation.

Capers

Capers were very widespread in the south of Europe and have been used the same way as olives. They are usually eaten as an appetizer, macerated in vinegar, and in salads. Occasionally, they can be also found in some stews and sauces.

Carob Pods

Throughout history, carobs have been widely used as a food in the Iberian Peninsula and the Mediterranean area in general. These fruits have been (and still are) a popular, inexpensive chocolate surrogate.

Cherries

The Romans improved cherry cultivation—also in Spain—although these fruits grew wild in most parts of Europe. Cherries are very popular, and are known to be diuretic and depurative, especially the Mediterranean varieties. The Valle del Jerte (Extremadura) is the largest area in Europe (more than 50 square miles) devoted to the cultivation of cherries (particularly the "picota" variety, very red and sweet). The cherry picking begins in April, and the fruit is ready to eat from the middle of May onward. June is the peak month for flavor, and the harvest continues into early August.

Chirimoyas

The fruits of the chirimoya tree come from Central America. These berries have a green rind and a white pulp, sweet taste, and a slightly rough texture. Chirimoyas are cultivated in warm countries and their cultivation in Spain, especially in the south, has been particularly successful.

Citrus Fruits

Oranges were bitter in ancient times; the sweet fruit that is known nowadays is the result of a later evolution of orange crops (which took place from the sixteenth century onward). The Mediterranean area, and Spain in particular, is now one of the largest European producers. Oranges are widely eaten for dessert and their freshly squeezed juice is very popular. The orange flavor has turned into the base of numberless variations: soft drinks, ice creams, candies, syrups, and so forth. Oranges have also been profusely used in some dishes (such as salads: Andalusian style, for example) and as a garnish. Orange trees, as well as lemon trees, also turned into ornamental plants and they still are, in many streets and squares or in private and public gardens, especially in the Mediterranean area and the south of the peninsula.

Lemons have also been cultivated in the Mediterranean regions. Lemons are considered healthy and their juice has been traditionally used as a dressing for diverse foods—such as seafood and fish, for example—or salads. Lemon juice mixed with water is a traditional refreshing drink. Grapefruit has not prospered much in Spain until recent times and is less important than oranges and lemons.

Dates

Dates are the very sweet fruits of the date palm. Normally eaten dried, they are a sweet dessert but are also eaten as an appetizer or, like plums, are used as a garnish for certain meat stews.

Figs

Mediterranean peoples have eaten the fruit of these trees throughout history. In Spain, fig trees are common in all the Mediterranean areas, from Catalonia and the Balearic Islands to Andalusia. Figs are eaten both fresh as a dessert and dried as a garnish for certain meat stews, cakes, and sweet desserts; and also macerated in liquor. Fig trees are normally culti-vated for fig production, but also, lately, as a decorative tree in private and public gardens, public squares, and so forth.

Grapes and Raisins

Together with wheat and olive trees, grapes belong in the famous Mediterranean trilogy. Grapes, apart from providing the juice from which wine is made, are also eaten as table fruit, although in the past they were scarce in areas where they were not produced, such as those European re-gions that were further north. Grapes are produced almost all over Spain, where almost every region has a wine with designation of origin. They are eaten as dessert and may occasionally be found in some stews, especially meat- and poultry-based ones. Dried grapes, known as raisins, are also very popular and have a sweet and intense taste. Must, which is pressed grape juice not yet fermented into wine, is drunk fresh. From the end of the nineteenth century, but especially in the twentieth century, it became a traditional custom to celebrate New Year's Eve eating grapes at the stroke of midnight, one for each chime. It is said that this celebrating will bring luck during the incoming year. This tradition is still popular nowadays and is followed all over the country.

There are many different varieties of grapes, and every wine is made with a special grape or, normally, with a special combination of different grapes. We can find, for example, among white grapes: Airén (La Mancha), Malvasía (north), Palomino (Andalusia), Pedro Ximénez (Andalusia), Parellada (Catalonia), Viura or Macabeo (Rioja and Mediterranean area), Xarel·lo (Catalonia), and Moscatel (Andalusia and Mediterranean area). Among black grapes are: Cariñena (Aragon and north), Garnacha (Aragón and north), Graciano (Rioja), Monastrell (Mediterranean area), and Tempranillo (north).

Melons

Melons are related to cucumbers, but the current sweet variety of melons are more recent and have come to be considered a fruit rather than a vegetable, and they have acquired a large size through specialized cultivation. Melons and watermelons are very popular, and they are commonly eaten as a dessert. Melons, except for watermelons, are thought to be best eaten during the day.

Membrillos (Quinces)

Membrillos were very popular in Roman Hispania and, later on, in Al-Andalus. The Al-Andalus king of the Mediterranean island of Menorca (Balearic Islands), Saïd Ibn Hakam, even dedicated a poem to quinces:

> Five maids, dressed in yellow,
>
> Their color does not change if they undress.
>
> Their skin is hard and smooth, like virgins are.
>
> They are prisoners in my hands.
>
> Eager to touch the moon,
>
> They go out in their grey cloaks at night,
>
> But as they watch the moonlight shining,
>
> Their skin turns into gold...like virgins are.[3]

Candied quinces are popularly used to make the famous *dulce de membrillo* ("quince jelly"), a well-known dessert that can be eaten plain, with fresh or soft cheese, and with other sweets and fruits.

Olives and Olive Oil

Together with wine and wheat, the olive tree belongs in the famous Mediterranean trilogy. Olives are the tasty fruit of olive trees. They are small, though their size varies depending on the species, and they are usually eaten after being treated in solutions of water, salt, and other ingredients (such as aromatic herbs, spices, vinegars, etc.) that help reduce their bitter taste. Olives are usually various shades of green, black, or brown. Their consumption has extended from the Mediterranean (chiefly from Spain, Italy, and Greece) to the rest of Europe. They are popular as an appetizer and a garnish and can be commonly found in salads and some stews. In Spain, more than 250 varieties of olives are grown; for example: *Hojiblanca, Picudo, Picual, Verdial,* and *Lechín* from Andalusia; *Empeltre* (black) from Aragon; *Cornicabra* from La Mancha; *Manzanilla* and *Verdial* (Extremadura); and the very small and tasty *Arbequina* are from Catalonia.

Olive oil, which is so famous and commonly used nowadays, is extracted from olives. In the Golden Age in Spain (the fifteenth to the seventeenth century) it was associated with the Arabs and the Jews, while Christians used animal fat (especially lard) for cooking. However, over the centuries olive oil became the predominant edible fat and spread toward the inland and northern regions of the peninsula. Olive oil can also be said to mark the difference between the Mediterranean—Catholic or Orthodox—territories, where the olive oil is predominant, and the Protestant north, where the use of animal fat and butter becomes predominant. There are many different olive oils, depending on the different varieties of olives and different processes used. Spain is (with other European countries such as Italy, Greece, and France, but also other Mediterranean countries such as Tunisia) one of the most important producers of olive oil in the world.

Today raw olive oil is a special dressing for salads and other foods, as well as an important preserving ingredient for diverse foodstuffs, such as fish, vegetables, and even meats. In the past decades, cardio-healthy and dietetic properties have been attributed to olive oil, which has turned into one of the pillars of the food regimen known and promoted as the "Mediterranean diet."

Peaches and Apricots

Peaches and apricots were both introduced into Hispania by the Romans. Peaches are a popular food and they are used in the elaboration of well-known desserts, such as peaches in wine or in syrup. The Spanish name *albaricoque* is of Arabic origin. Both fruits, especially peaches, are commonly used in the making of jam.

Pears

The Romans also introduced pear cultivation into the Iberian Peninsula. The traditional indigenous varieties are eaten all over Spain and can be found on the Spanish market almost all year long, from the small and savory pears of San Juan to the fleshy, sweet, and grainy textured *Roman pears* (Rome pears), which were traditionally stored all through the winter. Pears are mainly eaten fresh as a dessert or in salads, although they are also used in some stews, mostly meat stews.

Pineapples

Tropical pineapples are native to the New World, where they were called *ananás*. Their cultivation requires very specific climatic conditions, similar to those of tropical latitudes (such as in the Canary Islands). The names of these fruits in some European languages, such as *piña* in Spanish or "pineapple" in English, show an attempt to assimilate this strange new fruit to some familiar food, in this case the cone produced by pine trees. Other languages, such as French, adopted the original name, *ananás*. Pineapple consumption has spread over the last century, and this fruit is now eaten both fresh and preserved in syrup.

Plums

In Roman times, plums were called *cereola*, which later gave the Castillian name: *ciruela*. The laxative properties of plums are well known. They are eaten fresh, dried, and also macerated in liquor. Occasionally, prunes (dried plums) are used as a garnish for certain meat stews, particularly in Catalonia.

Pomegranates

Pomegranates are produced from the pomegranate tree. They are round, some varieties are sweet and others bittersweet, and their red pulp contains many seeds. In Spain, pomegranate crops can be found in the Mediterranean area in general. The sweeter varieties are eaten fresh, either plain or as ingredients of certain popular recipes (with wine, sugar, and cinnamon, for example). From the most bittersweet and bitter varieties a refreshing syrup is made, which is known as grenadine. It is mixed with water or other drinks.

Prickly Pears

The spiny fruit produced from the nopal or prickly pear cactus are called prickly pears. They originated in America, and when they started to be cultivated in southern Spain, their growth became nearly spontaneous, and they spread across the Mediterranean area as well. Prickly pears are sometimes also called *barbary figs* (referred to *Berbería*, the land of the Berbers, in North Africa) or *Indian figs*.

Strawberries

Small-size varieties of wild strawberries were eaten in Europe in the past, but they became popular when larger-size American varieties started to be imported. Producers and researchers have now come up with a new top-tier variety of Spanish strawberry called "Aguedilla," which has been accorded a higher quality rating in studies than other foreign varieties.

Strawberries are very common ingredients of preserves and jam, and nowadays they are usually eaten as dessert and used in various cakes and sweets. There are important strawberry fields in western Andalusia (at Palos de la Frontera or Lepe, in the province of Huelva) as well as on the Mediterranean Catalan coast (at Calella in the county of Maresme, in Barcelona).

NUTS

Acorns

Acorns are the fruits of the oak tree, also called *árbol bellotero* (acorn tree), and have traditionally been used as cattle feed. They are particularly utilized as a natural food for hogs, which once grew wild in the surroundings of farms. The famous *jamón de bellota* (acorn ham) is actually made from the meat of pigs that feed on this nut. The use of acorns as human food, in the form of flour, was also common in the past.

Almonds

Almonds are among the most popular nuts and Spain is one of the largest almond producers, together with Italy, the United States, Portugal, and Turkey. Production is mainly centered in the Mediterranean area and the Balearic Islands. The city of Reus, in Catalonia, is the most important world trade center of almonds. Almonds are eaten whole, toasted, or salted. Almonds are the basic ingredients of different sweets, such as *turrón* (a nougat of Hispanic-Arabic origin, usually eaten at Christmas) and almond milk, and also in stews and as a basic ingredient for sauces and preparations (such as the *picada,* made with almonds—or hazelnuts—crushed with other ingredients, such as bread, parsley, olive oil, garlic, or saffron). They are also eaten as an appetizer, toasted, and salted.

Chestnuts

Since ancient times, chestnuts have been an important food in the Spanish diet, especially in the north of the Peninsula. Before the arrival of food from the Americas, chestnuts played the role that is played by potatoes today; they were used for making flour and purées and as ingredients of various stews. Chestnuts are still used in many homes in regions such as Galicia—one of the large chestnut producers in Spain. Chestnuts are harvested in autumn (September–October). Traditionally, with the onset of winter, around All Saints Day (November 1), chestnut sellers make their appearance in all Spanish cities, offering brazed chestnuts and sweet potatoes. Chestnuts are used in many desserts and sweets, such as *pure de castañas* (chestnut purée) or *marron glacé* (crystallized chestnut), and are also preserved in syrup.

Hazelnuts

Hazelnut trees are largely cultivated in the Mediterranean area. Hazelnuts were already well liked by the Romans, and they are currently eaten toasted, as an appetizer or snack, as well as in various stews, especially also in the form of *picada* (crushed with other ingredients, such as olive oil, garlic, and parsley). In Spain the largest hazelnut production is centered in the Mediterranean area, especially in Catalonia. There, the city of Reus is, as in the case of almonds and nuts, the capital of hazelnut international trade.

Lupines

Lupines are soaked and commonly eaten in many Spanish regions as an appetizer or a snack, and they are usually eaten after being treated in solutions of water and salt.

Peanuts

Peanuts are native to South America and they were brought to Europe (to the Iberian Peninsula) by the Spaniards and the Portuguese. These nuts are eaten natural or salted, mainly as an appetizer. Among nuts, peanuts have a relatively low price, unlike almonds and hazelnuts.

Pine Nuts

Pine nuts are the seeds of the pine tree. They are small and savory and are eaten fresh or toasted. They are also the ingredient of some meat- and fish-based stews and dishes, sauces and desserts (e.g., the popular Catalan *coca de pinyons*—pine nut pastry). The price of pine nuts is usually higher than that of other nuts.

Pistachios

Pistachios were commonly used by the Arabs, who left their influence in the peninsular cuisines through this product. Their shells are reddish and they are green inside. Fresh pistachios have a very pleasant taste. They are also used in the flavoring of cakes, as a dressing, and as ingredients for anticough syrups. Like other nuts, dried pistachios are eaten as an appetizer or a snack and can be preserved for a long time.

Walnuts

Walnuts are produced from the walnut tree and are very popular either plain or as ingredients of various dishes, stews, sauces, and desserts. To the same family belong other species, such as the valued spice known as nutmeg.

DAIRY PRODUCTS

Milk, both fresh and in the form of dairy products, is a basic and a highly valued foodstuff. In Spain, four main milk-processing techniques can be distinguished:

Milk

- Liquid milk: it is cooled (raw milk); processed (pasteurized, sterilized, UHT); concentrated (elimination of water); fermented (yogurt and other preparations); jellied (thickened); and coagulated.

- Curdled milk: removal of casein; curdling; whey/water removal process; cheese.
- Fat removal: skim milk and butter.
- Utilization of milk by-products (whey, lactoserum): they are concentrated and dried, used as cattle feed.

In Spain, milk has been historically regarded as a complete food and it has been consumed whenever possible, especially by children. In any case, it is worth remembering that the populations that have developed higher tolerance to lactose are the northern ones, while the tolerance degree decreases as one moves toward southern Europe. Spain, one of the most mountainous states of Europe, is a large milk, cheese, and dairy producer, despite the fact that upon entering the European Union, where milk is an excess product, Spain was obliged to reduce milk production. Important milk producing areas in Spain are, in the north, Galicia, Asturias, Cantabria, the Basque Country, Castilla-León, and Catalonia, and in the south, Andalusia.

Cheese

Cheese is a product made from curdled milk, which may subsequently be treated in various ways (drying, salting, smoking, ripening, etc.) and may be molded in many different shapes. In Spain, cheese is mainly made from goat, cow, and sheep milk.

Cheese was made by hand on country farms until the nineteenth century, when the first important industries were created. More than 120 different kinds of cheese are made all over Spain. Some of them are of very high quality, belong to the local or regional gastronomic heritage, and are very much appreciated and popular all over the national territory, even beyond Spanish borders.

In some areas of Spain, specific methods of cheese making, using specific kinds of milk, have come under protection (acquiring the so-called designation of origin). This system has enabled producers to *fix* the way of making cheese, preventing change in the production of that specific area. Every designation of origin is ruled by a board that sees to it that the product manufacturing norms are maintained unaltered. Among the most renowned Spanish cheeses are: *Manchego* (Castilla-La Mancha), *La Serena* (Extremadura), *Burgos* (Castilla y León), *Mahón* (Menorca and Balearic Islands), *Idiazábal* (Basque Country), *Roncal* (Navarra), *Tetilla gallega* (Galicia), *Cabrales* (Asturias), *Tronchón* (Aragon, Catalonia, and Valencia), and *Tupí* (Catalonia), to list a few.

Yogurt

Yogurt is a dairy product obtained from the fermentation of milk, which has been previously pasteurized and concentrated. Native to Asia, yogurt was introduced into Western Europe from Turkey and the Balkans. Today, it is industrially made from cow milk (although not exclusively) and, especially from the second half of the twentieth century on, it has become an element of the Spanish diet in its own right. Yogurt is largely regarded as a healthful food, to the extent that, during the first four decades of the twentieth century, it was sold in pharmacies as a highly nutritional dairy product.

MEAT AND SAUSAGE

Chickens and Hens

Today, chicken is an everyday food. It is raised industrially and sold at a very affordable price, although this has not always been so. Only 50 years ago, chicken was a scarce and appreciated meat that the lower classes reserved for special occasions. It was eaten by ill people because it was considered a healthful and light food, especially if it was boiled, and it was also eaten for festivities, even as a Christmas dish. There are countless chicken-based recipes. Noteworthy among them is chicken or hen fricassee (stewed with egg yolks and saffron), a dish that dates to the seventeenth century, as well as many other preparations, such as roasted, boiled, and fried chicken, chicken soup, chicken *chilindrón*, and *al ajillo*.

Ham

Ham, the salted and dried leg or shoulder of the pig, can be also considered a kind of pork sausage. *Jamón serrano* is very popular, and *jamones* are seen hanging in stores, bars, and often in private homes. In a farmhouse, there is very often a room, windy and dry, where the cool winds blow through, curing hams. Like a connoisseur of wine who sniffs the cork, and savors the bouquet, the whiff of ham on the splinter is how a fine *jamón serrano* (or Ibérico) is determined.

Other similar products exist in Europe (Parma ham from Italy, or Bayonne ham from France, for example), even the Smithfield country ham,

Dish (*ración*) of Serrano ham.

from the United States, but the different flavor sets the *jamón serrano* apart. It is cured like a country ham, yet it has 300 percent less salt and is never smoked.

But the king of Spanish hams is the internationally renowned *pata negra* ham. *Pata negra* is the famous Spanish "black hoofed" ham, produced from an ancient breed of Iberian hog. *Pata negra* ham came, normally, from animals that were only fed acorns (*bellotas*) to fatten them up before they were butchered. Acorns provide this *bellota* ham with a wonderful marbling and give them their fabled texture, smell, and taste. As an added bonus, the fat is unusually high in oleic acid, which is known to lower cholesterol levels. *Bellota* ham should be produced from Iberian pork or other Spanish breeds.

Horse and Foal

Although the meat of horses and of their young has been traditionally eaten in the Iberian Peninsula, it is not very popular nowadays. For many centuries, horses were, in fact, very useful for transportation and as cart-animals. Horsemeat consumption was reintroduced into Europe in the nineteenth century. Despite the fact that it was not as popular as it is in other European countries, such as France and Italy, horsemeat has been eaten in Spain during the nineteenth and twentieth centuries, and today it is still possible to purchase it, although it is not commonly eaten. Horsemeat, which is slightly sweeter than beef, is appreciated for its nutritional qualities.

Oxen, Cows, Bulls, and Calves

The cow and the bull are, respectively, the female and the male of their bovine species; the ox is a castrated and tame bull; the calf is the young of the cow that still has milk teeth. While cows are mainly destined for milk production and breeding, and only secondarily for consumption, oxen are chiefly raised for their red meat, although in the past they were employed on the farms as cart animals and beasts of burden. Though less tasty than beef and ox meat, veal is preferred because it is more tender; its offal is also eaten (a well-known dish is made from veal tripe in almost all Spain: the so-called *callos*: chopped tripe stewed with a sauce and other ingredients). Together with ox, veal is the most eaten of the four meats listed here. The case of bull (wild or fighting bull) is different. Bulls are wild, grazing the pastures of the southern half of Spain (especially in Extremadura and Andalucia) and their meat used to be sold and eaten after the animal had died in the bullring. It has never been a popular meat, and its consumption has decreased through the years. Today it is still a rather uncommon food. Because bull meat is much tougher than ox meat, it is chiefly stewed ("bull's tail stew" is a dish that is still cooked nowadays, mainly in restaurants, because bull's tail is becoming increasingly difficult to purchase for home consumption).

Tripe Madrid Style

Ingredients
- 1/4 lb. diced veal tripe
- 1 lb. lamb leg, diced
- 1/2 lb. ham, diced
- 2 *chorizo* sausages, diced
- 2 *morcilla* sausages (blood sausage), diced
- 1 ham bone

- 1 onion
- 1 garlic head
- 1 tbs. flour
- 1 parsley bunch
- 1 bay leaf
- 2 chili peppers
- 1 pinch salt
- 1 tsp. sweet red *pimentón* (smoked paprika) powder
- 1 tsp. hot red paprika powder
- 1/3 cup oil
- 1 cup vinegar
- salt to taste

Preparation

Wash the tripe and lamb leg chunks thoroughly. Put them into a pot and cover in cold water and vinegar. Let them sit for 15–20 minutes and drain. Cover them with fresh water again and heat until the water boils. Remove the pot from the heat and change the water once more. Add the parsley, bay leaf, garlic, half onion (keep the other half for frying), chili peppers, ham, ham bone, and *chorizo* and *morcilla* sausages and cook on low heat for about two and half hours. Fry the remaining onion and stir in the flour and the hot paprika and sweet *pimentón*. Add the resulting sauce to the tripe stew, add salt to taste and let simmer on low heat for about another 15 minutes.

Partridges and Quail

Partridges are small game birds and their meat has been highly valued ever since Roman times. The most abundant species in the Iberian Peninsula is the red partridge. It was usually hunted with decoys, imitating the characteristic call. Partridge meat is usually left to sit for some time after the animal has been killed. According to a popular saying "partridges are to be eaten when they hit your nose," meaning that the meat (as is true of most game) must be eaten when it starts "going off" and smelling, a sign that it has become more tender.

Quail are also very popular. They are smaller than partridges and are usually seasoned with salt and pepper and baked. Their attractive spotted eggs are eaten as an appetizer or as ingredients in various *tapas*, hors d'oeuvres, and salads. They are also used (with their shells) as a garnish for some dishes.

Pork and Wild Boar

Through history, pork has been, perhaps, the most popular meat in Western Europe. In Spain, as the popular saying has it, "everything that comes from pig is used." Spanish breeds are very appreciated, chiefly the Iberian one. Lard was used for cooking in Spanish homes until the nineteenth century and even later, except during Lent, when it was replaced by olive oil. In Spain, nine main parts of pork meat can be distinguished: ham, sirloin, chine, ribs, shoulder, brisket, head, neck, and feet. Suckling pigs (called *lechón* or *cochinillo*) are also a popular dish, especially, although not exclusively, in Castilla, where the city of Segovia is particularly famous for its roast suckling pig, which is cooked only a few days after its birth.[4] Roast suckling pig (known under many different names in Spain, such as *tostón, cochifrito, rostrizo*) is the most widespread recipe, although there are many others that are also popular (stuffed and stewed piglet, piglet in sauce, etc.).

Wild boars are all over the peninsula. Boar meat has a stronger taste than pork and it is considered tastier, although it is also tougher and must be cooked after being previously macerated, as in the case of other large game, such as deer. A well-known sausage is made from the boar's head and other ingredients, which bears the same name ("boar's head").

Rabbit and Hare

Rabbit meat is very popular and is widely eaten all over Spain. Rabbit meat is best eaten during the winter, preferably when the animal is between three and nine months old. Rabbit meat is the base for various typical regional dishes and stews, such as braised rabbit with *allioli* (garlic sauce), rabbit hunter-style, rabbit *al ajillo* (with garlic), and so forth. Hares, which are also small game, but much larger in size than rabbits, are common in Iberian mountains. Unlike other meats, hare meat must be eaten fresh, soon after the animal has been killed, and the hare must be young, between three and six weeks old. However, the meat keeps its quality until the hare is more or less one year old, and, in the case of female hares, up to their second year of age.

Sausage

Pork has traditionally been an important food supply in Spain through the centuries, because it could be preserved all year long. Sausage consists of pork seasoned with spices, dried or fresh, which can be preserved for

Market stand with different *embutidos* (pork products and sausages: ham, *chorizos*, etc.).

much longer than fresh meat. The name *embutido* (sausage, literally "cased/stuffed") alludes to the traditional technique used for preserving meat. The animal's intestines are thoroughly washed and stuffed with the seasoned meat, following various recipes. There is a wide variety of sausage in the peninsula, each having specific ingredients and drying degrees: *butifarra* (raw or cooked, white or black), *morcilla* (made from blood and onion or rice), *salchichón* and *longaniza* (made from lean salted meat, dried and seasoned), the famous *chorizo* (with hot/sweet red *pimentón*), and *lomo embuchado* (cased chine, made from dried and seasoned chine).

Stag and Deer

Deer venison is among the most appreciated wild game meats and has always been abundant in the Iberian Peninsula. Traditionally, deer hunting during the Middle Ages and the modern age was the prerogative of the nobles. Deer meat is tough and difficult to digest, which is natural for an animal that lives wild in the mountains, and its taste, like that of game in general, is stronger than that of livestock and farm animals. The favorite parts of deer are the hind legs, although the ribs and fore legs are also appreciated. Deer meat is usually roasted, but it is often left to sit in wine, vinegar, oil, or other ingredients (onion, bay leaf, herbs, berries, etc.) for five to seven days, for it to become more tender. Fallow and roe deer venison are usually more tender than stag venison. Deer meat is not eaten much nowadays, and the law currently protects some species. In any case, venison is quite common on the market, especially during the large game hunting season. Its price is higher than that of farm animals in general.

Turkey

Turkey originated in North America and reached the Old World (more specifically France, from where it spread to the rest of the countries) well into the modern age. The custom of having turkey for Christmas lunch or dinner dates to the eighteenth century and originated in France. In Spain, however, turkey did not become a Christmas Eve food until the nineteenth century, and even today, this practice is not very common.

FISH AND SEAFOOD

Fish has been always a prominent food in Spain. There were important salting factories in the south and the east in ancient times (during the Phoenician, Greek, Roman, and Arabic periods) and fish preserves (such as the Roman *garum* mentioned in the previous chapter) were renowned. Nowadays, Spain has one of the world's largest fishing fleets; undoubtedly the largest of the European Union, and it is one of the main fish consumers and importers in the world. However, fish consumption was limited in the past. Due to the fact that it could not be easily preserved and transported, fresh fish was only eaten in coastal areas or in regions that were close to the coast. In the past, fish was less valued than meat and was regarded as a food of little substance, frequently associated with Lent and ecclesiastical prohibitions and bans. Cod is a special case. This fish, despite the fact that it was not native to the waters of the peninsula, has been captured by Iberian fishermen in the northern European seas for ages (the Basque people gained fame as fishermen and whalers during the Middle Ages). This is due to the fact that cod was salted, which guaranteed its preservation for a long time.

Anchovies

Anchovies are blue fish. In Spain two different names are given to anchovies, depending on whether they are fresh or cured. *Boquerón* is eaten fresh or in vinegar marinade (according to the popular recipe: fresh anchovies are cleaned, cut into fillets, and macerated in a marinade of vinegar, water, garlic, or spices). *Anchoas* are anchovies that have been blended and salted. Fresh anchovy recipes are famous in areas that are very different, such as the Basque Country and Andalusia. Among the most renowned anchovies are those of L'Escala, on the Catalan Costa Brava.

Anglerfish

This is a white fish that is fished for all year long. It was a favorite of ancient Greek and Roman cooks. Subsequently, however, the anglerfish's popularity with the Spanish population dwindled and was not recovered until the second half of the twentieth century. Nowadays, anglerfish can be said to be one of the most popular species in the Spanish gastronomy, especially along the coast. Anglerfish dishes include the Balearic anglerfish stew, the Catalan "Anglerfish with potatoes and *allioli*," anglerfish with potatoes and peppers from Eastern Andalucía, Galician *calderada*, Asturian anglerfish with cider, and the Basque anglerfish in green sauce.

Codfish *(Bacalao)*

Cod *(bacalao)* cannot be found in the waters close to the Spanish coasts. It lives in the cold North and Baltic Seas, Iceland, and Newfoundland, where it was fished in the past by Iberian fishermen. Basque whalers came across it while chasing whales in the North Sea, on their way to the coasts of Newfoundland.

Cod is preserved in salt and it was and still is largely eaten and prepared in countless ways in the peninsula, both in Spain and in Portugal. This fish was particularly popular during Lent, when people abstained from eating meat. Today, although religious practices are not as common any longer, codfish is still eaten in many ways by part of the population during Lent. The Spanish cod fishing fleet has gained importance again recently, and this fish is commonly eaten. There are famous cod-based recipes almost all over Spain (cod *ajo arriero*, with *allioli*, with raisins and pine nuts, with honey) but the ones from the Basque Country are perhaps the most renowned: codfish *pil pil* and codfish *vizcaína* style.

Different pieces of salt cod (*bacalao*).

Spanish codfish is never fresh but traditionally preserved in salt (for a long voyage from the North Atlantic to the Iberian Peninsula). This kind of preparation confers to Spanish (and also Portuguese) codfish a special flavor, but it is always necessary to desalt the codfish before cooking (except in a few popular preparations, such as salads), changing the water two, three, or even four times.

Codfish *Pil Pil*

Ingredients
- 2 lb. codfish
- 6 garlic cloves
- olive oil
- salt to taste

Preparation
Desalt the cod by soaking for 24 hours, changing the water frequently. Cook it on low heat. Put some oil and three garlic cloves into a separate earthen skillet. Fry

the remaining three garlic cloves in some oil in a frying pan and remove from heat. Place the cod chunks into the skillet and pour over some of the stock obtained by boiling the fish. Cook on low heat, gently shaking the skillet until the sauce thickens, to prevent sticking. Add the frying oil that was left in the pan little by little as the sauce becomes thick (about 15 minutes).

Eels and Elvers

Eels and elvers (baby eels) are bluefish. Their names stem from the Latin *anguilla* (whip), which alludes to their elongated shape. These fatty fishes were much appreciated by the ancient Greeks and Romans and were regarded as a choice morsel during the Middle Ages. Later on, eel consumption decreased and this fish became less common. Elvers are currently considered a delicacy and are highly valued, especially in the Basque gastronomy.

Hake

This white fish is fished all year long and is abundant along the coasts of Europe, northern Africa, and northeast Africa. This fish is highly valued by Spanish consumers, though in most areas (except for the Basque Country and the Cantabrian cornice), it has become popular only since the beginning of the twentieth century. The fact that hake can be easily preserved by freezing them at sea has favored the consumption of this fish at a price that is more affordable than that of fresh hake. Almost all its body is used: the tail fin and the central part (cut in slices or whole) are particularly appreciated. The *kokotxas* (Basque term that indicates the throat area of the fish) and the eggs are also popular. Even their head is used to add flavor to fish soups and stocks. The most famous hake recipes come from the Basque and Cantabrian areas (hake with cider, hake Basque style, *kokotxas*, etc.).

Herring

This bluefish cannot be found on the Mediterranean or the Atlantic Iberian coasts, but has been fished since ancient times, especially by the Basques, in the northern Atlantic latitudes. Pressed and salted herring have almost always been popular and affordable for the common people. During the nineteenth century and part of the twentieth century, herring were still a common food on the humblest tables.

Sea Bream

This white fish has a white and soft meat. It is renowned all over the peninsula, especially along the Cantabrian cornice. Roast bream was (and partly still is) a traditional dish in many inner regions (such as Castille and Aragon) on Christmas Eve.

Tuna

Tuna are migratory fish, common both in the Atlantic and in the Mediterranean seas, where they breed (red tuna breed along the Western Mediterranean coasts and white tuna in the bay of Cadiz, in Eastern Andalusia, Galicia, and the Atlantic area).

Tuna are still an important ingredient in the contemporary Spanish gastronomies. Many exquisite ancient dishes, in their essence, are continued in current Spanish cuisines. These include salted tuna steak, preserved in oil, and *mojama* (dried and salted tuna). Tuna has triggered the creation of many preserving industries: it is mainly preserved in olive oil. Spain is the main consumer and exporter of tuna.

Marmitako

This typical Basque dish gets its name from the receptacle in which it is prepared: the *marmita* (pot). This full-bodied stew, which is normally eaten during the summer months, is a highly coveted specialty and often requested in the finest restaurants.

Ingredients
- 2-1/2 lbs. fresh tuna
- 2 lbs. potatoes
- 1 lb. tomatoes
- 3–4 red peppers
- 6 green peppers
- 1 onion
- 8 garlic cloves
- 1 generous dash of olive oil
- 1 tbs. flour
- 1 tbs. smoked paprika
- 6 bread slices
- 1 hot chili pepper

Preparation

Bake the two kinds of peppers, peel them, and cut them vertically into strips. Fry them on a low heat together with a garlic clove. Peel and chop the remaining garlic and the onion, fry them in oil, always stirring, to prevent burning. When the mixture is golden brown, add the flour, the smoked paprika, and the tomatoes, seeded and chopped. Simmer for 20 minutes and add the fried peppers. Let cook for another five minutes.

Peel and dice the potatoes and boil them in a pot. Remove the skin from the tuna, cut it into chunks, and add these into the pot when the potatoes are nearly cooked. Five minutes later, add the fried vegetable preparation, the chili pepper, and the bread slices and let cook for another 20 minutes.

Whale

Whales are not fish, but marine mammals. Since prehistoric times, whale meat has been popular in all Atlantic Europe. Whales provided meat as well as oil, skin, and fat. Basque whalers, who plied the northern European seas since in the Middle Ages, are legendary. From the late Middle Ages on, whale meat was commonly eaten not only in the Atlantic regions of Spain, but also the inner Meseta, where it was eaten smoked. From the modern age onward, however, both whale consumption and fishing dramatically and progressively decreased, and today it is not possible to purchase whale meat. In 1986, Spain agreed to give up whaling before the International Whaling Commission.

DRINKS AND HERBAL TEAS

Absinthe

Absinthe was allegedly invented in Switzerland by Pierre Ordinaire in 1792 as an all-purpose remedy made with "Artemisia absintum," considered a drug in large quantities, and prepared as a commercial liquor by Henri L. Pernod in France. It was nicknamed in French *La Fée Verte* (The Green Fairy); a nickname that has stuck. Absinthe is a symbol of inspiration and daring, associated with the artistic life (as it was in France in the nineteenth century) and is sometimes used as an aphrodisiac. A ban on the drink was imposed in almost every European country and in the United States after World War I, except in Spain and Portugal, where absinthe has been always legal and produced following the traditional formula, even if it is not a popular liquor, as it was in France. Absinthe's production is controlled and has long been considered a toxic substance that causes degenerative brain damage. It is always made in the French way: sugar is placed on a spoon and suspended over a tall glass filled with a shot of green absinthe. Then ice-cold water is dripped over the sugar and allowed to fall in beads into the drink. Absinthe is mainly produced in the Mediterranean area and the Balearic Islands.

Anise

Anise spirit (widely known as *anís*) is a highly alcoholic drink distilled from the aromatic herb that bears the same name. There are two main varieties of anise: dry and sweet. It has traditionally been consumed as a digestive drink, at the end of meals.

Beer

Curiously enough, the most ancient remains of beer in Western Europe have been found in the Iberian Peninsula: in Catalonia.[5] But beer would remain ignored in Spain for a long time. From the nineteenth century on, important beer breweries were created in Spain, and beer consumption started to increase. Beer really became established in the second half of the twentieth century and Spaniards are currently some of the largest beer drinkers in the Mediterranean area, although well behind central and northern Europeans. Spanish beers have a good reputation all over Europe.

Brandy

Brandy, a distilled form of wine, acquires a higher alcoholic content. Usually it is left to rest in wooden barrels. It is normally consumed at the end of meals or in bars and has turned into a typical accompaniment to coffee. In Spain, the main brandy-producing areas are Andalusia (Jerez) and Catalonia (Penedès). Unlike other similar spirits, such as French cognac, Spanish brandy has a characteristically dark color.

Cava

The term *cava* indicates quality sparkling wine fermented in the bottle after a traditional method (also known as "champenoise"; in other words *cava* is the Spanish equivalent of the French designation of origin "Champagne"). *Cava* has been made in Catalonia since the nineteenth century;

more specifically, it is made from the white wines of the Penedès area. The quality of Catalan *cava* is excellent and this wine is exported internationally. Some of the largest multinational sparkling wine companies are Catalan. *Cava* is also produced in other Spanish areas such as Aragon, Valencia, Extremadura, and La Rioja, but not in as large quantities and it is not as popular. This sparkling wine is a traditional drink on festive occasions. Nowadays, it is difficult to conceive of a celebration without *cava*, and its consumption is currently increasing, to the extent that *cava* has begun to replace wine during meals.

Chocolate

Cocoa is native to the Americas, from where the Spaniards brought it into the Iberian Peninsula at the beginning of the sixteenth century. It soon became popular, especially among the wealthy classes and the clergy. Chocolate spread swiftly as soon as sugar was added to its preparations. Chocolate became so popular in Spain that at the beginning of the eighteenth century there were already some factories that specialized in its production. When consumed as a hot drink, it was particularly appreciated thick. When, in the eighteenth century, King Philip V sold the, until then, secret formula of chocolate, it became widely popular in the rest of Europe, especially through Italy and France. This preparation became known as "chocolate Spanish style." However, chocolate consumption was not a mass phenomenon and it remained the prerogative of certain social elites. Despite the fact that the use of chocolate for cake making dates to as early as the modern age, chocolate bars, as they are eaten nowadays, were invented much later, in the nineteenth century. Aphrodisiac and invigorating properties have traditionally been attributed to chocolate and it is also considered to be a remedy against depressive symptoms.

Cider

Cider is made from apple juice and is low in alcohol. In Spain, cider is mainly produced in the Cantabrian area, the most renowned ciders being the Asturian and the Basque ones. A soft and tasty vinegar cider is also produced.

Coffee

In the nineteenth century, coffee replaced beer and wine as a morning drink, providing a higher degree of alertness during the day. It is a highly social drink, popular in cafés both in Spain and in the rest of Europe, drunk after meals, and on social occasions and meetings. Coffee is consumed in various ways in Spain: it is drunk plain and black, aromatic, and with abundant milk. A popular way of drinking coffee in Spain is in the form of *cortado* ("cut"), a sort of espresso with a dash of milk, which softens its bitter taste.

Must

Must is the natural juice obtained from grapes (that is, it is not fermented or turned into wine). It is a very common drink, especially in the north of the Iberian Peninsula.

Orujo (Aquavit)

Orujo is a spirit distilled from the remains of the skin, seeds, and stems of grapes left after pressing. *Orujo* is traditionally homemade and has a high alcoholic content. The *Orujos* from Galicia are particularly renowned; they are either white (with no added ingredients) or flavored with herbs or honey.

Rum

This spirit is distilled from sugarcane, and its Spanish consumption and production are bound to Cuba, which remained under Spanish domination until 1898, and more specifically, to the Catalan emigrants who resided on the island. The product distilled from sugarcane was commonly consumed in Cuba, and it was a handmade, bitter, and strong drink. Some of the most important rum distilleries today were created during the Spanish rule, just like other distilleries of the peninsula, which made rum from Cuban sugarcane (the most ancient ones were also located in Catalonia). It is worth highlighting, in this respect, that rum was an important drink for the "Indians" (name for Spaniards who left Cuba and went back to Spain at the end of the nineteenth and beginning of the twentieth century). Rum is commonly drunk with coffee; some *quemados* (*cremats*, in Catalan, which literally means, "burnt ones")[6] made from this spirit even contain some toasted coffee beans.

Water

Spain, as a member of the European Union, is subjected to a common legislation with respect to water production and commercialization.

Spain, together with Italy and France, is an important producer and consumer of bottled mineral water. The main producing areas usually coincide with mountainous regions: Catalonia and Aragon, Andalusia, Galicia, and the Cantabrian area.

Wine

Spain is currently one of the main producers and consumers of red, white, and rosé wine in the world (as well as the aromatic wines from Andalusia). Today, Spain has (together with France and Italy) some of the most valued wine designations of origin in the world. Among them, the most internationally renowned are Rioja, Ribera del Duero, Penedès, and Priorat. As for aromatic wines, the most popular are those from Jerez (the famous *Sherry*), Manzanilla (from san Lúcar de Barrameda, Cadis) and also Montilla-Moriles (Cordova); whereas among sweet wines, the most distinctive ones are *Malaga* wine together with Muscat and *garnacha* wines. On the northern peninsular coast, fine white and fresh wines are produced: *Ribeiro*, the Galician *Rías Baixas*, and the Basque *Txacolín*. Other prominent designations of origin are those of Costers del Segre (Catalonia), Toro and Valladolid (Castilla y León), and the wines from Navarra, Somontano, Borja and Cariñena (Aragon), Jumilla (Murcia), aromatic wines from Montilla and Moriles (Andalusia), Castilla-La Mancha, and the white wines from Rueda (Castilla-La Mancha), Extremadura, Valencia, or the wines from Binissalem or Pla i Llevant (Mallorca and Balearic islands).

NOTES

1. The Spanish term *companaje,* which stems from the Latin *companatium* (that is, *cum panis* = with bread). The same word appears in various Romance languages.

2. The expressions referred to are, for example, *no me importa un comino* (literally "it bothers me less than a cumin seed" that is, "I couldn't care less"; and "no vale un comino" (it's not worth a cumin seed).

3. From Josep Piera, "El oriente de al-Ándalus, una cocina de frontera," in *La alimentación mediterránea: Historia, cultura, nutrición,* ed. F. Xavier Medina (Barcelona: Icaria, 1996).

4. According to the Roman author Pliny, piglets were ready to be consumed as early as four days after they had been born.

5. More specifically at the Iberian site of Cova Sant Sadurni (Barcelona), which dates from the Bronze Age, about 5000 B.C. (See: Edo, M., Banco, A., and Villalla, P. "Cova Sant Sadurni," in *International Congress on Beer in Prehistory and*

Antiquity. Barcelona, October 3–5th, 2004 (forthcoming). See also: Jordi Juan-Tresserras, "La cerveza prehistórica: Investigaciones arqueobotánicas y experimentales," in *Genó: Un poblado del Bronce final en el Bajo Segre,* ed. J.L. Maya, F. Cuesta, and J. López Cachero. (Barcelona: Publicacions de la Universitat de Barcelona, 1998).

6. Method whereby rum is heated (burnt) together with other ingredients, such as sugar, coffee beans, or lemon, to obtain a less alcoholic drink, which is thought to be beneficial for some minor ailments, such as colds.

3

Cooking

Since the early twentieth century Spain has changed from a prominently rural and agricultural country into a modern industrialized nation that ranks among the top 10 world's economies, and into one of the pillars of the European Union.[1] This process has brought along deep cultural and social transformations, which have affected both the structure of families and the distribution of working and leisure time, and consequently, the timing of all those activities related to food, both inside and outside the home.

THE TRANSFORMATION OF WOMEN'S ROLES IN THE HOME AND AT WORK

At the onset of the twentieth century Spain was undergoing a crisis: it had just lost a war against the United States (1898) as well as its last American and Asian colonies (Cuba, Puerto Rico, and the Philippines). In general terms, Spanish society was chiefly agricultural and women occupied a subordinate position within the home, where they were responsible for house chores and child raising. However, women's activities were not confined to household duties, as they also worked in the fields and tended farm animals. In some cases, they worked in factories, as maids, or even doing extra piecework at home to contribute to the household income.

Women were in charge of household chores, and among these, cooking was a primary activity. On one hand, women did the shopping and the cooking, managing the scarce economic resources of the lower strata of the population. On the other, over generations they were the repositories and transmitters of culinary lore, family culinary recipes, and traditions.

During the Second Spanish Republic (1931–1936), women acquired a modern and urban role and Spain was one of the first European countries to allow female suffrage and to rely on various female deputies and ministers. Yet, this was only a brief parenthesis, which ended with the establishment of a fascist dictatorship after the bloody Civil War (1936–1939). The new government brought back a more traditionalist conception of women, emphasizing their role as "queens of the house," wives, and mothers. The kitchen again was the place where women carried out their main household activities, and they continued to be the ones in charge of buying and cooking food. In this period, the nurturing and caretaking role was reflected and endorsed by the advertisements related to food and household chores, which exclusively addressed women, emphasizing the tasks and duties that housewives were expected to carry out.

Women's confinement to the domestic milieu would continue until the 1960s and 1970s, with the imposition of democracy. Then, women recuperated their place within the public sphere of life, entering the political, social, cultural, and labor worlds. All this would trigger important changes in the domestic environment, and consequently, in what was related to food and cooking practices.

With the incorporation of women into the paid workforce, the time that used to be devoted to buying and cooking food was spent on public and productive work. From this time onward, as in other industrialized Western countries, women spent less time buying and preparing food. In recent decades, household appliances have become increasingly essential in the kitchen as timesaving devices. The elaborate dishes of grandmothers and mothers have now been replaced by ready-made dishes or simpler recipes. In addition, children, who some years earlier used to eat in their homes, have started to eat their lunch at school with ever-increasing frequency, because their mothers work outside the home. In homes where extended families live together (something that has become less common) the role of grandmothers with respect to the preservation of eating habits and to family nurturing is very important. Another change was that dinner became the one meal that all the family members ate together (women were still mostly in charge of preparing it), though after working all day, families would now appreciate quick and easy-to-prepare dishes.

While women are responsible for preparing food, men (in various parts of the country) are often in charge of outdoor cooking and of special celebrations that involve roasting and grilling chops and sardines, and cooking *paella*. Outdoor cooking is usually done for holidays, either for family or guests. Domestic cooking is still a woman's task, while "exterior" or "public" cooking traditionally falls within the masculine range of activities.

An interesting phenomenon relative to gendered cooking practice is that of the gastronomic societies of the Basque Country, created in the nineteenth century, where men cook for their fellow members (see also the Basque Country section in Chapter 4). It is highly significant that, until very recently, these gastronomic societies have not admitted female members (except as occasional guests on specific holidays). This practice is still maintained in the most traditional societies.

Nowadays, complete equality between the sexes, as far as domestic duties are concerned, has not been yet reached. However, much as been achieved, and it can be foreseen that such equality will certainly be reached in the future. The incorporation of women into the public world implied a slow, but significant, incorporation of men into domestic activities, including cooking. Other changes include the transformation of the familial unit, traditionally made up of a married couple, children, and grandparents, into a wider variety of family forms: heterosexual and gay married and unmarried couples, with or without children (incidentally, Spain has one of the lowest birth rates in Europe), one-parent families (singles, widow/widowers, divorcees), and so forth. All this has had important repercussions on shopping and food preferences, as well as on who is in charge of cooking. In the urban milieu, although not exclusively there, food comfort, quickness, and food security have become of primary importance.

It is worth noting that, like other industrialized societies, Spain is witnessing a revaluation of cooking and resurgence of traditional products and dishes, possibly as a reaction against the increasingly industrialized and uniform ready-made cuisine. The widespread renewed taste for home-made food, family recipes, and so forth is taking place within a global context of rapid social change toward gender equality in all aspects of life.

COOKBOOKS

Cookbooks have always been important in Spain. In general, it can be observed that from the eighteenth century onward, Spanish cookbooks would faithfully include recipes and methods by great cooks of the previous century, and that French innovations would be introduced much later. The book *Arte de Cocina (The Art of Cuisine)* by Martínez Montiño, written in the seventeenth century (1611), was re-edited a number of times during this century, while new culinary books were scarce. Among them are the works of Juan de Altamiras like *Nuevo arte de cocina sacado de la esuela de experiencia económica* (*New Art of Cuisine from the School of Economic Experience*; 1786). Also the cookbook of Domingo Hernández de Maceras was important and also re-edited (less than Martínez Montiño's cookbook) in this period. Published in 1607, this cookbook describes dishes that go back to the "big culinary Spanish tradition" of the sixteenth century.

The French influence was strong from the nineteenth century on and resulted in a large quantity of cookbooks, mostly anonymous, that were translated or copied all over Spain. However, as a reaction against this tendency, especially in the second half of the nineteenth century, there was a revaluation of folklore and of the products of popular culture, including food. As a result, various cookbooks were written that illustrated the peculiarities of the diverse Spanish gastronomies.[2]

The most complete and influential recipe book published in Spain in this period was the work of the marchioness of Parabere, and it was re-edited countless times after its first 1933 edition. The book includes the outstanding work of cook Ignacio Doménech. Throughout the century male and female cooks wrote a number of books on popular cuisine that were addressed to housewives; they provided recipes, tips, and advice on household economics.

As the century advanced and "women's magazines" became widespread, especially from the 1960s onward, recipes became an essential element of such publications and both local and international cuisine became popular. Likewise, the number of cookbooks progressively increased, and they broadened their scope, including more information on exotic and foreign gastronomies, as well as practical, traditional, monastic, healthy, Spanish, regional, and Mediterranean cuisines.

PROFESSIONAL COOKS AND CHEFS

While during the twentieth century the home had been mainly a female space, the "public sphere" and thus, commercial cooking, as mentioned, has been a typical male environment. Whereas housewives were great, unknown cooks, professional male cooks became the trademark of their own restaurants and publicly exhibited their gastronomic skills. Conversely, women who worked in restaurants occupied a secondary and largely ignored position.[3] Female authors who wrote quality cookbooks were an exception.

Although the gastronomic activities of hotels and restaurants have been famous ever since the nineteenth century, it was only well into the twentieth century that the fame of chefs started to transcend their own kitchens, and that they became socially prominent. Toward the late twentieth century, some Spanish cooks started to gain international renown. The success of famous chefs (such as Ferran Adrià, Juan Maria Arzak, Santi Santamaria, or Karlos Arguiñano) is due to traditional cooking on one hand (Basque and Catalan cuisines, to mention the most prominent ones), and investigation into new culinary techniques on the other. In recent years, however, women have joined the ranks of famous international cooks (e.g., Carme Ruscalleda and Elena Arzak). Recently, cuisine has also invaded the media. Various cooks conduct radio and TV programs, write articles, and are in charge of specific magazine sections, reports, and so forth. This is due to the fact that the Spanish population is greatly interested in cuisine and gastronomy; but at the same time, such programs reflect the Spanish society with its changes and new needs. For example, some of them deal with homemade and popular dishes, others with *haute cuisine*, and others are addressed to particular groups, with themes such as "cooking for singles" or "easy and quick cooking."

PROCEDURES AND EQUIPMENT

The Iberian Peninsula occupies a strategic position between the Mediterranean Sea and the Atlantic Ocean, between Europe and North Africa; thus, it is culturally and historically at the crossroads between Asia and America. Over the centuries, as a result of the influence of various civilizations, the exchange and distribution of diverse culinary traditions and products took place in the peninsula, and its gastronomy became a combination of many different cuisines. It is worth noting that a cuisine is made of procedures rather than recipes; and that new products are assimilated or rejected by "culinary lore" depending on whether or not they are accepted into existing cooking practices. Thus, foods are either easily integrated into traditional eating habits or excluded by the culinary corpus in question.[4]

Procedures

Despite the wide variety of products and dishes of the various Spanish cuisines, some common culinary procedures, with major or minor variations, can be found all over the Iberian Peninsula. Sometimes, the same methods can be found in Europe or the greater Mediterranean area. Some of the most common Spanish cooking procedures are addressed in the following sections.

Roasting, Grilling, and Pan Broiling

Roasting, grilling, and broiling have been mainly used to cook meat, although fish, vegetables, and dried fruits are also prepared in these ways. Roast meats are quite popular all over Spain in all their varieties: roast lamb, roast piglet, grilled rabbit, and lamb ribs (in various sauces, for example, in *allioli* sauce). For fish, *sardinadas* (sardine barbecues) are very common in the Cantabrian area, and in the north of the peninsula in general, where this fish is consumed fresh and grilled. Vegetables are also grilled, such as Catalan *calçots* (grilled tender onions), for example, which people usually eat when spending a day in the countryside. In the north of the Peninsula various restaurants are known as *asadores*, after the name of the spit used for roasting *(asador)*. The most renowned ones are in the province of Burgos and Castilla León, and they specialize in roast meat.

Pan broiling consists of cooking food (meat, fish) on a metal pan that has been heated until red hot.

Pickling

Pickling is a popular way of preserving food in Spain, avoiding contact with air and bacteria. Certain foodstuffs, mainly vegetables, such as cucumbers, onions, carrots, and peppers, are easily preserved with this procedure. Olives are usually marinated in salt, water, and herbs. Meat and fish may also be preserved by pickling.

Marinade

Escabeche is a very popular marinade in which fish and meat are macerated. It is made of olive oil, vinegar, garlic cloves, and various spices and herbs (laurel, thyme, fennel, dill, etc.). The most common pickled foods are tuna, mackerel, sardines, and game, which become more tender in a marinade. Occasionally, marinades are also used as sauces and added to food while cooking.

Stews

Stews differ from soups and stocks in that the juices of the cooked ingredients are more concentrated and turn into a liquid sauce that is used to accompany the dish and add flavor. During the Spanish Golden Age (sixteenth and seventeenth centuries), there was a very popular stew called *olla podrida* ("rotten pot"): various foods were boiled in the same pot for some time (even for a few days), and more ingredients and water were added as the stew thickened and the stock evaporated. Nowadays, stews are a very common dish in Spanish cuisines; they are chiefly made with meat and vegetables (such as the popular bean or lentil stews, for example, to which meat chops, pork ribs, sausage, etc. are added).

Frying and Deep Frying

In Spain, frying consists of cooking food in a pan, almost always in boiling oil, and mainly olive oil (less often in fat or lard). Fried dishes have been popular in Spain since early times, as Diego Velázquez's famous seventeenth-century painting "Old Woman Frying Eggs" (in the National Gallery of Scotland, Edinburgh) demonstrates. Until the twentieth century, most foods were fried in pork lard. Olive oil, a lighter fat, became predominant in the last century, though it had already been used in the past, mainly during Lent, when meat and animal products were prohibited for religious reasons. In the Golden Age, Jews and Muslims cooked with olive oil because their religions forbade pork consumption. Thus, using pork lard turned into an important marker of religious identity. As Bachelor Andrés Bernáldez (sixteenth century) observed in his work *Historia de los Reyes Católicos, don Fernando y doña Isabel:* "they cooked meat with oil, which they used instead of pork fat [...] and oil together with meat causes breath to smell; thus, their homes and doors stank of such foods".[5]

Today, food is fried almost all over the Spanish territory, and almost always in olive oil, either directly (potatoes, eggs, vegetables, meat, and fish), or as part of more elaborated dishes (as in the case of the Spanish omelette, or potato omelette, which is made with potatoes that have been previously fried). A popular dish in southern Spain, especially in Andalusia, is *pescaditos fritos*, small-size fish that are deep fried.

Another popular frying method in Spain is frying in batter. Food is first dipped into beaten egg, then coated in flour or breadcrumbs, and last deep fried in boiling oil. Batter is used for frying meat, fish, and vegetables.

Boiling, Bain-Marie, Soups, and Stews

Boiling is a common method for cooking vegetables, eggs, grain, fish, and meat in Spain. It is also regarded as one of the healthiest methods because no fat or other substitutes are added. The fish and seafood soups made in many regions of Spain, especially in the coastal areas, deserve special mention for their variety and richness. Also worth mentioning are the diverse stews (such as the well-known stew Madrid style, or the Catalan *escudella y carn d'olla*) that are a combination of boiled food, soups, and braised dishes. Stews are made by throwing various ingredients into a pot and bringing them to a boil. Commonly used foods include vegetables, different kinds of meat, chicken, chickpeas, and so forth. When the stew is ready, different dishes are served with the main ingredients separated: a bowl of soup first (to which some kind of pasta may be added) and then, separately, vegetables and pulses (if there are any) and the boiled meat (some of it previously seasoned with spices, to make it tastier). A similar procedure to boiling is bain-marie cooking. In this case, food is put into a double boiler so that it is only indirectly heated. This method is used for foods that cannot be heated directly, that are not desirable to boil, or that change if warmed up (such as solid chocolate for example, which would melt).

Baking

The first baking ovens were used for baking bread and were traditionally heated with wood. In the course of time, ovens have turned into one of the almost omnipresent elements in the Spanish kitchen, especially among the middle and upper classes and later on, after the modern age, also among the lower classes. Ovens were either placed in one of the kitchen walls, near the floor, or else they were an independent cavity, leaning against the wall or fixed to it. Sometimes they were in a separate room, inside or outside the house (in the yard, for example, if there was one). Ancient wood ovens were replaced, already in the nineteenth century, by charcoal ones, and later on by electric and gas ovens. A wide variety of foods can be cooked in the oven: from bread and cakes to meats and various kinds of fish and foods, such as pasta, purees, and even snails. Bread ovens are particularly popular, to the extent that in some areas of Spain, bakeries are known as "ovens." The microwave oven is quite popular today. In 1988, 1.6 percent of Spanish families had a microwave oven at home; in 1997, this number was increased to 39.2 percent.[6]

Jams, Jellies, Honey, and Alcohol Preserves

Jam is a preserve made with fresh fruit or other similar products, such as tomato for example, cooked with sugar or honey. As in other countries, jams and jellies are very popular in Spain, particularly because this method allows the preservation of fruit, a food that is highly perishable, for a long time. The candying process, that is, coating fruit in sugar, also facilitates preservation; besides, it turns fruit into a tasty sweet, which is common throughout Spain. In Spain, as in all Europe, both techniques became widespread from the sixteenth century on, due to a greater availability of sugar, and the foods, thus prepared, gained some fame as medical and healthful preparations. In any case, in Spain, since early times, it was common to coat fruit and other kinds of food in honey to isolate them from air and bacteria. Also worth mentioning is the introduction of fruit (and other foods) into spirits or liquors made from those very fruits (cherries, raisins, plums, etc.).

Drying and Salting

The drying technique is generally used in combination with others, such as salting. Common salted foods in Spanish cuisines are fish (codfish, or the renowned *mojama*, that is, dried and salted tuna), mushrooms, various kinds of sausage, and hams. Special places in the mountains are particularly renowned for drying and salting sausage: Mount Moncayo in Aragon and Alpujarra in the province of Granada, for example. In combination with drying, salting—which consists of covering food in various layers of salt—helps remove the liquids, facilitating the drying process and, thus, leading to better and longer preservation.

Salads

In Spain, and particularly in the Mediterranean area, salads are more than a recipe. They are a very typical combination of great-tasting ingredients (vegetables, olives, legumes, but also fish, seafood, ham, sausages, and fresh and dried fruits) and easy preparation. Variety, simplicity, and freshness and also flavor and color are essential. Salads are made and consumed every day with fresh products bought in local markets and are present at almost every table. The usual dressing is also easy, but tasty: olive oil, vinegar, and salt, with or without black pepper.

Kitchens and Equipment

Cookware and kitchen utensils have evolved notably in Spain in the last century. A brief general account of the most common materials and

instruments will be offered here, together with a description of more specific Spanish utensils.

The Culinary-Domestic Space

Between the 1950s and the 1960s, during Francisco Franco's dictatorship, Spain (chiefly in the north) reached its apogee in terms of development and industrialization. During the 1960s, Spain lived a kind of
"technological revolution" in the home (mostly urban, but not exclusively) and particularly in the kitchen, saving time and effort.

Maybe the biggest and most rapidly introduced "technological" element in Spanish kitchens is the refrigerator, popularly adopted in the
1960s. Home freezers became common in the 1970s. Both are now standard in Spanish kitchens. The use of frozen produce has also increased. In
rural areas, the freezer has largely replaced the older tradition of home
canning fruits, vegetables, and meat for storage. The freezer in country
households is quite large and it contains the produce of the garden and
meat when home raised or bought from friends or neighbors.

Gas was introduced as a cooking fuel for commercial kitchens in the
late nineteenth and twentieth century, when electricity also made an appearance. Fireplaces and hearths were first replaced in homes by the "eco-
nomical stoves" with various hobs or rings, fueled by wood at first, then by
coal (mainly coque), petrol, and finally electricity and gas. Gas and electricity are now the most important fuels for cookery. In many homes—
mostly urban—the typical gas is butane. Gas (butane or, chiefly, "natural"
gas, as it is called in Spain) or electricity is now preferred for cooking and
is standard in most Spanish kitchens. A few additions have also been
made in the last years, such as timers, automatic ignition systems, and
vitro-ceramics stoves: 35.5 percent of Spanish homes have an electric,
vitro-ceramics stove.[7]

In urban contexts, the kitchen replaced the older, moveable furniture,
such as dressers and freestanding cupboards with a marble top (or similar surface), replacing very often the ancient tables. During the 1960s,
other consumer goods were progressively acquired: mixers, pressure
cookers, electric coffee grinders, coffee makers, espresso machines; and
in the early 1970s other appliances were obtained, such as freezers (first,
a refrigerator with a freezer in the same item, and later separate or special items), smoke extractors, electric toasters, meat grinders, electric
juicers; and later (1980s) yogurt makers, electric knives and can open-
ers, and so forth. Many of them, such as the electric mixer, are useful for

popular preparations or sauces, such as the traditional mayonnaise or *allioli*.[8]

The microwave oven was introduced in the 1980s and developed in the 1990s. It has become a popular item in many kitchens, mainly for defrosting and reheating.

The slowest to become established is the dishwasher, more and more present in Spanish homes (in 42.4% of Spanish homes, up from 10% in 2003), particularly in the new apartments, flats, or houses. The percentage of Spanish kitchens that have a deep fryer is 49.4 percent.[9]

A well-designed kitchen made with fashionable materials has become a status symbol. Spanish kitchens are normally decorated with "traditional" tiles, ceramics, and ornamental objects. In the nineteenth century, and following the new fashion, the inner walls of a building were covered with tiles, with domestic and culinary scenes, flowers, and so forth. Today, this is still the most common decoration in Spanish kitchens.

Normally, people prefer to eat in the dining room and not in the kitchen (except for a "lonely meal" or a snack, or maybe for a quick coffee in the morning). For that reason, many kitchens do not have a table to eat at (but sometimes, in big kitchens, a table is there for preparing food, even in quite modest houses). Kitchen-offices (popularly called *cocina americana*— "American kitchen") are only found in small, urban apartments or in summer apartments.

Earthenware Utensils

Earthenware objects of all shapes and sizes have always been used in Spain. Pitchers, pots, stewpots, casseroles, *escudillas* (bowls), and jars can be porous—for refreshing water or wine—or waterproof. They have traditionally been used to carry and to keep water, oil, fruits, meat, and spices; and also to stew and eat. Most kitchenware is still used. However, tableware is now made of glazed and decorated ceramics, or even glass.

Earthenware is still made in potteries—*ollerías* or *obradores*—thanks to ancient techniques that have been preserved. However, the art began to decline in the second half of the last century.

Casserole Dishes

Clay *cazuelas* (terra-cotta dishes or casseroles) have been used in Spain for hundreds of years. *Cazuelas* are made with moistened clay, low fired with an interior glaze so it can hold liquids. *Cazuelas* are one of the origi-

Popular red clay casserole dishes.

nal vessels used for a developing cuisine. They may be brought to the table straight from the oven. The glaze on the *cazuelas* contains no lead, so it is safe for all cooking applications.

Due to its excellent quality and the special flavor that it gives to stews, the *cazuela* (also a generic name for casserole) is the most important piece, and it is normally placed directly over the heat source. Terra-cotta holds the heat and keeps food at its best for a long time.

Made in several sizes and shapes, the most widely known is the round one, which comes in different sizes:

- A 4-inch diameter dish is a handy size to serve *tapas* such as olives, almonds, capers, and so forth.
- A 6-inch diameter is a handy size to cook and serve many dishes directly to the table; also for serving *tapas*.
- A 7.5–8, 12–13, and 15-inch diameters are some common sizes to cook many dishes, such as rice, pulses (such as beans or peas), and so forth.

Before using a terra-cotta *cazuela* for the first time over stovetop burners, it must be presoaked in water.

In addition to the traditional (round) casserole, there are oval and rectangular ones (also known as *asadores* "spits") adapted for ovens.

Pucheros (stewpots) are large pots of clay used mainly for stews, as they give them a special taste and retain heat longer.

Serving Bowl for Olives

This (very recent) bowl solves the age-old problem of what to do with the pit of the olive one just ate. It is just a ceramic bowl (very often hand-painted) with a small side (or inside) bowl for pits, and very often also another small holder for toothpicks *(palillos)*. One puts the olives in the bowl, a bunch of toothpicks in the small holder or side bowl, and the remaining small bowl is for the pits (called "olive bones"—*huesos de oliva*).

Tortilla Flipper/Server

The tortilla server is a big ceramic plate used to flip the *tortilla de patatas* (Spanish omelette or potato omelette) to cook the other side.

Stand of red clay casserole dishes in a popular market, Salamanca.

Porcelain Casseroles

Porcelain casseroles are actually made of red, enameled metal.

Metal Cookware

Aluminum is used for all sorts of pots, casseroles, and particularly frying pans. Copper is the best heat-conducting metal and it is ideal for cooking jams, sugar syrups, or even chocolate, such as in the ancient *chocolateras*. Currently, copper is not used very much, particularly because it is expensive and difficult to clean. Cast iron is still very popular. It is heavy, durable, and an excellent conductor of heat. Although enameled iron, aluminum, or other materials are actually better than cast iron, many housewives prefer the old-fashioned *sartenes* (frying pans) made of this metal. Stainless steel is now the most popular material for stewing, boiling, and so forth. It is "modern," clean, and durable.

Casserole dishes come in a variety of shapes and sizes. They have lids and are useful for slow and prolonged stewing or baking in the oven.

Frying pans are usually made of aluminum with a nonstick coating. There is also the traditional cast iron pan. The cast iron frying pans are ideal for egg omelettes (*tortillas*), and particularly for Spanish omelettes. After using them, they must not be washed, but rather cleaned with a paper tissue.

Tortilla de Patatas (Potato Omelette or Spanish Omelette)

Ingredients
- 1 cup olive oil
- 4 large potatoes (peeled and cut into small cubes)
- 1 large onion, thinly sliced (optional but typical)
- 4 eggs
- salt to taste

Preparation
Heat the oil in a frying pan and add potato cubes. After a few seconds, add the slices of onion, cooking slowly on medium heat. Turn occasionally until potatoes are tender, but not brown. Simultaneously, beat eggs in a large bowl with a fork, and add salt to taste.

Drain the potatoes, and add potatoes to beaten eggs (in the bowl), pressing them so that eggs cover them completely. Pour the potato-egg mixture into the frying pan, spreading quickly. Increase the heat to medium-high. Shake pan to prevent sticking. When potatoes start to brown, put a plate (or a tortilla flipper) on top of the frying pan and flip to cook other side. Brown on the other side and flip up to two more times, and the "tortilla" is ready.

Ollas (pots), which have higher sides than casseroles, have traditionally been used to cook vegetables, pasta, stews and so forth.

The *paella* pan is a round, metal pan with two lateral, symmetrical handles traditional and essential in homes and restaurants alike for cooking the popular rice dish bearing the same name, as well as other derived dishes, such as *fideuà* (a noodle-based dish). They come in different sizes, normally: 10, 13, 15, 18, or 22 inches (for 2, 4, 6, 8, or 12 people, respectively). The traditional *paella* pan is made of cast aluminum that weds the virtue of the traditional *paella* pan with modern nonstick technology. The coating prohibits the crispy crusting on the bottom of the pan, which some people savor. The normal steel *paella* pan will change color and absorb flavor as it is used. There is also a stainless steel *paella* pan. For cooking at home, if the *paella* pan is bigger than the heat source (18 or 22 inches, for example) it is also necessary to have a special burner that cooks rice (or noodles, in the case of cooking *fideuà*) uniformly.

Pan for cooking *paella*.

Utensils

In Spanish kitchens, many different types of spoons are used. Wooden spoons are adequate for cooking different stews, pulses, or vegetable *potajes*, and so forth (metal utensils are not recommended in those cases because their metallic flavor can be transferred to the stew). Metal, round spoons (stainless steel is very common) are normally used for scooping and stirring (useful in many dishes, such as popular *paella* or *migas*), serving spoons are for serving dry dishes, and ladles (*cucharones*) are used for serving soups or stews.

Wooden forks are very useful also in stews, thick soups, rice, pasta, and other kinds of similar preparations. Metal forks and skewers are used particularly for meat.

Glass

From the Middle Ages on, glass work became more widespread, too, and luxury items made of glass and gold reached a high level of sophistication. At the end of the nineteenth century and the beginning of the twentieth century, it became fashionable to cut glassware out of colored glass. However, connoisseurs would progressively replace these colored glasses with colorless ones, which allowed one to appreciate the quality of the liquids they contained, especially wine. Thus, special glasses were created for each kind of wine: white, red, *cava* (or champagne), dessert wine, brandy, fine wines, such as *fino*, *manzanilla* or sherry, and other liquors.

Other Interesting Drinking Vessels

Porrón

In many homes, but also in popular restaurants and bars in Spain one will find the drinking vessel known as *porrón*, a glass wine container with a narrow, pointed spout that shoots a stream of wine directly into a drinker's mouth. The *porrón* is probably of Catalonian origin. It is passed around the table. Normally, it is filled with table wine or sweet wine (the smallest models). Drinking from it takes skill and good guzzling ability to keep up with the steady stream of wine. It is never brought to the mouth, but lifted and aimed toward it. For the adept drinkers, the arm should eventually be straightened.

Bota (Bota Bag)

The *bota* is a typical goatskin bag that holds about a liter of wine. The interior is coated with pitch in the traditional way. The *bota* is also made for sharing the wine and has a nozzle on one end; when the bag is squeezed, the wine is forced out and into one's mouth. Drinking from this also takes skill and good guzzling ability to keep up with the wine directly shot into the mouth. It is used in the countryside, but also in many urban homes and popular restaurants (particularly in the countryside).

NOTES

1. Specific areas like Catalonia or the Basque Country, though, had already undergone a process of industrialization in the nineteenth century, at the beginning of the industrial revolution.

2. Among the numerous publications are the cookbooks by Doctor Trebussem (*La mesa moderna*), José Altamiras (*Novísimo arte de cocina*), Ángel Muro (*Diccionario general de cocina* and *El Practicón*), Pere Alcántara (*La cuyna mallorquina*), and the anonymous *La cuynera catalana*. This cuisine would be revalued throughout the twentieth century, with remarkable works like *La cocina española antigua*, written by Countess Pardo Bazán (1914).

3. The case of the sisters Úrsula, Sira, and Vicenta de Azcaray, owners of a famous restaurant of Bilbao was different: they spent their whole lives in the restaurant kitchen but their books and recipe manuscripts became known thanks to their posthumous publication.

4. Such was the case of maize, for example; this plant was very successful in France and northern Italy but has never had a major role in Spanish cuisines.

5. Andrés Bernáldez, *Memorias del Reinado de los Reyes Católicos*, ed. Manuel Gómez and Juan de Mata (Madrid: Carríazo, 1962).

6. F. Xavier Medina, *La Cocina en España: Anotaciones* (Barcelona: unpublished report, 1999).

7. Redaction, "La Mitad de los Hogares de las Ciudades Españolas Tienen un Ordenador," Master-Net, http://www.masterdisseny.com/master-net/atrasadas/155.php3.

8. Popularly, a very expanded theory in Spain says that mayonnaise (*mayonesa* or *mahonesa* in Spanish) was invented in Mahón, the city capital of Menorca, in the Balearic Islands, under the French domination (eighteenth century) and this is the origin of the name *mahonesa* (sauce from Mahón).

9. Redaction, "Uso de Electrodomésticos en los Hogares Españoles," Electro-Imagen, http://www.electro-imagen.com/es/noticia/15.

4

Typical Meals and Cuisine by Region

The Spanish climate is generally mild and there are a good number of hours with sunshine daily; this directly affects mealtimes and lifestyles in general.

Although food consumption varies depending on age, gender, social class, and so forth, it is possible to define certain general social patterns.

MEAL TIMES

Eating hours in Spain underwent significant changes in the twentieth century; the most important ones concerned lunch and dinner, which were shifted to a later time of day. Generally, the daily meals are as follows:

- *Desayuno* (breakfast, approximately between 5 and 8 A.M.) Both in the country, where people traditionally get up at the crack of dawn, and in the city, where factory work starts quite early as well, breakfast has never been a big meal. It usually consists of a hot drink, such as coffee, white coffee (with milk or cream), chocolate, or herbal teas (and more recently other beverages such as fruit juice), together with some solid food, either sweet (cookies or *magdalenas*) or salted. Before coffee use spread in the nineteenth century, providing caffeine and thus facilitating an early start in the morning, in some areas it was common (especially for men) to drink a small glass of alcohol, which provided a high amount of calories. Breakfast is usually eaten at home, before leaving, or more quickly in some of the bars that open very early in the morning.

- *Almuerzo* (midmorning meal, approximately between 10 and 12 A.M.) For *almuerzo*, more food is eaten than at breakfast, and less than at lunch. *Almuerzo* may consist of various kinds of rolls (with sausage, cheese, etc.) or even small portions of some kind of stew, accompanied by a glass of wine or other drinks (and currently also by beer). Alternatively, people also drink white and black coffee together with sweet food (this is a variant of the so-called continental breakfast).[1] On holidays and weekends, breakfast and mid-morning snack merge into one meal.

- Aperitif and *tapeo* (approximately between 1 and 3 P.M.) This eating habit is particularly common on festive days and usually consists of a snack, prepared at home and shared with one's family and friends. It usually includes some drinks (wine, vermouth, beer, soft drinks, etc.) and homemade *tapas* (olives, sausage, cheese, seafood, etc.). Alternatively, people go to bars and restaurants to drink and eat *tapas*, which are small portions of food that are different in each bar. *Tapas* include cold cuts and sausage, cheese, seafood, fish, and so forth, as well as more elaborate dishes such as *paella* and *migas*.[2]

    In some areas of Spain, especially in the last century, aperitif has been renamed *vermut* (distilled herb wine), as so much of this is drunk.

- *Comida* (lunch, between 2 and 4 P.M.) Together with dinner, this is one of the main daily meals. In Spain, unlike other European countries where very little time is devoted to lunch, lunchtime generally lasts from one to two hours and the meal is usually a complete one (starter, main course, and dessert). Those who have time to return home for lunch habitually eat with their family. Nowadays, the working time and the distance between the workplace and home make it difficult for people to have lunch at home. As a consequence, most restaurants offer the so-called midday menus (based on the three-course pattern), which provide a complete meal at low cost. This meal has been traditionally considered a social occasion, so it is common for people to meet for lunch, either with relatives, friends, or coworkers. Wine, together with water, is the traditional drink. Today, however, the consumption of beer and soft drinks has increased considerably.

- *Merienda* (mid-afternoon snack, approximately between 5 and 7 P.M.) The Spanish term *merienda* stems from Latin *merenda*. It consists of a small amount of food, generally a roll or a cake and a drink, to bridge the time period between lunch and dinner. Although everybody has *merienda*, it is more commonly associated with children, who eat it as soon as they finish their afternoon classes.

- *Tapeo* (between 7 and 9 P.M.) Whereas midday aperitif and *tapeo* are limited to holidays and weekends, the *tapeo* that precedes dinner is a widespread weekday practice. In various areas of Spain, in fact, it is common to meet friends, relatives, and colleagues for a drink and a *tapa* after work and before dinner.

- *Cena* (dinner, between 8 and 11 P.M.) Dinner is usually the last meal of the day. On weekdays it is confined to the family and is actually the time when the different members of a family can get together. The typical structure of a dinner coincides with that of lunch: a light starter, such as soup, salad, or omelet, followed by fish or meat, and a dessert, such as fruit. Yet, at home and on weekdays, dinner is usually lighter and simpler, due to its proximity to bedtime. Holidays and celebrations are a different matter. On these occasions, dinner may turn into the heaviest meal of the day, both in the home and in restaurants, which become crowded with people.

Spaniards usually eat much later than other Europeans. The difference is particularly evident in regard to lunch and dinner, which are eaten about two hours later than in other European countries. Whereas in places such as France and Switzerland, lunch is at about 12 P.M., in Spain it is around 2 or 3 P.M. (even later on weekends and on holidays). Likewise, in certain European countries dinner is at about 7 or 8 P.M. (and earlier in places further north, such as Norway, where people may have dinner at 4 P.M.), but in Spain it is had between 9 and 10:30 P.M. (and even later on holidays and weekends). A recent study shows that the daily distribution of meals in Spain corresponds to a different distribution of the working hours; the Spaniards' workday may stretch until 7 or 8 P.M., yet, they go to bed later and wake up at the same time as other European workers.[3] In other words, Spanish people sleep fewer hours than other Europeans. This is only a twentieth-century phenomenon. In the nineteenth century, lunch was around 12 or 1 P.M. and dinner at 7 or 8 P.M., depending on the season. These mealtimes progressively shifted into the current pattern during the twentieth century.

Another aspect related to Spanish eating habits is worth highlighting: the *siesta* is a custom that has become an international stereotype. This practice is a consequence of specific climatic and physiological conditions. Lunchtime usually coincides with the hottest hours of the day, especially in central and southern Spain. In rural areas, for example, people commonly wait until the sun is lower in the sky before resuming work. From a physiological perspective, because lunch is one of the main meals, a large quantity of food is ingested, and this causes sleepiness. A *siesta* may last between 10 minutes and 1 hour. In any case, it must be noted that in an urban environment, with productivity concerns, the afternoon nap is confined to weekends and holidays, and not everyone has the chance to rest.

SOME OBSERVATIONS ON DRINKS

An important characteristic of the Spanish food system is that drink and food are considered a unity, rather than two separate elements, as happens conversely in other European countries. Spaniards mainly drink while they have food, be it at lunchtime, dinner, or during *tapeos* (*tapas* were created precisely to avoid drinking alcoholic beverages on an empty stomach). Drinks are taken without any food only after dinner (thus, with a full stomach). Both during lunch and dinner, wine has been, and still is, the traditional drink, together with water. Only recently, since the 1960s, has beer found its prominent place within these drinking practices and so have soft drinks. Even so, wine is still the drink par excellence when it comes to lunch and dinner: red wine for meat, stews, and main courses, and white wine and rosé for starters and fish. *Cava,* sparkling wine, is the chief festive drink and it became so popular in the twentieth century that nowadays celebrations cannot be conceived of without this drink. Last, coffee, in all its variations, also occupies an important role in daily life. It is consumed at breakfast, with the mid-morning snack, at the end of lunch and dinner, and in between meals. Coffee is clearly the most consumed drink in Spain, whereas tea and herbal infusions are not as popular.

CUISINE BY REGION

Spain boasts a great cultural, geographical, and gastronomical diversity. It is a country with high potential both in terms of cultural relationships and of geographical and environmental resources: from the Mediterranean coast, with a mild climate, to the Atlantic coast, which is colder, wetter, and has more vegetation; from the flat and dry Castilian Meseta to the high mountainous ranges. These diverse features make each Spanish cuisine different and unique, as each of them specializes in specific products, flavors, and cooking methods.

The culinary peculiarities of each area also result from the various gastronomic encounters that took place through the centuries in the Iberian Peninsula. As previously discussed, the peninsula has always been a cultural crossroads. Since ancient times, the Mediterranean area has been the main importer of new foods and cultures. Products from the Americas mainly entered through western regions (western Andalusia, for example); the south was closer to North African culture; the north, especially the Cantabrian area, was open to the Atlantic and established trade with northern Europe (Great Britain, for example); last, the central area of the peninsula (mainly Madrid, but also other places related to the Spanish Court) was influenced by the courtly fashions of countries such as Austria, Germany, and France).

All these factors marked a particular evolution in the various Spanish cuisines, giving each of them a specific character and individual features that not only distinguish them from each other and from the cuisines of other countries, but place them (as is the case of the Basque and Catalan cuisines) among the most famous gastronomies in the world. The following sections offer a brief summary of the main characteristics of Spanish cuisines.

Andalusia and Extremadura

Andalusia is a large territory.[4] Its political capital is the city of Seville, and the region is characterized by very different climates and lands, hence, by different foods and dishes. Andalusia has both a Mediterranean and an Atlantic coast, mountains, countryside, and even the largest desert in Europe.[5] In this region grain fields mingle with olive tree groves and what are called truck farms (those that take produce to sell at farmers' markets), and the Mediterranean and Atlantic coasts provide a wide variety of high-quality fish. Tuna is very common, but sole, sea bass, hake, red mullet, tope shark, sardines, anchovies, prawns, and shrimp are also abundant. As for cooking methods, frying in olive oil is among the most common (fried small-size fish is a popular dish in Andalusia), but pan broiling, marinating, and stewing are also widespread methods.

Truck farm products, both seasonal and greenhouse, are abundant and varied (the greenhouses located in the province of Almería, in eastern Andalusia, are particularly outstanding; they supply the main international markets all year long). Andalusia also boasts abundant fruit plants, trees, and bushes that produce oranges, medlars, pomegranates, figs, prickly pears, cherimoyas, strawberries, and more recently, tropical fruits such as papaya and kiwi. Native and refreshing dishes are made from vegetables: *gazpacho*, a soup made of various vegetables, served cold, especially in the summer, for example, which is the most famous dish of Andalusian gastronomy, in all its varieties: *ajoblanco* (with garlic and almonds), *salmorejo* (with tomatoes, bread, olive oil, a little vinegar, garlic, and salt), *pipirrana* (no bread, but tomatoes, peppers, and onions). Among the most popular stews are the chickpea stew, spinach and codfish stew, and bean stew, with their high caloric value. As for meat products, pork preparations are particularly outstanding. Among the most renowned Andalusian sausage products are *jamón Iberico de bellota* (Iberian acorn ham) from the Sierras of Huelva and Cordoba, and *chorizos* and blood sausage from Granada and Jaén. There are a variety of meat stews:

these are made with pork (which is actually eaten more in the form of sausage than as fresh meat), bovine (bull's tail stew, for example), lamb (*ajillo*—with garlic, *calderetas*—a kind of stew), poultry (hen and turkey fricassee, duck Sevillian style), and offal (kidney with *jerez*, tripe Andalusian style) all seasoned with aromatic herbs. *Tapas* deserve special mention—small food portions that are eaten as snacks and as an accompaniment to drinks, usually consumed before meals (see also chapters 1 and 5). Some bars offer *tapas* menus with more than 100 specialties, which are eaten while consuming wine or the drink that better suits each of these appetizers. Among the most remarkable *tapas* are ham-based ones, small-size fried fish, prawns, shrimp, and omelets, many of which are typically Andalusian.

As for sweets, cakes are still made with almond and honey, following the Arabic tradition. Some typical sweets, such as *dulce de membrillo* (quince jelly—made with the flesh of this fruit), *alfajores* (made with milk, sugar, flour, cinnamon, and lemon rind), *polvorones* (made with sugar, almonds, lard, flour, egg, and cinnamon), and *mantecados* (similar to *polvorones*, but made without flour and eggs), were traditionally homemade, whereas today they are commercially manufactured. However, the cake-making tradition has been preserved in convents (as happens in other parts of Spain), where various specialties are produced: *yemas* (sweets made of sugar and egg yolks), fritters, pumpkin cakes, puff pastries with candied pumpkin pulp, fruit in syrup, *pestiños*, and so forth.

Andalusian wines are internationally renowned, especially the ones from Jerez (*fino*, *manzanilla*, aromatic wines, *amontillado*, and sweet wine), Málaga, Huelva, and Montilla-Moriles regions, which have their own designation of origin.

The cuisine from Extremadura is, like the Andalusian one, tasty and varied. Among the most famous products of this region are Iberian pork, and more specifically the *jamónes de bellota* (acorn hams) and other sausages. Lamb is one of the top dishes in Extremadura, and it is cooked in various tasty ways. Large and small game (partridges, pigeons, rabbits and hares, wild boars, and deer) are also abundant in this region. Historically, the fields of Extremadura have always been appreciated by members of the Spanish royal family and nobles, who used them as private game preserves. There are still large rural estates that, among other things, are still used for large and small game hunting.

As Extremadura has no direct access to the sea, the fish is mainly freshwater: the tench, for example, is very popular and competes with trout in quality; it is prepared in various ways (in a marinade, fried, or in sauce). The cheeses from Extremadura are also worth mentioning: among the most remarkable ones are *Torta del Casar*, the cheeses from La Serena, and the goat cheese from Tiétar. The production of honey (both the aromatic and flower varieties) is also important in this region. The most popular desserts are *rosquillas* (small doughnuts), *técula/mécula* (a highly caloric and tasty dessert made of almonds, eggs, sugar, and lard), as well as other local sweets and pastries that are not well known outside the region. The fruits produced in Extremadura are many and varied: cherries (from the Jerte River valley), melons, apples, peaches, figs, and so forth. As for wine, there is only one designation of origin—Ribera del Guadiana. The wines from Extremadura are not well known, but their quality has improved recently and they have lost their local character, entering the national Spanish market.

Aragon

The region of Aragon, with its capital Zaragoza, lies halfway between the Mediterranean coast and the Castillian Meseta. It is a dry land and the most popular dishes are usually meat based. Lamb is the star product in this region (the famous *ternasco*, or Aragonese suckling lamb, has its own designation of origin). Chicken is another important meat; in the past it was reserved for festivities and it became the base of an important Aragonese dish, chicken *chilindrón* (in Aragon this is a popular way of preparing lamb as well, using tomatoes and red peppers). Among sausage preparations, the ham from Teruel and the Aragonese *longaniza* (typical sausage) deserve special mention. Among the most commonly eaten game are rabbits and hares, stewed in their own blood (*civet*), partridges, deer, and wild boar. Fish, which is mainly freshwater, includes trout and eels, among other kinds. Bread is a basic element of this cuisine and takes many shapes and names in the different Aragonese counties. Traditional cakes, pastries, and other sweets are also popular, such as *guirlache* (nougat made of toasted almond and sugar), chestnuts, candied fruit (such as the "Fruits of Aragon," pieces of candied fruit coated in chocolate), and *magdalenas* (small sponge tea cakes).

As for wine, there are four designations of origin in Aragon: Cariñena, Campo de Borja, Calatayud, and Somontano (all areas that have a long-established wine-producing tradition). Other alcoholic drinks made in Aragon are spirits, fruit liquors (cherry and wild blackberry liquor, for example), and walnut *ratafias*, which are excellent digestive drinks.

Asturias and Cantabria

Asturias and Cantabria are in the north of the Iberian Peninsula, on the Cantabrian seacoast. They both have a remarkably unique cuisine, mainly based on stews, such as the popular Asturias *fabada*, which is cooked very slowly, almost without spices or seasoning, in order to preserve the natural taste of the ingredients. Asturian *fabada* is made with white beans (*fabes*), accompanied by sausage (*chorizo*, *morcilla*, shoulder ham, etc.) and other ingredients, such as potatoes. There are various recipes for this dish, because the ingredients may vary according to personal taste; some of them include fish (clams and lobster), small game (rabbit or partridge), poultry, and so forth. *Fabada* is the signature Asturian dish, but not the only one: *potes* (a type of thick vegetable soup) are also popular; they are made with diverse foods, depending on the basic ingredient: *fabes*, *chorizo*, potatoes, or chestnuts.

Fish—both marine and freshwater—and seafood are also very important in these coastal territories: anglerfish, hake, conger, tuna, sea urchins, salmon, trout, goose barnacles, and clams are only a few of the countless species provided by the sea and the rivers of this region. Meats are also a remarkable in this area: both cattle meat (among the most popular dishes are sirloin cooked with strong local cheeses, such as Cabrales and stewed ox), pork (a basic ingredient of the Cantabrian "mountain stew"), game (wild boar and venison), and poultry (especially chicken).[6] Among all these foods, cheese surely plays an outstanding role in the gastronomy of northern Spain. Asturian specialties include various local cheeses (*Gamonedo*, *Pría*, *Porrúa*, *Casín*, etc., made from cow, sheep, or goat milk), the star product being Cabrales, a designation of origin blue cheese of very strong taste, which is internationally renowned. In the mountainous region of Cantabria, milk is high quality, too, and it is used to make highly appreciated cheese and butter. Cantabrian cheeses are strong, and they are carefully manufactured and seasoned. The most popular ones are *Picón*, smoked cheese, and cream cheese.

The Asturian dessert par excellence is milk rice (rice boiled in milk, sugar, cinnamon, and lemon rind), but there are also many other sweet preparations, such as almond cakes, custard millefeuille, *brazo de gitano* (literally "gypsy arm," a kind of roll filled with custard, whipped cream, or chocolate), *tocinos de cielo* (small cakes made with egg yolk and sugar), and *huesos de santo* (literally, "Saints' bones," sweets eaten on All Saints' Day). Cantabria, on its part, is renowned for desserts, such as *quesadas pasiegas* (fresh cheesecakes) and puff pastries.

Asturias and Cantabria are also wine areas. Cider is the Asturian drink par excellence. It is drunk in cider bars or in restaurants and, when possible, on the site where it is produced. Cider is poured from a great height (which requires some skill and marksmanship) into a large and wide glass that is only filled with a very small amount of the drink. It is a convivial drink that fosters conversation and celebration. An outstanding Cantabrian drink is *orujo* (spirit), which is traditionally made and has digestive qualities.

Balearic Islands

The autonomous region of the Balearic Islands consists of two different archipelagos: the Balearic Islands proper (Mallorca and Menorca, the largest islands) and the Pitiusas (Ibiza and Formentera). Discussing Balearic gastronomy is tantamount to speaking of a cuisine that fully exploits the natural insular resources, as well as the various cultures that influenced the archipelago through its history: Greeks, Phoenicians, Romans, Arabs, French, and English, all this on a cultural Catalan base with strong social and political influences of the Spanish state in general (through immigration, for example).

The most outstanding crops in the Balearic Islands are almond trees (which bloom in February and March); almonds have been, and still are, an essential element within the insular traditional cuisine, and so are bread, olive oil, and tomatoes (the Catalan influence can be observed in the preparation of the typical "bread with tomato"). These elements, ably combined, may be a tasty starter to any meal, as well as a nutritive breakfast or afternoon snack. The most renowned cheese in the islands is Mahón, which has a designation of origin. Despite the fact that this cheese was made in various parts of the island of Menorca, it acquired this generic name because it was from the harbor of Mahón from which it was exported. Other products worth mentioning are *cocas*, of Catalan origin and very similar to pizza; they have an elongated shape and are made with fine bread dough. *Cocas* are topped with a wide variety of ingredients and may be eaten both sweet or salted, hot or cold.

Other popular foods are the potatoes from Sa Pobla, the insular "fair peppers" (of yellow color), the purple carrot, and other typical vegetables of this land. Yet, the base of the Balearic cuisine is seafood and meat— together with the omnipresent bread. Traditional Balearic gastronomy results from the intensive fishing and agricultural activities that were carried out before the tourist boom.

Long ago, pork became an almost essential product, and sausage preparations have become quite famous, especially the one known as *sobrasada*. This sausage, which has a designation of origin, is made with spiced pork, mainly seasoned with *pimentón* (smoked paprika), which gives it the unique red color.

Balearic fish is rich in taste and varied, and it is widely used for fish broth, soups, and *suquets* (luscious, brothy fish stews), such as the lobster stew, a specialty of the isle of Menorca. Another fish-based dish is the remarkable *frita de calamar*, made with fried squid and potatoes. Small game and bird game are also particularly appreciated; among popular game dishes are rabbit with onion and duck with olives. Offal dishes also play an important role in Balearic gastronomy, with preparations such as the *frit de freixura* (fried offal).

Delicious desserts can be found on all the islands: cottage cheese casserole and sweet *cocas* with apricot, for example. However, the traditional *ensaïmada* (with the designation of origin Ensaïmada de Mallorca) is the most famous dessert of these islands: it is round and made from sweet bread dough and lard (the so-called *saïm*, which gives the cake its name). It may be plain or filled with candied pumpkin pulp, custard, or whipped cream, with powdered sugar icing on top. Other typical desserts are the small sponge cakes called *quartos*, *flaó* (made with fresh cheese), or almond *gató* (cake).

These delicious desserts are accompanied by a wide variety of traditional liquors (which are also drunk as aperitifs), the most important ones being *Palo de Mallorca* (sweet liquor made with marinated cinchona bark and gentian roots), the typical herb liquors from Mallorca or Ibiza, and the gin from Menorca (legacy of the English occupation during the eighteenth century). There are currently two wines with designations of origin: *Binissalem* and *Pla i Llevant de Mallorca*, examples of the millenary wine culture of the islands. Red wines are more commercialized than white and rosé wines. Also worth mentioning is the designation of origin *Vins de la Terra d'Eivissa*, which protects the highly valued wines made on the isle of Ibiza.

Canary Islands

The Canaries are an archipelago consisting of seven islands located off the coast of northwest Africa and they have a tropical, year-round, sunny climate. Although natural resources are abundant and the islands have been influenced by various cuisines, especially by the Andalusian one, local gastronomy is marked by great simplicity.

One of the basic ingredients of the Canary cuisine is *gofio*, toasted wheat or corn, which may be either the essential part of breakfast, an accompaniment to the various insular stews, or even the base for a unique variety of local nougat. Other simple but tasty preparations are *mojos* (from the Portuguese "molho," meaning "sauce"), sauces that accompany most dishes. *Mojo picón* (hot sauce made with peppers, vinegar, olive oil, garlic, cumin, salt, and paprika) and green *mojo* (a lighter sauce, made with parsley and coriander) are the most renowned. Other kinds of *mojos* are coriander sauce, garlic sauce, saffron sauce (to serve with fish), cheese sauce, and *palmero* sauce (pepper sauce).

Since the Middle Ages, the Canary Islands served as a testing ground for the establishment of new crops, such as sugar cane, intensively cultivated in this area under the Castilian Crown. Subsequently, from the sixteenth century onward, new products were introduced into the islands, which were on the navigation route toward the Americas: tomatoes, bananas, and potatoes or *papas* (which gave way to a smaller local variety, of distinctive taste). These tubers are the base of one of the most famous Canary dishes: *papas arrugadas* (literally "wrinkled potatoes"), which are boiled in their skins in highly salted water, preferably seawater. The *papas* are served with red or green *mojo*. The Canary climate, which is rather different from that of other parts of Spain, is particularly propitious for the cultivation of diverse tropical fruits such as bananas (the most representative product of these islands), papayas, mangoes, avocadoes, and pineapples.

The high quality fish of this area is eaten in stews, salted, or *jareado* (sun-dried and seasoned). Typical fish dishes are *tollos*, made with tope shark, and the traditional *Sancocho* (salted fish that is soaked all night and then boiled together with *papas* and sweet potatoes, served with green or hot sauce). Seafood is also an important product: the most common seafood are limpets, which are grilled during the summer months, and clams. Small game is very popular, such as rabbit (used in the preparation of the typical marinade known as *salmorejo*), kid, and veal.

As for as desserts, the most common ones are *Bienmesabe* (made with honey and ground almonds), *ñames* (pies filled with sweet potatoes, almonds, raisins, or candied pumpkin pulp), *quesadillas* (made with fresh cheese) from the Hierro island, *tortas* (small and tasty cakes), marzipan, and almond cakes.

The Canary islands have ten wines with designations of origin; the most remarkable are El Hierro, Tacoronte-Acentejo, Valle de Güimar, and Valle de la Orotava. Typical drinks are banana liquor and honey-rum.

Castilla y León

Castilla y León is the largest autonomous region in Spain and occupies most of the northern inland territory. It includes the central areas that, in the Middle Ages, were the original kingdom of León and the County (and subsequently Kingdom) of Castile. This area is culturally and historically rich, as it was situated on the pilgrims' route to Santiago; thus, over the centuries, it was constantly crossed by pilgrims on their way to Galicia. Gastronomically speaking, it is characterized by roast meat dishes, mainly suckling pigs and lambs, which are the standout food of this cuisine. In Castilla, the main meat dishes include lamb, hare, rabbit, partridges, and the omnipresent pork. Segovia is famous for its roast piglets and Burgos for its veal chops.

In Castilla y León, which is rather cold in winter, stews and hot soups play an important role. Among the most popular ones are garlic soup, onion soup, trout soup, and *zamorana* soup, made with garlic, ripe tomatoes, and hot chili. Stews are made with a wide variety of pulses: white, black, and red beans, chickpeas, lentils, and so forth, and they are enriched with poultry and pork meat. The *batillo* from León, for example, is made with the pig's backbone, ribs, tail, and abundant meat, all stuffed into the animal's stomach, and this is boiled with potatoes. Sausage, pork product par excellence, occupies the most important position within the gastronomy of this area: ham (from Guijuelo and Ledrada, in the province of Salamanca, and acorn ham, considered one of the best hams of Spain), blood sausage from Burgos, the *farinato*—sweet-tasting sausage that is commonly scrambled with eggs—from the Salamanca area, and *chorizos* (such as the famous Cantimpalo, in Segovia). Among dried and salted meats, the jerked beef from León is particularly popular.

A special place in the gastronomy is occupied by poultry, more specifically by pigeons and partridges. Other special products from the León area are the *empanadas* (pies) of Galician origin and the *hornazos*, a sort of pie filled with abundant sausage and other ingredients, typical of Ávila, Segovia, and especially Salamanca. These foods, which used to be typical of the country, have now became a very "urban" dish. Fish (apart from the inevitable salted codfish) is mainly freshwater. The trout from the rivers of the areas of León and Zamora, small in size and outstandingly tasty, are particularly renowned. Cakes are traditional preparations typical of monasteries and convents, many of which are still active. The most famous are Santa Teresa's yolks, made with egg yolks and sugar. The wines deserve special mention. There are five with designations of origin, but the most distinctive is the one from Ribera del Duero, internationally renowned for its red and top quality wines.

Castilla La Mancha and Madrid

In the center of the Iberian Peninsula are Castilla La Mancha and Madrid, with gastronomies that comprise a wide variety of dishes, made with simple ingredients.

All the natural elements of La Mancha are reflected in its cuisine: the country, the mountains, the small lakes, and the rivers. This flat land has always been a land of farmers; thus, vegetables play a primary role in cooking. The most popular vegetables are eggplants, garlic, peppers, and tomatoes. Green and red peppers, tomatoes, and zucchini are the main ingredients of a popular dish called *pisto manchego*, which can be served hot or cold. Other typical dishes are the *asadillo* (red peppers, chopped and roasted with garlic, tomatoes, and olive oil) or the popular *ajoarriero*. The latter is made with shredded codfish, which is slightly grilled and then cooked in an earthenware pot with peppers, onion, tomato, and garlic. Another common dish is garlic soup (as in Castilla León) and the *migas de pastor* (shepherd's breadcrumbs)—based on fried breadcrumbs, which can be also found in other areas such as Andalusia, Extremadura, Murcia, and Aragon. Breadcrumbs are combined with various ingredients such as sausage, sardines, pickles, and even grapes and chocolate.

As in the rest of Spain, meat is also important in this region; a popular local meat dish is *galiano* or *La Mancha gazpacho* (which should not be confused with Andalusian *gazpacho*), a sort of poultry or rabbit pie made with unleavened, toasted bread. Small game, especially rabbit and partridges, are well liked; and among meats, roast kid is the most popular. The most outstanding desserts and cakes are *mantecados* (lard buns), rum babas, marzipan, and the popular *bizcochá* from Alcázar—a cake soaked in milk, sugar, vanilla, and cinnamon. Cheese deserves special mention: the *manchego* is one of the most well known cheeses. It is eaten all over Spain and it is also the most exported Spanish cheese. Sheep cheese, if preserved in oil, can be eaten even after two years. Wine is the drink par excellence in this region (which boasts the largest wine cooperative in Europe). The most famous wines are the designations of origin of La Mancha and Valdepeñas. Madrid, historically, was close to Castilla La Mancha, as it became the capital of this state in the mid-sixteenth century, and it exerted a unifying influence on the rest of the Spanish regions. The presence of the Spanish monarchy affected Madrid since the Renaissance, both economically and politically and, thus, gastronomically as well. Furthermore, toward the end of the nineteenth through the twentieth century migrants from other regions of Spain left their mark in the form of various culinary influences. This is how Madrid developed its own cuisine, food preparations, lifestyle, and eating habits. Distinctive food practices from Madrid include the typical breakfast, which can be had in local bars, based on white coffee, butter or oil on toast, and the characteristic thin *churros* (long loop-shaped doughnuts that are fried and sometimes coated in superfine sugar) or the thicker *porras* (bigger than *churros*, and made from the same dough). Later in the day, *tapas* (small portions that accompany drinks) are also very popular.

Churros con Chocolate (Churros with Chocolate)

Ingredients
- Olive oil to fry (or other vegetable oil, but never butter or shortening)

Churros
- 1 cup water
- 1 cup all-purpose flour
- 3 eggs
- 1/4 cup sugar
- salt to taste

Chocolate
- 4–6 oz. bittersweet chocolate, chopped
- 2 oz. margarine or butter
- 2 cups of milk
- 2 tbs. sugar

Preparation
Prepare to fry the *churros* by heating olive oil in a pan (1 to 1 1/2 inches) to 360 degrees.

To make *churro* dough: heat water, olive oil, and salt to rolling boil in 3-quart saucepan; stir in flour. Stir vigorously over low heat until mixture forms a ball (about 1–2 minutes); remove from heat. Beat eggs all at once; continue beating until smooth and then add to saucepan while stirring mixture.

Spoon mixture into cake decorators' tube with large star tip. Squeeze 4-inch strips of dough into hot oil. Fry 3 or 4 strips at a time until golden brown, turning once, about 2 minutes on each side. Drain on paper towels. Roll *churros* in sugar or dump the sugar on the pile of *churros*, like the pros.

To prepare chocolate for *churro* dunking:

Put the margarine or butter into a double boiler; after a few seconds, add the chocolate (so that the chocolate is only indirectly heated) and half the milk, stirring, until the chocolate has melted. Add some more milk and sugar, whisking constantly, until the chocolate is thickened. Remove and whisk smooth. Pour and serve in cups or bowls for dunking *churros*. Do not pour over *churros*, but use the mix for dunking *churros* after every bite. Always serve warm.

The dishes par excellence in this area are stew Madrid style and tripe Madrid style. Stew Madrid style can be defined as a synthesis of the various stews prepared in the rest of Spain and even in the United States; recipes vary according to the availability of the ingredients and to climatic conditions. Chickpeas are the most popular pulses in this area. They are not only used in stews, but also in a variety of dishes, most of them homemade, such as chickpeas *potaje* (thick soup), made with chickpeas, spinach, and codfish—a classic dish for Lent. Lentils with *chorizo* and beans also play a special role within the cuisine of this area. The tripe is usually from beef and it is also stewed and habitually accompanied by chickpeas. The establishment of the Spanish Court in Madrid brought a taste for game: wild boar and deer, but especially partridges and pheasants were mainly the prerogative of the nobles. Among fowl, the most popular were hens. Last, offal-based dishes were also very common.

The most distinctive dessert of this area is Easter *torrija* (bread slices soaked in milk, fried, and coated in superfine sugar). As for wine, some of them became popular with the Spanish Court during the modern age, such as those from San Martín de Valdeiglesias. Yet, wine production declined in the course of time, and only toward the end of the twentieth century was a designation of origin created in this area (Vinos de Madrid). The Chinchón anise liquor (which owes its name to a place in the province of Madrid) is worth mentioning as well.

Catalonia

Catalan cuisine has a clear Mediterranean character. Catalonia, with its capital the cosmopolitan city of Barcelona, has always been a cultural melting pot. Thus, it is no wonder that Catalan cuisine should be closely related to other gastronomies; more specifically to those of eastern Spain, the French Mediterranean area, and the south of Italy, regions that Catalonia has had important ties with ever since the late Middle Ages. As in other Mediterranean areas, vegetables such as tomatoes, garlic, onions, and fresh herbs are very important in Catalonia, as well as the omnipresent olive oil, which is the main cooking fat.[7] One of the signature dishes of this region is *escalivada* (a salad of chopped, grilled peppers and eggplant seasoned with salt and olive oil), but Catalonia boasts many other foods that correspond to the different geographical features of the region: from pork and other meat products to fish, fruit (cherries and pears), and what can be collected from the woods (such as mushrooms). The top product on the coast is Mediterranean fish: sea urchins, rock fish, and fishermen stews (also called *suquets*, see also the Balearic Islands section). Codfish is also a common food in Catalonia, although, as previously observed, it is not captured in nearby waters; typical cod-based dishes are *esqueixada* (with shredded desalted codfish, combined with minced vegetables and olive oil) and cod with raisins, pine nuts, and honey. Mushrooms, grilled or stewed, are among the most popular foods in Catalonia during autumn and a wide variety of them may be found in the woods of this region. Typical of the northern territory of Catalonia (especially in the area of Empordà and the famous Costa Brava) are the dishes that combine sea and land products, such as rabbit with lobster and snails, and chicken with spiny lobster or scampi with pears and plums. Some believe these combinations to be the legacy of Roman cuisine.

During winter and up to the beginning of spring, Catalans ritually eat *calçots* (grilled tender onions dressed with a special almond and tomato sauce), in the company of friends and family, particularly in the province

Mortar with wood handle, cruet (*aceitera*), and garlic cloves (instruments and ingredients for *allioli* sauce).

of Tarragona. These popular meals are called *calçotades*, and their reputation is increasing to such an extent that a number of restaurants all over Catalonia (and not only in the south of the region where this eating practice originated) offer this product as a seasonal gastronomic attraction. Rice dishes are also popular in Catalonia. The delta of the Ebro River is an important, protected rice-producing area. Common rice dishes are *arrossejat* with squid, rice with shrimp and conger, and rice with rabbit and mushrooms. Meat also occupies a privileged place in Catalan cuisine, especially in the northern area. The most common meat dishes are the beef chops from Girona, rabbit and fowl stews, and, of course, pork products. Some of the numerous Catalan sausage preparations were already famous in Roman times, such as the hams from Cerdaña. Other popular, present-day sausages are *fuet* (long-shaped sausage stuffed with lean pork meat), *butifarra* (big spicy sausage, usually grilled and accompanied by dry beans), and the sweeter *butifarra dolça* from Girona.

Creativity combined with simplicity in what is perhaps the most important and renowned Catalan dish: *pa amb tomàquet* (bread with tomato). This preparation is simple but tasty, and it consists of a slice of bread rubbed with tomato, olive oil, and salt, and accompanied by a slice of ham or any kind of sausage or cheese on top. Bread and tomato, which is very close to the famous Mediterranean pizza, may be said to have acquired the status of "national dish" in Catalonia. Within this rich culinary panorama, Barcelona, the capital of this region, has turned into the showcase of Catalan (and international) gastronomic diversity. It was in Barcelona that the emerging bourgeoisie adopted and transformed typical country dishes in the nineteenth century, and it was also here that popular taste was incorporated into the menus of many good restaurants, turning the city into the place with the best gastronomic offerings in Spain. Fine Catalan cuisine is not only a monopoly of Barcelona; excellent restaurants can be found all over the Catalan territory, even in small towns.[8] One of the largest culinary attractions of the Catalan capital is its unique markets: *La Boquería*, the most popular one, originated in the Middle Ages and still preserves the original structure to a certain extent. Other important markets are those of Sant Antoni and Santa Caterina, and the most remarkable of them all: the Born market, which is currently being transformed into a cultural center. Another example of the gastronomic sensibility of Barcelona are the *colmados*; they were initially started as grocery stores, but nowadays they sell food and other products.

Wine is also an outstanding product of Catalonia. Through the ancient Greek settlements of Empúries and Roses, wine crops became part of the local Iberian food culture and, later on, they were extended and improved by the Romans. Catalonia has always produced red wines. From the 1860s on, production was extended to *cava*, with three different local varieties: *Xarel·lo*, *Macabeo*, and *Parellada*. Today, 11 designations of origin are found in Catalonia, making it the wine region with the largest geographical diversity and variety in Spain. Along with production areas as wide as Penedés (which is the most important one), there are many smaller and more specialized areas. Catalan wine heritage ranges from fresh, light wines to high-quality red wines and sparkling wine of international renown (the famous *cava*).

Valencia and Murcia

The region of Valencia, and its capital city Valencia, have a rich gastronomy, but rice is its foremost product. Rice dishes from Valencia are, indeed, countless. Rice can be prepared in many ways and it can be combined with numberless foods; the cooking method is not only determined by the ingredients, but also by the type of pan/pot used to cook it. If rice is cooked in a deep pot it will be brothy, if it is cooked in the oven it will be drier, and if the famous *paella*—typical flat metallic pan with two handles—is used, the result will be the most international Valencia dish: *paella* Valencia style.

A number of pulse and vegetable stews are typical in Valencia. Some stews are also prepared with meat: cattle meat (ox and beef, which only some decades ago were reserved for festivities), game (rabbit and duck, which are common complements to rice), fowl (mainly chicken), and roast lamb.

The Valencia region comprises a long stretch of Mediterranean coast, which encompasses almost all of eastern Spain. Consequently, the region is rich in fish (conger, hake, sea bass, sea brim, red mullet, anglerfish, etc.), which is fried, roasted, cooked in salt, or with onion. Salting is a common method of preparing fish, such as sardines and dried tuna.

Market gardens are also of prime importance in Valencia. The main products are citrus fruit, vegetables, and potherbs, which this region exports in large quantities (oranges are particularly renowned and even have a designation of origin).

As for desserts, the most internationally renowned is *turrón* (a kind of nougat mostly made with honey and almonds and commonly eaten at Christmas): the most famous nougats are the one from Jijona (soft nougat made with ground almonds) and the one from Alicante (hard nougat, made with whole or coarsely chopped almonds). Both of these specialties are classified under a designation of origin. Other popular desserts are *arnadíes* (made with pumpkin and sweet potato), typical Easter cakes, *orelletes* ("small ears"), and fritters that come in various shapes.

One of the most distinctive beverages in Valencia is *horchata*, a sweet drink made from pressed tigernuts mixed with water and sugar. There are also a number of designation of origin wines.

Discussing the gastronomy of Murcia means mentioning vegetables, which can be found in most dishes. The cuisine of Murcia, close to that of Valencia, is based on its vegetables, fruits, rice, and wine. Pulse and vegetable stews are popular and are made with a wide variety of ingredients, such as fresh or dry broad beans, fresh garlic, thistle, artichokes, peppers, cauliflower, and green beans. Also worth mentioning are dishes such as the gypsy pot (pumpkin stew) or the wheat stews. Rice is also an outstanding food in Murcia and it is prepared in various ways; the most typical preparation is rice with vegetables, but many other rice dishes deserve special mention, such as rice with rabbit and snails, rice with lean meat and ribs, or *caldero*, a typical coastal dish, made with rice boiled in various kind of fish stock. The most common meat dishes are baked suckling goat, lamb chops with *ajo cabañil*, a mixture of chopped garlic, vinegar and a bayleaf, small game (rabbit, hare, partridges, and quails), large game (deer), and poultry (for example, the "stock with balls," a turkey stew with meatballs, a traditional Christmas dish).

As in the region of Valencia, fish also play an important part in the gastronomy of Murcia, especially the gray mullet, whose roe are considered exquisite, the sea bass, the sea bream, and the small and tasty prawns.

Mediterranean fruit is the main dessert, although there are also some typical sweet preparations, such as *tocinos de cielo* and *yemas de Caravaca* (made with egg yolks and sugar), marzipan, candied pumpkin pulp, rum babas, *tortada* Murcia style (a meringue-based cake), and the *papajotes*, a dessert of Arabic origin made with lemon tree leaves battered in a fine sweet dough and coated in sugar and cinnamon. As for as wine, red wines are prominent. There are three designations of origin—*Jumilla, Yecla,* and *Bullas*—and some other local varieties of good quality.

Galicia

The autonomous region of Galicia is located in the farthest northwestern part of the Iberian Peninsula, on the Atlantic ocean. Its coastline stretches about 250 miles and consists of alternating high cliffs and calm

Dish with different pork products, Galicia.

firths, rich in seafood and fish. Galician fishermen are of prime importance for the economy of the region and likewise, fishing and marine
products are essential to Galician gastronomy.

The city of Vigo is currently the main fishing harbor of Europe, and
Galician firths are the largest producers of mussels in the world, as well as
of other shellfish: goose barnacles, scampi, scallops, mussels, cockles,
clams, octopus, sea brim, sardines, sea bass, and many other species. The
markets where fish is auctioned present a wide variety of deep-sea species,
such as tuna, hake, codfish, pollock, and the savory blue jack mackerel.

The importance that Galician people attach to food is shown by the
more than 300 gastronomic festivals held through the year in this region.
These celebrations are mainly related to land products and originate from
local holidays and all kinds of fairs. Celebrations often coincide with harvesting and religious festivals, such as the pilgrimages to local shrines,
usually accompanied by traditional meals.

The coast is surely rich in products, but inland areas equally provide a
wide variety of foods: *pimientos de Padrón* (designation of origin peppers),
potatoes, turnip tops (tender turnip sprouts exclusively eaten in this part

of the peninsula), different kinds of bread, chestnuts, walnuts, hazelnuts, and almonds, as well as wild mushrooms, blueberries, and wood honey. Farm products are the base of dishes, such as Galician soup, made with different vegetables: chard, green beans, cabbage, turnip tops, potatoes, and beans. Of all Galician meats, bovine products are the most popular ones. Veal is controlled by the designation of origin Ternera gallega. Countless veal recipes can be found in Galicia, such as tenderloin and stew Galicia style. Ox and kid (which is usually roasted) are also very appreciated, and among poultry, roosters and capons, which were traditionally eaten during Christmas season, are popular. Pork is an essential food in Galician gastronomy: *lacón* (a kind of savory cooked ham) is used in the preparation of the famous *lacón* with turnip tops. In the interior of the region, sausages, both dried and smoked, are highly popular, too. Other parts of the pig are used in various Galician stews (bacon, snout, the meat around the vertebrae, feet, etc.). Another important preparation is *empanada*: puff pastry filled with various local products, such as pork rib or sirloin, veal sirloin, sausage, sardines, octopus, codfish, or tuna.

As for cheeses, most of them are made from cow milk. The most distinctive is the *tetilla* or *teta gallega*. The most internationally famous Galician dessert is the popular *tarta de Santiago*, an almond cake. As for alcoholic drinks, there are five designations of origin in Galicia, the most outstanding one being Ribeiro. Among liquors, the most popular one is a Galician spirit (*orujo*), which is also used in the recipe for the traditional *queimada* (flamed spirit with sugar).

Tarta de Santiago (Galician Almond Cake)

Ingredients
- 2 cups of blanched almonds
- 1 cup of sugar
- 2–3 tbs. of butter
- 6 eggs
- grated rind of 1 lemon
- 1/4 tbs. powdered cinnamon
- Powdered sugar for topping

Preparation
Preheat oven to 425 degrees. Mix butter with sugar and cinnamon. Separately beat eggs with grated lemon rind until foamy. Grind almonds to fine paste in a mortar or electric blender. Add almonds and beaten eggs to butter and sugar. Mix only enough to blend well. Pour into 9-inch round cake pan that has been lightly

buttered and sprinkled with flour. Bake 25 to 30 minutes in 425 degree oven. Cake is done when a toothpick inserted in the middle comes out clean and cake springs back if pressed with a finger. Invert cake until it cools before removing from pan.

Place cooled cake on cookie sheet, and coat top of cake with the powdered sugar. The cake should be of a rich brown color and "snowed."

Basque Country, Navarra, and La Rioja

The Basque Country, or Euskadi, is a coastal region that borders France. Its culinary richness and variety are due to the combination of fishermen's traditions with a deep rooted mountain culture. Nowadays,

Pintxos in a bar, Basque Country.

both of these features mingle to create a modern *cusine d'auteur* (author's cuisine) of very high quality, which made its appearance in the last decades with the so-called New Basque Cuisine. Such distinguishing culinary traits are due, above all, to the cultural specificity of the Basque people, who have maintained and improved their tradition and their ancestral language: *Euskera*. The Basque are fond of good food and a large part of their social life revolves around meals. An example of the cultural importance of food in this country are the various gastronomic associations, traditional meeting places, mainly restricted to men, that were created toward the end of the nineteenth century. The members of the associations compete in the preparation of special dishes, contributing to the preservation and recovering of old recipes and bringing fresh energy into the Basque cuisine by revaluing dishes of humble origin but of high culinary value. Until very recently, gastronomic societies did not admit women, except, perhaps, on specific festive occasions. The most traditional associations still do not.

Living on the Gulf of Bizkaia, the Basque people have historically been great fishermen. Their constant fishing expeditions to Newfoundland, ever since the Middle Ages, are reflected nowadays in the massive consumption of cod, a fish that, through the Basque harbors, also reached the rest of Spain. The sauces that were created to go with this fish (for example, *pil pil* is made with olive oil, garlic, and chili pepper; *vizcaína* is made with olive oil, tomatoes, peppers, onion, and garlic; and green sauce is made with olive oil, parsley, green pepper, and garlic) are the particular heritage of Basque gastronomy. Other kinds of fish, such as hake, tuna, sea bream, *txangurro* (lobster), baby squid, anchovies, and the highly valued elvers, are also a must within the culinary offering of this region, and they have inspired the creation of fishermen's stews as popular as *marmitako* (with tuna), baby squid in its own ink, or the particular *kokotxas*, which are traditionally eaten in small coastal villages or public canteens belonging to fishermen's associations. Tuna belly and sardines are mainly eaten roasted. In Euskadi, roasted food, fish, and bovine meat are very popular; the meat is preferred rare and as large chops.

Mushrooms, called *perretxikos* (especially the boletus species) and small game (pigeons, woodcocks, turtle doves) are characteristic of autumn; as in the case of local vegetables. They have become the ingredients of diverse local dishes, such as the peppers from Gernika or the renowned beans from Tolosa. Most traditional dishes are prepared with local products, considering that this is a mountainous region with many isolated farms and valleys.

Many desserts are based on milk: fried milk, *cuajada, intxaursalsa* (dairy dessert with walnuts), custard *canutillos* (tube shaped fritters), and *franchipán* (puff pastry cake filled with custard and almonds). Among cheeses, *Idiazábal* deserves special mention. This is usually eaten before dessert. The most popular alcoholic drinks are wine and apple cider. In many cider bars, especially in the province of Gipuzkoa, cider is served directly from huge barrels and the meals consist of dishes, such as codfish omelette or beef chop, served on large, common tables. Yet, the main drink in the Basque country is wine; part of the internationally renowned designation of origin La Rioja is located in the inner Basque province of Alava, a subarea called Rioja Alavesa, which boasts some of the most ancient wineries. Together with *Rioja*, the Basque wine par excellence is *txakoli*, a local white wine, light and aromatic. The practice of *tapeo* (here known as *txiquiteo*[9]) in the Basque country is almost a daily social ritual. In the old areas of the cities, such as the historic areas of Bilbao, Donostia-San Sebastaían, Vitoria, or even in smaller towns, bars are packed one next to the other. Groups of friends successively visit each bar and have some of the different *pintxos* (like *tapas*—small portions) offered on the counter, accompanying them with *txikitos*. Customers seldom take a seat, eating the food and drinks while standing by the counter.

The kingdom of Navarra was the last one to join the union of kingdoms that shaped Spain in the sixteenth century, actually after the kingdom of Granada had been reconquered (1492). Thus, the autonomous region of Navarra shares some cultural and historical characteristics with the Basque country, as well as the language (*Euskera*, the Basque language is spoken in the whole northern mountainous territory of Navarra) and landscape, although it has no coastal area (it stretches southward, toward the inner land). In Navarra, valleys alternate with thick woods and rivers. These geographical features are reflected in the gastronomy, and the dishes change depending on whether one approaches the Pyrenean area, the river shores, or the midterritories, with their green valleys and plains. Typical products of the mountainous territory are milk, cheese (*Roncal* is the most famous), meat (bovine and ovine), chestnuts, hazelnuts, potatoes, abundant tomatoes, borrage, peas, lettuce, peppers, thistle, curly cole, cabbage, and chard. Apart from this variety of food, Navarra is famous for three specific products: the asparagus from the river area, *piquillo pimientos* (peppers roasted over beechwood and peeled by hand), and the artichokes from Tudela.

Most fish is freshwater, mainly trout and salmon. For meat, Navarra shares some eating practices with Aragon, for example, lamb *chilindrón*. Other popular meats include beef, pork, and game (doves, deer, hare, partridge, and quail).

As for wine, although some local wines share with La Rioja and the Basque Country the Rioja designation of origin, Navarra also has its own designation of origin with excellent red wines. Another particularly outstanding alcoholic drink is *pacharán*, typically made by mixing sloe berries with aniseed liquor: this liquor, which was conceived as a medical remedy, is nowadays industrially made, though in Navarra traditional homemade preparations are still frequent.

La Rioja is a small inland region located along Santiago's Way, both a traveler destination and an exchange area and, importantly, the producer of excellent wines (classified under the *Rioja* designation of origin). Its gastronomy has been strongly influenced by that of its neighbors. The cuisine of La Rioja, traditionally an agricultural area, is characterized by vegetables, herbs, pulses, peppers, garlic, onion, artichokes, asparaguses, lettuce, chard, and borrage. Among the most popular La Rioja dishes are the stews based on *pochas* (beans), which preserve the taste of beans, absorbing at the same time that of the quail and *chorizo* that accompany them. Pigs, the symbol of Christian culture, are raised both in the wild and on farms. Lamb chops are a must at the evening meals eaten in the wineries and gastronomic societies and a frequent dish on the menus of restaurants, where they are grilled over fruit canes, acquiring a special flavor.[10] The most typical sausages are sweet blood sausage and *chorizo* Rioja style. Another remarkable dish is potatoes Rioja style, with chorizo or pork ribs.

Fish are a highly traditional food, despite the fact that La Rioja is an interior region. Codfish is surely outstanding (cooked Rioja style, with tomatoes and peppers), as well as sea bream in sauce, mainly eaten on Christmas Eve (as in many other interior regions of Spain). Other remarkable fish dishes are the delicious river crayfish with *fritada* and hake in green sauce. Snails and mushrooms are also a common food in La Rioja and are often combined into one dish.

What has most contributed to giving La Rioja an international reputation is the quality of its wines. La Rioja occupies the center, and the largest part, of the designation of origin area that, as previously seen, it shares with the Basque Country and Navarra. La Rioja produces excellent red wines that are aged in casks for a minimum of 24 months (*crianza*) or 36 months (*reserva*).

NOTES

1. All over Spain there are many traditional ways of drinking coffee: black, *cortado* (coffee with a dash of milk), "stained milk"(milk with a dash of coffee), and *carajllo* (coffee with brandy). Names, quantities, and cup size may vary depending on the region considered.

2. Dish made with flour or breadcrumbs, eaten in various Spanish regions (see the following section on "Cuisine by Region").

3. Carried out by the Fundación Independiente, *La hora de Europa, la hora de España* (Madrid: Fundación Independiente, 2002).

4. The North African autonomous towns of Ceuta and Melilla are included within the Andalusian area of influence. Their cuisines, halfway between the Andalusian and Moroccan ones, are especially renowned for fish preparations and for Moroccan spices and aromas.

5. The Tabernas desert, in the province of Almería, on the Oriental Mediterranean coast of the peninsula.

6. The most important national livestock fair, that of Torrelavega, is held in Cantabria.

7. There are two designations of origin for olive oil in Catalonia: Garrigues and Siurana, both obtained from a fruity and small olive species known as *arbequina*.

8. As is the case of *El Bulli* in Roses (Girona), run by Ferran Adrià, considered internationally as the most creative cook of our time, or of *El Racó de Can Fabes* of Sant Celoni, managed by Santi Santamaria.

9. Term indicating the consumption of *txikitos*, small glasses of red wine or *txakolí*, but also of beer. *Txikitos* accompany the local *pintxos*, small portions of various kinds of food (similar to *tapas*), placed on a slice of bread. *Pintxos* have recently turned into sophisticated gastronomic creations.

10. On festive occasions it is traditional for friends and family to meet in the household cellars where wine is kept to mature, in order to eat an afternoon snack or have dinner.

5

Eating Out

At present, eating out is a much-discussed mass phenomenon in all Europe. In general, Spaniards are keen on eating and drinking out, as their lifestyle and traditions show. The Iberian Peninsula encompasses a wide variety of climates, but the temperatures, typical of a southern European country, are never extreme. A mild climate allows for outings and outdoor celebrations almost any time of the year, which results into a lifestyle where "going out," sociability, and commensality are held in high esteem.

It appears that the Spanish consumption pattern, in general, falls within the Mediterranean consumption profile, as in France and Italy.[1] Thus, in terms of time devoted to leisure and personal relationships, Spaniards, unlike the rest of the Europeans, spend a great deal of money on eating out and drinking, especially in bars and restaurants. So much so, that Spain, together with Ireland and Italy, is the country with the highest food budget in the European Union. Among the daily practices connected with leisure, social meetings in bars and restaurants are the most important spare-time activity in Spain, especially for men, while for women it is only a secondary activity. "Eating out" implies kinds of sociability and commensality that can be associated with different spaces, institutions, and groups, characterized by a high sociocultural content. Some of these features are discussed in the following sections.

Fondas and inns (*posadas*) that provide accommodation and food have a long established tradition in Spain, and their services have been usually

Sign in a bar listing different typical foods.

aimed at foreigners and "guests" (tourists).[2] The nineteenth century brought, at least in the main Spanish cities, a consolidation of the bourgeoisie and, above all, of the middle classes; this would strongly affect the consumption pattern and would lead to a consolidation of restaurants.[3] The latter would become established as such, and under this name, at the beginning of the century; they were either new, elitist initiatives or transformations of the dining rooms in the already existing inns and hotels.

In the main Spanish cities (Madrid, Barcelona, and Bilbao, and later on Seville and Valencia) restaurants soon started to proliferate. As for taverns (predecessors of today's bars) and food and drink stalls, they also played an important role on a popular level. They used to be located near markets and offered drinks (mostly wine) and local food specialties at a very low cost (toward the end of the eighteenth century these facilities started to include tables and long benches for common meals). In Seville, around the mid-nineteenth century there were 446 taverns in the city but only 36 restaurants and cafés.[4]

The kind of food that could be eaten in inns, cafés, and restaurants may be classified thus: local, Spanish, "French," and "foreign."[5] As has been observed in previous chapters, the French influence was particularly strong in Spain from the nineteenth century onward. French *haute cuisine* became the model to follow in the best restaurants, which imitated French recipes and style to satisfy an incipient influx of wealthy tourists. Local cuisine, however, was appreciated mostly by the populace. On some occasions, French recipes were adapted to local products and techniques; the result, far from being genuine French cuisine, was yet promoted as such. For a long time, the terms *fonda* and *restaurante* were confused by the population and they were used to indicate similar establishments. Yet, little by little, the word *restaurante* became distinguished from *fonda* because

Popular tavern (*taberna*) in the center of Seville.

it denoted a place where wealthier customers could enjoy more sophisticated dishes and better service, as well as a novelty: wine menus that included better quality products, imported from different places and even from abroad.

In the nineteenth century, the first gastronomic societies or *txokos* were founded in the Basque Country. In these places, which were exclusively for men, members cooked and shared meals; they recreated recipes and investigated, creating new dishes.

Another novelty in the Spanish panorama of the late nineteenth century were beer pubs, initially like cafés, which specialized in serving cool beer.[6] At this time, the first beer breweries were created in Spain, but their number dramatically increased from the 1920s on, and through the rest of the twentieth century. Taverns, which would later evolve into bars, also proliferated in this period. In Madrid, in the 1920s, already more than 2,000 establishments sold alcoholic drinks. *Tapas,* which are now considered traditional, were a novelty introduced at the beginning of the twentieth century. Although their historical antecedents date back to earlier times, during this period *tapas* became part of the public and popular gastronomic offering and multiplied into many different specialties.

The 1930s were marked by the deposition of the monarchy and the restoration of the second Spanish Republic as well as by the Spanish civil war (1936–1939). This was a time of crisis and conflict that would be followed by the postwar era and by a general scarcity of food. Consequently, catering establishments did not fare well and many of them shut down, while others survived after overcoming great difficulties. The postwar period was characterized by lack of food, a dictatorial regime, and the predominance of the Catholic Church, which imposed restrictions on entertainment facilities (such as dancing halls, for example). Although the visits to restaurants decreased, due to lack of resources, bars and the practice of *tapeo* enjoyed greater success during these years of scarcity, especially in the south and the center of Spain, because a few small *tapas* could replace lunch or dinner. All over Spain there were internal migrations from the country to the cities, especially to Barcelona and Madrid. Various restaurants, which were opened as a consequence of the increased population, specialized in local cuisine and in other Spanish gastronomies. The number of new bars multiplied by approximately 150 between the 1960s and the end of the 1980s. The phenomenon of mass tourism also started in this period; tourists were attracted by the Spanish sun and beaches and this triggered a transformation of coastal areas, which became crowded with hotels, restaurants, bars, and leisure facilities. Tourist menus made their appearance, as well as the "typical" dishes, such as *paella* and *sangría*, which would turn into tourist banners of Spanish gastronomy. New dishes were invented in this period, such as the mixed *paella* (which combines fish and meat), a specialty that was created exclusively for tourists and subsequently became successful with the local population as well.

Since the restoration of democracy, toward the mid-1970s, and Spain's entry into the European Community in the mid-1980s, there has been a burgeoning social and economic advance. Not only has tourism been increasing, but it has evolved to include cultural, sports, adventure, urban, and congress-related services (besides the traditional offer of sunny resorts and beaches). Accommodation and catering services have also developed in measure, seeking to achieve higher quality and targeting wealthier consumers. Spain currently ranks third among the countries with accommodation capacity, following the United States and Italy, and it has the second highest number of foreign visitors, after France.

EATING OUT TODAY

Bars

Bars are, perhaps, the most popular establishments in Spain and there are about 200,000 of them. They provide drinks and meals (the latter usually on a small scale). People mainly visit bars to have breakfast, *almuerzo* (white coffee, cakes, rolls, etc.), aperitif and *tapas*, and in general, all day long in order to have coffee, drinks, and snacks. Bars offer a wide selection of products and prices. Some of them also offer inexpensive lunches (fixed-price menus including starter, main course, dessert, and coffee) chiefly aimed at those who eat outside the home. As far as *tapas* are concerned, it is worth mentioning that Basque taverns (some of them are recently created franchises) have recently become quite popular almost all over Spain. Here customers can have diverse *pintxos* (Basque variety of *tapas*) at inexpensive prices, together with beer and wine. *Terrazas* (outdoor patios) are very popular in the spring and summer.

The tip is never included in the bill (not only in bars, but also in cafés and restaurants), and this is always a personal option solely if the customer has been satisfied.

Cafés

As in other European countries, cafés have been socially important ever since the nineteenth century. In some cases, their fare was similar to that of inns and taverns. Cafés were also the places for artistic and literary get-togethers, and some of them, such as Els quatre gats, which reopened, or Les set portes, today a very popular restaurant in Barcelona, or the coffee shops of Gijón and Pombo in Madrid, are still popular meeting places.

The service and hours of business of cafés mostly coincide with those of bars; yet, they mainly specialize in drinks (coffee, liquors, etc.) and snacks (cakes, sweets, delicatessen), and they are more for social gatherings, quiet, and conversation, especially in the afternoon. The most classic coffee shops have a higher status than bars; however, since the 1990s, some coffee shop franchises have been created and are rapidly spreading all over Spain. Their appearance is that of traditional Italian cafés and they combine rather inexpensive prices with a popular appeal.

Restaurants

In Spain there are a wide variety of restaurants that may be classified according to the various kinds of cuisine they offer. They usually open at lunchtime and in the evening, or only in the evening. At lunchtime most establishments (except top-tier restaurants), with a wide variety of food offered, provide inexpensive, fixed-price menus. In the evening, prices are higher. On weekends, especially in big cities where demand is great, dinners are served in two shifts: about 9 P.M. and 11 P.M. Families and friends commonly have lunch and dinner in restaurants on holidays and weekends, a phenomenon that is facilitated by the great variety of restaurants and prices that are affordable to most of the population.

The most basic restaurants offer various Spanish dishes, either local preparations or specialties from other regions. Other establishments include in their menus a number of well-known Spanish dishes, although they are not oriented toward any specific kind of cuisine. This panorama is completed by specialty restaurants, such as vegetarian and macrobiotic ones.

In the mid-1980s, when foreign immigration to Spain increased, ethnic restaurants (Chinese, South American, Pakistani, Indian, Moroccan, Lebanese, etc.) became more numerous, especially in urban areas, adding to other restaurants that already offered other kinds of food, mainly European (Italian, Greek, French, German, etc.). In recent years, ethnic fast food, such as warm donner kebab (Turkish-German style), in restaurants or also as a food in the street or take-out, is very popular at reasonable prices.

Restaurants that specialize in new cuisine deserve special mention. Spain, together with France, is currently the leading country for cutting-edge, creative cuisine. Some of the best chefs and restaurants in the world are located in Spain, more specifically in Catalonia, the Basque Country, and, to a lesser degree, in Madrid. The Catalan Ferran Adrià (internationally regarded as the most innovative chef at the moment), Santi Santamaría, Carme Ruscalleda, the Basque Juan María Arzak, and Pedro Subijana belong to the international cooking elite. This has triggered a proliferation of high-level cooking schools and the consolidation of an outstanding generation of chefs who have turned their restaurants into an impressive feature of the current Spanish gastronomy.

Basque Gastronomic Societies or *Txokos*

The relationship of Basques with cooking and eating is very close, to the extent that it is claimed to be one of their own cultural features. Private Basque gastronomic societies were started in the nineteenth century. They are usually reserved for men, although some of them have admitted women as members in the last decades. The only way to visit one is by invitation and in the company of a member. All the activities of these societies revolve around food and their members compete in the preparation of special dishes for their brethren. The societies' members have contributed to preserving and recovering old recipes, and to innovating cuisine. Some of the most renowned Basque chefs of the moment have belonged to a gastronomic society.

Fast Food and Take Out

Since the 1970s, Spain experienced a boom of pizzerias and later on, under the influence of North America, of fast-food outlets, which have enjoyed increasing success from the 1980s on. Most of the popular international fast-food chains can be found in Spain, although, unlike in other European countries the market penetration rate of this kind of establishment in Spain is less than 5 percent.[7] Some local fast-food franchises have been created to counteract this phenomenon, supporting Spanish food, such as sandwiches (*bocadillos*) made with long Spanish loaves and filled with various local products (ham, *chorizo*, cheese, meat, peppers, etc.). Take-out food has also become more popular in the last decades, especially in the cities. Pizzerias and ethnic take-out provide quick, hot meals at low prices. In the case of pizzerias, it is worth distinguishing between those that are fast-food chains, which usually deliver and provide take-out pizzas, and the popular pizzerias (mainly Italian and Argentinean), which prepare pizzas to be eaten on the premises, and thus, must be regarded as restaurants.

Last, there are also fast-food establishments that offer all kinds of dishes (stews, pasta, vegetables, meat, fish) homemade style, saving customers' time and effort.

TRIPS AND OUTDOOR MEALS

Going out to the country, to meadows, rivers, and other places outside the city to have a country meal or a picnic has been a tradition for centuries, due to the favorable climate of the peninsula. In the twentieth century, at the end of the postwar period and in the subsequent years, going to the country with the extended family and friends became a leisure activity that could be afforded by the lower and working classes who could not always afford to gather in a restaurant. These outings involved taking food that had been prepared at home (Spanish potato omelette, sausage, etc.) and could be eaten cold. Alternatively, people carried along the necessary utensils to cook food in the open air (grilled meat was particularly popular, as well as other festive dishes, such as *paella,* if the place was suitable for its preparation). This kind of excursion involved carrying folding chairs and tables and camping cutlery sets; the main means of transportation were utilitarian cars, and the most popular sites were natural environments that were relatively close to the city.

Because of new legislation concerning fire making in natural environments, picnic sites and suitable common spots were created for this type of gathering; they included stone tables and benches, and barbecues for meat roasting. Although this kind of outing is less popular nowadays, some picnic sites are used sporadically.

SCHOOLS AND INSTITUTIONS

In the 1930s, companies were obliged by the law to provide their workers with a cafeteria in case lunch breaks lasted less than two hours; firms also had to subsidize most of the meal if there were more than 50 workers.[8] During the 1960s, costs were cut down by eliminating personnel and introducing self-service cafeterias. Currently, only large firms or those in industrial areas far away from the city have cafeterias. In urban areas, where food options at lunchtime are varied and abundant, cafeterias are not needed.

However, in recent decades there has been, in general terms, an important expansion of common dining halls in universities, schools, health centers, factories, and so forth. The food is inexpensive (they are usually publicly supported) and they address the increasing need of the population for eating their meals outside home at lunchtime and during night shifts. Recently, the menus have reflected a change in eating modes, including diet and vegetarian dishes, halal, and so forth. Schools are a special case. School dining halls have a double function: they provide a meal for children who cannot go home for lunch, and they are the place where table manners and food practices are learned. In recent years, the focus has been on nutritional balance and offering the healthiest possible foods.

NOTES

1. Data from Eurostat, the Statistical Office of the European Commission, which carries out surveys on diverse issues related to countries belonging to the European Union.

2. The term "hotel" would not become established until the beginning of the twentieth century.

3. The antecedents of restaurants date back to the end of the eighteenth century, to the time of the French Revolution. They were created in order to offer the population the same dishes as those consumed by the nobles. The first restaurant was opened in Paris in 1765. This model would rapidly spread to the rest of Europe and the world.

4. Isabel González Turmo, *Sevilla: Banquetes, cartas, tapas y menús* (Seville: Ayuntamiento de Sevilla, 1996).

5. While restaurants were more elitist, there was no clear difference between *fondas* and cafés. *Fondas* apparently offered accommodation and food, while cafés provided drinks and occasionally food as well. However, it was common for these terms to be confused.

6. Beer pubs had already made their appearance in the sixteenth century, due to the influence of Emperor Charles and his court, but they were not popular yet.

7. In Switzerland and the United Kingdom the fast-food market penetration rate is 20 percent; the market penetration rate in Germany, Sweden, and France is between 10 and 20 percent. In Belgium, Austria, Finland, and Ireland it is between 5 and 10 percent. In Spain, Portugal, Italy, and Greece it amounts to less than 5 percent.

8. González Turmo, *Sevilla: Banquetes, cartas, tapas y menús*.

6

Special Occasions: Holidays, Celebrations, and Religious Rituals

Celebrations are very popular in Spanish society, and food plays an important role on these occasions. We can distinguish between private celebrations and public ones; the latter can be further classified into local, regional, and national festivities. Most celebrations are associated with typical foods, which are always eaten and shared in social contexts.

Culturally, Spain has a long-established Catholic tradition, although currently, religious practice has decreased significantly. Despite this secularization, annual festivities, mostly of religious origin, are still observed and celebrated. In general, there is a renewed interest and a wish to recover traditions, although celebrations are informed nowadays by a different social and cultural meaning.

This chapter will discuss the most important festivities through the year. Only those celebrations that are of gastronomic interest and involve typical food preparations will be contemplated. In addition, some of the most important personal and familial celebrations—those related to the life cycle—in which food also plays an essential role, will be overviewed.

THE CHRISTMAS CYCLE

The Christmas season—the Christmas religious cycle—officially begins December 8, the day of the Immaculate Conception. In many Spanish cities (such as Seville, for example) and villages it is celebrated each year with dances, parades, or community banquets.

From Saint Lucia's Day (December 13, the prelude to Christmas celebrations) on until Christmas, there are many Christmas markets with stalls where one can find all kinds of Christmas decoration: from the *belenes*—the little figures that represent the birth of Christ—to Christmas trees. The variety of the stalls is expanding: one can find jewels, handmade crafts, and typical Christmas food and sweets. Christmas markets in Spain are scattered among villages and cities with booths filled with lots of different food, fresh and dried fruits, such as raisins, oranges, apples, and nuts. There are also cakes, marzipan candies, and other baked goods.

In Spain, big Christmas celebrations occur on Christmas Eve (December 24) and Christmas Day (December 25). Depending on the region, one day is celebrated more than the other. In the center and the west of the peninsula, for example, Christmas Eve is the most celebrated day, whereas in the east (and especially in Catalonia), Christmas Day is the most important one.

Christmas Eve

Christmas Eve is traditionally a family celebration, and until very recently, bars and restaurants used to be closed in the evening. It is commonly celebrated with a big dinner, usually in the home of one of the family members. Traditionally, baked sea brim has been the main dish in many areas of the interior of the peninsula, such as the Castilian Meseta. Stuffed chicken (*capon*) turned into the main Christmas Eve dish in the mid-twentieth century, when it was not as common as it is today.

Even though the tendency is to pull out all the stops for the Christmas meal, there is no one particular Christmas menu to speak of. The menu is much more varied and standardized (seafood, shrimps, prawns, sea bream, turkey, lamb, piglet, etc.). Until some decades ago, however, each region had its own typical Christmas Eve menu.

As for cakes and drinks, a few are more or less common to all tables: *turrón* (nougat) and marzipan (desserts of Arabic origin, made with almonds and honey), *polvorones* (made with almonds, lard, sugar, and cinnamon), and *mantecados* (made with almonds, lard, egg, flour, sugar, and cinnamon). The *turrón* is the most important Christmas dessert: a very tasty and sweet nougat of Arabic origin made with almonds and honey or sugar, without which it would just not be Christmas in Spain. There are innumerable variations—chocolate, coconut, orange, praline—but the oldest and authentic recipes are those for "soft" (Jijona) *turrón*, made with ground almonds, or "hard" (Alicante) *turrón*, made with whole almonds,

Cava.

or, recently, also served as an ice cream. Besides sweets, people also eat dried fruits and nuts: almonds, walnuts, hazelnuts, figs, and raisins.

Drinks usually include Spanish wines (red for meat and white for fish and seafood), cider, and especially *cava*, the festive drink par excellence, which became widespread during the twentieth century and is a must for all celebrations nowadays.

Catholics usually attend midnight Mass (*Misa del Gallo*, literally, "Cock Mass" or Mass of the Rooster). According to the Catholic tradition, this animal was the first one to witness Jesus' birth and announce it to the world. The family members attend midnight mass together and after that they have a snack (sweet wine, dried fruits, Christmas sweets, etc.).

Young people usually go out with their friends after they have had the "typical" dinner at home with their families.

Christmas Day

As on Christmas Eve, the Christmas Day table is set with the best tablecloth, cutlery, and glasses. As for the Christmas menu, although there has been a certain homogenization with prestige food (meat, seafood, etc.) taking center stage, each region has its own dishes. These include varieties of stew (such as Catalan *escudella y carn d'olla* or stew with meatballs from Valencia), *capon* (chicken), and roast lamb. Desserts are similar to those served on Christmas Eve: *turrón* (nougat), marzipan, *polvorones*, *mantecados*, and dried fruits. And also important on Christmas day is wine, and finally *cava*—must-haves for Spanish celebrations.

Saint Stephen's Day

In Catalonia and some areas of the Levant, Saint Stephen's Day (December 26) is also a holiday. This traditional festivity is still maintained in Catalonia, whereas it has been lost in other places such as the Valencia region. On this day people usually consume the same dishes as on Christmas (very often, the abundant leftovers).

New Year's Eve

The last day of the year is celebrated all over Spain with a very special dinner. After dinner, at midnight, millions of Spaniards eat grapes while the big clocks of cities and towns chime twelve strokes (the most popular clock on this night is in the *Puerta del Sol* in Madrid, which is shown on TV for all to see). They eat one grape for each stroke and tradition has it that those who manage to eat the twelve grapes at the rhythm of the strokes will have a good year. This is a happy moment, pregnant with good intentions for the year that has just started. Spaniards celebrate the New Year toasting with *cava*. Afterward, most people go to the several parties, balls, and cotillions, public or private, organized everywhere.

New Year's Day

Lunch on the first day of the year is usually a family meal and it is rather late (about 3 P.M. or later), because everybody, especially young people, has been celebrating the New Year until early morning hours. Lunch is served again on a festively decorated table and the menu is quite elaborate, but also in this case, there is no one particular New Year's Day menu to speak of.

Three Kings' Day

In Anglo-Saxon countries Santa Claus brings gifts to children on Christmas Eve. Spaniards, however, celebrate Three Kings' Day (Twelfth Night) on January 6. January 5, the Feast of the Epiphany, is heralded with parades in cities where candy and sweets are distributed to throngs of children. On the night of January 5, children go to bed hoping to find, the following morning, the gifts left by the Three Eastern Kings. On January 6, after a family lunch, the typical Epiphany cake is eaten: *Roscón de Reyes*, a ring-shaped cake made with fine dough and decorated with little pieces of candied fruits symbolizing the rubies and emeralds that, according to the popular imagination, adorned the cloaks of the Three Kings. A little surprise is hidden inside the dough, usually a small figurine, and the one who finds it is crowned king of the house with a golden cardboard crown (which usually comes with the cake). The *roscón* may also contain a dry broad bean, and traditionally, the person who finds it must pay for the cake (though this is not usually enforced).

Saint Agatha's Eve and Day

In the north of Spain (particularly in the Basque Country, Navarra, and La Rioja) on Saint Agatha's Eve (February 4), many choirs (children and also adults, but particularly young people) gather in the street to sing to this patron saint of young people and also women.[1]

In the villages, the choirs are frequently dressed in the typical local style and they also carry big wooden sticks with them to keep the rhythm. Neighbors give the choirs some food (eggs, bacon, sausages, wine) or, recently, also some money for a shared banquet.

CARNIVAL AND LENT

Carnival and Lent belong to the Easter cycle of holidays. Carnival goes back to the fifteenth century and became popular in Spain in the sixteenth. It is the celebration of excess and entertainment. Although it has almost completely lost its religious meaning, it is also the time when people "take their leave" from meat for Lent.

Carnival celebration was banned in Spain during the last dictatorship. The reason is clear: Carnival is the most irreverent, subversive, authority-defying of festivals. Since it was legalized under democracy, in all Spain the Carnival has progressed as a feast that is both of the street and for the street. Many Carnival celebrations and parades are renowned all over Spain: Tenerife (said to be second only to that in Rio de Janeiro); Las Palmas, in the Canary Islands; Cadis, in Andalusia; Sitges, in Catalonia (the most important gay carnival in Europe); or the carnivals in many small villages in the Pyrenean area (in Navarre, Aragon, or even in Catalonia).

In the past, since Lent was associated with contrition and abstention from meat, people tried to enjoy food (especially meat) as much as they could during Carnival. This was not only because during the next 40 days meat was forbidden by religion (to commemorate Christ's 40 days in the desert), but also because people were eager to consume a food that was otherwise scarce throughout the rest of the year. Fat Thursday was the first day of this period before Lent, characterized by abundant and communal meals that are still had in some places. For example, a typical food was crackling omelette and, more specifically potato omelette, eaten above all

Market stand with salt cod and other salted preparations.

by schoolchildren who enjoyed this holiday very much. In certain areas, such as Catalonia, another typical dish is *butifarra* with egg. The last day of Carnival is also known as *fiesta* or *entierro de la sardina* ("sardine holiday"); a sardine is buried as a sign that Carnival festivities are over. That day is still celebrated in various Spanish areas with a popular sardine feast (different historical and artistic representations of that day in Madrid are renowned, as, for example, Goya or Gutiérrez Solana's masterpieces with this title: *El entierro de la sardina*).

Lent is a period of contrition and reduction of food; although the religious meaning is not as important as is once was, some traditions are still maintained and fish consumption, for example, increases. The most popular fish is cod, which is cooked in countless tasty and imaginative ways. The typical Lent cakes are *buñuelos* (spongy fritters made with dough and aniseed, which are fried and coated in sugar).

Carnival traditions persist. For example, in Barcelona's food markets, a new "tradition" was born also a few years ago: for the Shrove Tuesday Carnival, shopkeepers come to work in fancy dress, and, in some markets, when they are selling food, they have also a glass of *cava* with their customers.

THE HOLY WEEK CYCLE

The Holy Week commemorates the passion of Christ. Religious celebrations were carried out all over Spain in the past, but the religious significance has been lost in most parts of the north of the peninsula. In the south, conversely, religious tradition is still very common, especially in Andalusia, where Holy Week processions are widely popular. On Palm Sunday (last Sunday before the Holy Week), people go to mass in the morning and carry laurel and herbs (adults, and particularly women) or palms (children) to be blessed by the priest. Boys carry a simple palm branch, and girls carry a branch that has been decorated. They often have sweets, tinsel, or other decorations hanging from them. Laurel and other herbs blessed by the priest seem to be very good to put in stews or other recipes during the year.

During Holy Week, meat was still prohibited from ancient times until the late twentieth century. The prominent dishes used to be garlic soup, thick soups (with chickpeas for example), and fish (more specifically codfish). Among the typical sweets were rice with milk and *torrijas*, a dessert made with bread slices soaked in milk, which are then fried in oil and coated with cinnamon and sugar (or honey). *Buñuelos* are also eaten. On

Easter Monday people eat decorated chocolate eggs. In Catalonia, this tradition is more spectacular because Easter *monas*—traditional chocolate shapes and decorations—may be enormous chocolate masterpieces.[2] Currently, *monas* are placed on top of a profusely decorated cake, which is served as dessert at the end of Easter Monday lunches.

Together with spring, the summer season is the period of festivities par excellence. Most local festivals and patron's holidays are celebrated in the summer. Some of these festivals have been shifted to the summer period, at least symbolically, because it is during these months that tourists and natives go back to the small villages where the festivals are celebrated. All over Spain, *romerías* (pilgrimages) are very common, as well as other kinds of celebrations that involve communal meals and sharing food.

San Juan's Day

The night of San Juan (Saint John) (June 24) is a festivity that opens the summer period. Its celebration coincides, in fact, with the summer solstice. It is common in most parts of Spain, especially on the Mediterranean coast, and it is widely known as "night of the fire" because people light bonfires that keep burning while everybody celebrates with typical summer dances, music, and communal meals. In Catalonia and some areas of the Levant, it is traditional to eat *cocas,* a typical cake made with dough and various ingredients: candied fruit, pine nuts, and cream crackling. A few decades ago the dances held on the nights of Saint Peter's and Saint James' Days (*Santiago*), the eve of June 28 and July 25, respectively, were also quite popular; *cocas* were also a traditional food on these occasions. Both festivities, however, especially that of *Santiago*, have disappeared.

FALL CYCLE

Celebrations of the Dead

Although it cannot be considered a festivity in the strict sense of the term, All Saints' Day (November 1) is also bound to special food practices. Before the arrival of winter it is common to see vendors offering roasted chestnuts and sweet potatoes. These foods are eaten on the eve of All Saints' Day during the traditional dinner called *castañada* ("chestnut feast"). This holiday is also celebrated in schools, where children have parties and eat chestnuts, sweet potatoes, and other typical foods.

In many villages, All Saints' Day is characterized by communal meals that include the following specialties: the already mentioned chestnuts and sweet potatoes, "Saints' bones" (made with marzipan and filled with chocolate, sweet potato, custard, etc.), *buñuelos de viento* (fine dough balls fried in olive oil and coated in sugar), or, in Catalonia, *panellets* (small cakes made with potato, sugar, almonds, and pine nuts). Other pastries also remind people of the dead.

In various Spanish localities, especially in the north, people (mainly the elderly) still keep the tradition of visiting cemeteries and eating there to honor the memory of their dead kin. This ritual practice is of Roman origin and consists in having a family feast by the tomb of the dead, symbolically sharing food and drink with them.

Life Cycle Celebrations

Various occasions in the life cycle are important socially and are celebrated in a special way with particular dishes. As previously mentioned, religious practices and feelings have dramatically decreased. Yet many traditions of religious origin are still preserved as festive occasions despite the fact that they have lost their primordial significance. Weddings have undergone a process of laicization without losing their festive component and the traditional banquets.

Baptism

In spite of the fact that it is not as popular as it used to be some decades ago, baptism (which celebrates the entry of the newborn into the church) is still practiced by wide sectors of the Spanish society. The ceremony is usually followed either by a modest banquet (sometimes not so modest, depending on the family's wealth) to which not only godparents, but also relatives and closest friends are invited: alternatively parents treat their guests to a snack, which consists of hot chocolate and some cakes or pastries. It is also common to give guests a gift, usually *peladillas* ("Jordan almonds," almonds coated with solid sugar) or candies.

First Communion

First Communion is intimately bound to the Catholic life cycle, even more than baptism, although its popularity is also diminishing nowadays. During this ceremony children receive Communion (they receive the consecrated host) in church for the first time. They wear special clothes, especially girls, who usually wear a long white dress, similar to that worn by a bride (a relatively recent practice). As is common with baptism, the first communion is also celebrated with a banquet together with family and friends. Until the 1950s, however, this religious ceremony was rather intimate and it was celebrated in schools, only with other children who were also receiving First Communion. Instead of celebrating it with a banquet, people had breakfast or an afternoon snack (*merienda*) of chocolate and cakes.

Weddings

A wedding is, perhaps, the most important and socially conspicuous event in a person's life. After the ceremony—religious or civil—guests are invited to a wedding banquet (it may be either a lunch or a dinner, attended by just a few people or by hundreds of guests). In the past, the banquet was usually paid for by the father of the bride, but nowadays it is common for families to share expenses, especially if the number of guests is very high. Currently, banquets are usually held in restaurants (some specialize in this kind of affair); here, guests sit within a near or far distance from the bride and bridegroom, depending on how close their bond with the married couple is. The bride and bridegroom sit at the bridal table with their parents and sometimes also with their grandparents. The rest of the relations are seated at nearby tables, and the guests who are least close to the family are seated at the farthest tables.

There is no typical menu for weddings. Usually, after an aperitif, four courses are served: a starter, soup or cream, the main course—red meat, fish, or something similar—and dessert. Drinks include wines (white and red), water, and finally *cava*. After the dessert, the bride and bridegroom symbolically cut the wedding cake before all their guests; coffee and liquors are served last. The wedding cake may consist of various ingredients, although it is usually a sponge cake filled with chocolate, custard, and so forth, and covered in custard, cream, or meringue. The cake usually has a light color and it is decorated with sugar, chocolate, and so forth. On top of it there are usually two figurines representing newlyweds.

Funerals

In urban Spain there is no social meal related to funerals. In the past, wakes were held in the homes and it was common to offer food and drink to those who had come to join the family bereavement. Today, this cultural aspect exists only in rural areas. On some occasions the family and relatives had lunch or dinner together, to honor the memory of the deceased. At present, however, it is rather uncommon for wakes to be held in houses—particularly in urban areas—and the dead are carried to funeral homes arranged for this purpose; after the wake the funeral party goes straight to cemeteries or crematories.

Birthdays

Most Spaniards celebrate birthdays. Children's birthdays are usually celebrated with a party (a *merienda*, where sandwiches, snacks, sweets, or, most popularly, hot chocolate and cakes are offered) to which other children are invited, either at home or, more recently, on some kind of public premises. For adults, the celebration may consist of a lunch or dinner at home or in a restaurant, together with the family and close friends. The chief gastronomic element of any birthday is a cake made from various ingredients (chocolate, custard, cream, etc.). It is topped by as many small candles as the age of the birthday person, who will blow them out and will subsequently cut the cake and serve it. Adults, as with most celebrations, usually toast with *cava*.

NOTES

1. In other places in Spain, such as the famous village called Zamarramala, in Toledo (Castila-La Mancha), Saint Agatha is the "patron" of women. The "ritual inversion" of gender roles in this day in Zamarramala, when women take all the local political power in the village, is world renowned.

2. Particularly after 1935–1940, when the Catalan pâtissier J. Santapau, from Barcelona, presented his first creations.

7

Diet and Health

RECENT CHANGES IN DIET

The Spanish diet changed remarkably throughout the twentieth century. At the beginning of the 1930s, before the Spanish civil war, the diet of the working class mainly consisted of carbohydrates (bread, potatoes, rice, pulses), milk, fish (chiefly cod), vegetables, fruit, and a little meat and fat, mainly from olive oil. This diet would be later known as the "Mediterranean diet." The civil war and the postwar period were characterized by scarcity of food and even by famine, which deeply affected the generations of the 1930s and 1940s. After the economic recovery of the 1960s and 1970s, the Spanish diet reverted to its previous pattern: grains and pulses, vegetables, potherbs, abundant fish (mainly sardines and cod), roast meat, olive oil, and eggs. Yet, since then the Spanish diet has varied greatly again: the rates of meat consumption per person have soared, and so have those relative to dairy products, while carbohydrate consumption has dropped significantly. In general, the consumption of sugar and commercially prepared cakes has also increased, alerting physicians about a possible progressive abandonment of Mediterranean food patterns, favoring less healthy practices, imported from central and northern Europe and from North America. Although there are not as many grounds for medical concern in Spain as in other countries, health has become a current issue. Increasingly greater attention is being devoted to illnesses caused by overnutrition, such as high cholesterol, cardiopathy, hypertension, obesity, and diabetes. As in other industrialized countries, the public health concern with food practices has led to a process of the "medicalization" of food.

THE SPANISH DIET

As the latest official survey has shown, after a period of decrease (between 1987 and 1999), the consumption of some foods groups, such as fruit, vegetables, and fish, has risen again.[1]

Meat consumption is steady (25% of the current Spanish food budget is spent on meat), and fish consumption has slightly increased, too. Milk consumption, after a notable increase in the last years, has now diminished, while dairy product consumption has increased remarkably. Olive oil, one of the pillars of Spanish gastronomy and the healthiest of all fats, is the most used fat in Spanish kitchens. There has been, however, an increase in pastry and cake consumption, while carbohydrates appear to have become less popular in the last years.

As for drinks, wine is still the alcoholic drink par excellence on Spanish tables. There has been an increase in the consumption of quality and designation of origin wines, while low-quality wine sales have dropped. Beer consumption rates are steady and rising, while the popularity of soft drinks has come to a standstill in the last years.

In new food trends, organic products are slowly finding their place on the Spanish market. Ready-made dishes have also become more popular because they are easy to prepare and save time. Companies making ready-made food are tending to reduce the fat contained in their products and to increase the amount of vegetables and grains. The average Spanish food-related expenses in 2003 amounted to about $1,100.

HEALTH

Food-related health concerns are a constant in present-day Spanish society. Not only health authorities, but also food companies have started to address health problems promoting "healthier," "balanced," and "Mediterranean" products.

The concern of Spanish institutions about health and diet must be understood in terms of the progressive change in food practices since the 1980s. There has been an increase in saturated fat consumption and a decrease in carbohydrates, fiber, and vitamin consumption, along with an increase of sedentary jobs (most of the population works in the service sector). Overeating has also directly affected the development of food-related pathologies.

Since the mid-1960s, when the Spanish diet corresponded to the Mediterranean diet pattern (considered the healthiest eating option), there has been an increase in the percentage of energy derived from fats; fat content increased from 32 percent in the 1960s to more than 42 percent in the 1990s, to the detriment of carbohydrates (which provided 53% of total calories in the 1960s and only 40% in the 1990s). All these changes in diet may have directly caused certain diseases and ailments.

Hypercholesterolemia and Cardiovascular Diseases

Hypercholesterolemia is among the cardiovascular risk factors that can be attenuated through diet. Various researches have proven that there is a direct connection between deaths by cardiovascular diseases and cholesterol concentration due to a diet rich in saturated fat. In Mediterranean countries like Spain, the intake of calories derived from fats is higher than 35 percent and sometimes it rises to 40 percent; saturated (animal) fat only amounts to 12 percent of the total fats, because olive oil is still the main fat source.[2]

Yet the Spanish diet is slowly changing and becoming increasingly rich in saturated fats, which, in most cases, are hidden. This change in diet might lead to an increase in cholesterol rates, and in fact hypercholesterolemia cases have increased in the last decades, especially due to new food practices and lifestyle (sedentary jobs, less physical exercise, etc.).

Circulatory system diseases are the number-one cause of death in Spain (they are responsible for 40% of total deaths), and they mainly affect the male population. Coronary diseases are the biggest killers. In geographical terms, the mortality rate due to such diseases is higher in the south of Spain and the Mediterranean area than in the north. In spite of all this, if compared with those of other countries, Spanish mortality rates are rather low. The number of deaths from coronary diseases is similar to that of other Mediterranean countries, and much lower than those of northern and central Europe and the United States.

Obesity

A person is considered to be obese if the amount of fat in his or her body is greater than 30 percent (according to the standard body mass index). Obesity is a recent health problem in Spain and it is evolving according to the same patterns as those of other industrialized countries. In comparative terms, between 1977 and 1997 there has been a 3.9 percent increase in cases of obesity.[3] Recent data show that the percentage of overweight Spaniards has increased to 30 percent; of this percentage, 12 percent corresponds to obese people. Obesity is predominant especially in Galicia, Andalusia, and the Canary Islands. Western European countries have significantly lower rates than eastern European ones and than the United States. Spain is basically at the same level as other Mediterranean countries, occupying a medium-low position within the statistics.

Diabetes

Diabetes occurs either when pancreas loses its ability to produce insulin, or when body cells develop a resistance to it. Since the late 1990s, the percentage of diabetic people in Spain has increased due to risk factors, such as obesity (around 80% of diabetic people are obese), sedentary life, and to the longer life span of the elderly population. At present, however, less than 5 percent of the Spanish population suffers from diabetes.

Cancer

In Spain, as in other industrialized countries, cancer causes 25 percent of deaths, and in 50 percent of these cases, diet may have had a direct influence. Breast, colon, and prostate cancer are the most frequent ones, and their appearance has been related mainly to the consumption of saturated fats, meat, and its by-products. Diets rich in fresh fruit and vegetables (mostly raw vegetables) may prevent various kinds of cancer, especially lung cancer and tumors of the digestive system.

Eating Disorders (Anorexia and Bulimia)

These pathologies have a psychological origin and reflect the social image, values, and cultural stereotypes to which teenagers are daily exposed. These disorders are relatively new in Spain, appearing only in the last decades.

The figures relative to anorexia cases correspond to 0.4 percent, those relative to bulimia to 1.2 percent, and cases of anorexia mixed with bulimia amount to 2.5 percent. Women between 14 and 22 years of age are the most affected group; out of the total of Spanish cases, 8 to 18 percent are adults. Eating behavior disorders are the leading psychiatric pathology in Spanish teenagers, and they currently affect 5 percent of the population.

Alcoholism

Alcohol consumption has usually had a social character in Spain. At the beginning of the 1990s, Spaniards were among the five biggest alcohol consumers in the world (following France, Portugal, Luxembourg, and Hungary). Yet alcoholic drink consumption per capita in Spain has now diminished by 25 percent since 1990 and it actually corresponds to approximately 2.5 gallons per person per year. By regions, the highest alcohol consumption is reported in the north (Galicia, Basque Country, Navarra, and La Rioja), while the regions reporting the lowest consumption are southern and Mediterranean ones (the Canary and Balearic Islands, Murcia, Valencia, Andalusia, Catalonia, and Madrid). Until the 1960s, the most consumed alcoholic drink in Spain was wine, but from the 1980s onward, beer and liquors with higher alcohol content became more popular.

Although there are still important gender differences (the number of male drinkers is twice that of female ones), the contrast notably diminishes when the group studied is that of young people; besides, youth start drinking at increasingly earlier ages.

Promotion of the "Mediterranean Diet" as a Healthy Eating Model

In general, the data relative to food-related diseases are still favorable in Spain if compared with those of its neighboring European countries. However, the increase in some of the health-related indexes have set off the prevention alarm, especially as far as the afore-mentioned eating habits and lifestyles are concerned. To address the increase in saturated fat, sugar, and calorie content recorded in the last decades, Spanish health authorities have started a campaign to promote foods that are considered healthier. Most of these foodstuffs are part of the Mediterranean diet, mainly based on a high consumption of grains, fruit, vegetables, pulses, olive oil, fish, moderate wine consumption, and small quantities of red meat, dairy, and sugar. This results in a diet rich in fiber, vitamins, and carbohydrates (through fruit, vegetables, grains, and pulses), polyunsaturated fats (mostly from vegetables and fish), and monounsaturated fats (olive oil).

Indeed, the foods that Spaniards have *traditionally* eaten, at least in the last 100 years, have an important healthy component, which is reflected in the food-related health figures exposed above. Yet, it cannot be forgotten that eating, as a concept, does not only amount to the food ingested, but is affected by other factors, such as lifestyle, eating habits, where, when, and with whom people eat, and physical exercise. The idea of eating as a social activity, sharing food, chatting after a meal, and sitting for longer after eating are all factors that contribute to better digestion and absorption of foodstuffs. Likewise, lack of exercise may often be as responsible for an increase in diseases as the ingestion of certain foods. To conclude, lifestyle can be said to be as essential to eating as food itself.

NOTES

1. *Panel de Consumo Alimentario 2003* (Madrid: Ministerio de Agricultura, Ganadería y Pesca, avance inédito, 2004). Survey carried out by the Ministry of Agriculture, Livestock, and Fisheries (unpublished).

2. See I. Plaza, et al., "Control de la colesterolemia en España, 2000: Un instrumento para la prevención cardiovascular," *Rev. Esp. Cardiol* 53, no. 6 (June 2000); F. Rodríguez, F. Villar, and J.R. Banegas, "Epidemiología de las enfermedades cardiovasculares y de sus factores de riesgo en España," Sociedad Española de Arteriosclerosis, 2004, http://www.searteriosclerosis.org/aula_searteriosclerosis/tema1/epidemiologia.html.

3. J.A. Martínez, et al., "Variables Independently Associated with Self-Reported Obesity in the European Union," *Public Health Nutr.* 2 (1999); and J. Aranceta et al., "Documento de consenso: Obesidad y riesgo cardiovascular," *Clin. Invest. Arteriosc.* 15, no. 5 (2003).

Glossary

Aceituna Olive.

Ajillo (or "al ajillo") Popular cooking method, with fried garlic and olive oil.

Almuerzo Midmorning meal.

Andalusi From *Al-Andalus*, the Muslim Arab-Berber medieval Spain.

Bacalao Codfish.

Brazo de gitano (Literally "gypsy arm") A kind of dessert roll filled with custard, whipped cream, or chocolate.

Butifarra (Catalan) Big, spicy sausage, usually grilled and accompanied by dry beans.

Calçots (Catalan) Grilled tender onions dressed with a special almond and tomato sauce.

Callos Tripe.

Cantabrian From the north of the Iberian Peninsula (Cantabric Sea).

Carajillo Typical coffee with brandy.

Carnaval Carnival.

Cena Dinner.

Chilindrón (Aragon) Popular way of preparing lamb, using tomatoes and red peppers.

Churros Long doughnuts that are fried and sometimes coated in super-fine sugar.

Cocido   Stew.

Colmado   Grocery store.

Comida   Lunch. Also, usually, generic word for "meal."

Cortado   Small coffee with a dash of milk.

Desayuno   Breakfast.

Embutidos   Sausages.

Ensaimada   (Catalan, Balearic Islands) Round in shape, like a brioche, made from sweet bread dough and lard.

Escalivada   Typical Catalan salad of chopped grilled peppers and eggplant seasoned with salt and olive oil.

Escudella   Catalan stew.

Esqueixada   Typical cod-based dish from Catalonia, with shredded de-salted codfish, combined with minced vegetables and olive oil.

Euskera   Basque language.

Fabada   (Asturias) Dish made with white beans, accompanied by different sausages.

Farinato   Sweet-tasting sausage that is commonly scrambled with eggs.

Fonda   Inn.

Freixura   (Catalan, Balearic Islands) Offal.

Garum   Roman sauce; liquid seasoning made from fermenting fish in saltwater.

Gazpacho   Soup made from various vegetables and served cool, especially during the summer. It is one of the most popular dishes of Andalusia and Murcia.

Gofio   Toasted wheat or corn, essential part of the gastronomy of the Canary Islands.

Hispania   (Latin) The Iberian Peninsula under the Roman Empire.

Horchata   Tigernut milk, made from the juice of the *cyperus esculentus sativus* tuber; a sweet drink typical of the area of Valencia.

Hornazo   (Castilla y León) A sort of pie filled with abundant sausage and other ingredients.

Huesos de santo   (Literally, "Saints' bones") Marzipan sweets eaten on All Saints' Day.

Iberia   Iberian Peninsula (politically, Spain and Portugal).

Jamón   Ham.

Jamón Ibérico de Bellota   Iberian acorn ham.

Jerez   Sherry.

Lacón   Local Galician savory cooked ham.

Magdalenas   Small sponge teacakes.

Manchego   From La Mancha region.

Mantecados   Lard buns—a dessert.

Marmitako   Basque stew made with tuna.

Membrillo   Quince jelly.

Merienda   Mid-afternoon snack.

Migas   Popular dish whose main ingredient is breadcrumbs, eaten in various Spanish regions.

Mojama   Dried and salted tuna.

Mojo   Sauce from the Canary Islands.

Mozarabic   Christians living in Muslim kingdoms in Medieval Spain.

Morisco   (medieval and modern ages) New Christian, converted after the *Reconquista* and living in a Spanish Christian kingdom.

Olla podrida   Stew.

Orujo   Local and popular spirit in northern Spain.

Pa amb tomàquet   Popular Catalan dish: bread slices rubbed with tomato, with or without garlic, and dressed with olive oil and salt.

Paella   Catalan word meaning frying pan and referring to the large pan where the rice was cooked. Also, the famous and international dish, made with rice and always cooked in this pan.

Patata, Papa   Potato.

Pacharán (or Patxaran)   (Navarre) Typical spirit obtained by mixing sloe berries with aniseed liquor.

Pimentón   Traditional Spanish smoked paprika.

Pintxos   In the Basque Country, small portions of various kinds of food (similar to *tapas*), placed on a slice of bread.

Potaje   Thick soup.

Puchero   Popular word for stew.

Reconquista   Christian reconquest of the Iberian Peninsula (seventh to fifteenth centuries).

Rosquillas   Small doughnuts.

Sobrasada   (Balearic Islands) Sausage made with spiced pork, mainly seasoned with paprika, which gives it the unique red color.

Suquet   (Catalan) Luscious, brothy fish stews.

Tapas   Popular kind of snack.

Tapeo   Going out for *tapas*.

Tarta   Cake.

Técula-mécula   (From Extremadura) Dessert made of almonds, eggs, sugar, and lard.

Ternasco   (Aragon and Navarre) Lamb.

Tocinos de cielo   Small cakes made with egg yolk and sugar.

Torrijas   Bread slices soaked in milk, fried, and coated in superfine sugar, eaten at Easter.

Turrón   Nougat.

Txangurro   (Basque) Lobster.

Txakolí   Local Basque white wine—young, fresh, and fruity.

Txikitos   In the Basque Country, small glasses of red wine or *txakolí*, but also of beer.

Txoko   In the Basque Country, a popular Gastronomic Society.

Vermut   Aperitif.

Yemas   (Literally: "egg yolks") Sweets made of sugar and egg yolks.

Resource Guide

RECOMMENDED READING

Albala, Ken. *Food in Early Modern Europe*. Westport, CT: Greenwood Press, 2003.

Dalby, Andrew. *Dangerous Tastes: The Story of Spices*. London: The British Museum Press, 2002.

Davidson, Alan. *The Oxford Companion to Food*. Oxford: Oxford University Press, 1999.

———. *The Penguin Companion to Food*. 2nd ed. New York: Penguin Books, 2002.

Defourneaux, Marcelin. *Daily Life in Spain in the Golden Age*. Stanford, CA: Stanford University Press, 1970.

Flandrin, Jean-Louis, and Massimo Montanari, eds. *Food: A Culinary History*. New York: Columbia University Press, 1999. (Many entries about Spain and Spanish products and cuisines.)

Foster, Nelson, and Linda S. Cordell, eds. *Chilies to Chocolate*. Tucson: University of Arizona Press, 1992.

Gamella, Juan F. "Spain." In *International Handbook on Alcohol and Culture*, ed. D. B. Heath. Westport, CT: Greenwood Press, 1995.

González Turmo, Isabel. "The Pathways of Taste: The West Andalusian Case." In *Food Preferences and Taste: Continuity and Change*, ed. Helen Macbeth. Oxford: Berghahn Books, 1997.

———. "Spain: The Evolution of Habits and Consumption (1925–1997)." In *Rivista di Antropologia*. Supl. 76. Rome: Istituto Italiano di Autropologia, 1998.

Hansen, Edward C. "Drinking to Prosperity: The Role of Bar Culture and Coalition Formation in the Modernization of Alto Penedès (Catalonia)." In

Economic Transformation and Steady-State Values: Essays in the Ethnography of Spain, ed. J. Aceves, E.C. Hansen, and G. Levitas. Flushing, NY: Queens College Press, 1975.

Kidgway, Judy. *The Olive Oil Companion: The Authoritative Connoisseur's Guide*. London: Apple Press, 1997.

Lellep-Fernandez, Renate. "Cheesemaking as a Living Cultural Resource in Covadonga National Park, Spain." In *Proceedings of First International Conference on Cultural Parks*. Denver, CO: National Park Service and The Colorado Historical Society, 1989.

March, Lourdes. "The Valencian Paella: Its Origin, Tradition, and Universality." In *Oxford Symposium on Food and Cookery 1988: The Cooking Pot*. London: Prospect Books, 1989.

Millán, Amado. "Tapeo: An Identity Model of Public Drink and Food Consumption in Spain." In *Drinking: Anthropological Approaches*, ed. Igor De Garine and Valerie De Garine. Oxford: Berghahn Books, 2001.

Montanari, Massimo. *The Culture of Food*. London: Blackwell, 1993. (Many references to Spain.)

Ríos, Alicia. "The *Cocido Madrileño*, A Case of Culinary Adhocism." In *Petits Propos Culinaires*. Vol. 18. London: Prospect Books, 1984.

Rooney, James F. "Patterns of Alcohol Use in Spanish Society." In *Society, Culture, and Drinking Patterns Reexamined*, ed. D.J. Pittman and H.R. White. New Brunswick, NJ: Rutgers Center for Alcohol Studies, 1991.

Rosenblum, Mort. *Olives*. New York: North Point Press, 1996.

Santich, Barbara. *The Original Mediterranean Cuisine: Medieval Recipes for Today*. Devon, UK: Prospect Books, 1995. (Medieval history and recipes, particularly from Catalonia.)

Sarasúa, Carmen. "Upholding Status: The Diet of a Noble Family in Early Nineteenth Century in La Mancha." In *Food, Drink, and Identity: Cooking, Eating, and Drinking in Europe since the Middle Ages*, ed. Peter Scholliers. Oxford, UK: Berg, 2001.

COOKBOOKS

Aris, Pepita. *The Essential Food and Drink: Spain*. Lincolnwood, IL: Passport Books, 2001.

———. *The Spanishwoman's Kitchen*. London: Cassell, 1992.

Butcher, Nicholas. *The Festive Food of Spain*. London: Kyle Cathie, 1991.

Casas, Penélope. *Delicioso! Regional Cooking of Spain*. New York: Alfred A. Knopf/Random House, 1996.

———. *Tapas, the Little Dishes of Spain*. New York: Knopf, 1985.

Dunlop, Fiona. *New Tapas: Today's Best Bar Food from Spain*. London: Mitchell Beazley, 2002.

MacMiadachain, Anna. *Spanish Regional Cookery*. London: Penguin, 1976.

Manjón, Maite. *The Gastronomy of Spain and Portugal*. New York: Prentice Hall, 1990.

Mendel, Janet. *My Kitchen in Spain: 225 Authentic Regional Recipes*. New York: HarperCollins, 2002.

——. *Traditional Spanish Cooking*. Reading, MA: Garnet Publishing, 1996.

Ríos, Alicia, and Lourdes March. *The Heritage of Spanish Cooking*. London: Limited Editions, 1993.

Saacs, Alicia. *The Best of Spain: A Cookbook*. San Francisco: Collins Publishers, 1993.

Santich, Barbara. *The Original Mediterranean Cuisine: Medieval Recipes for Today*. Devon, UK: Prospect Books, 1995.

Torres, Marimar. *The Spanish Table: The Cuisine and Wines of Spain*. Garden City, NY: Doubleday, 1986.

Walden, Hilaire. *The Book of Spanish Cooking*. Palo Alto, CA: H. P. Books, 1993.

——. *Tapas and Spanish Cooking*. Baltimore, MD: Salamander Books, 1993.

Wason, Betty. *The Art of Spanish Cooking*. Garden City, NY: Doubleday, 1963.

VIDEO/FILM

Smith, Jeff. *The Spanish Cooking*. 30 minutes. Oak Forest, IL: MPI Home Video, 1986. A production of WTTW Chicago, VHS.

The Tapas Buffet. 30 minutes. Oak Forest, IL: MPI Home Video, 1992. A production of WTTW Chicago, VHS.

WEB SITES

http://specialflavors.com/special/spanish/spanish.htm. Spanish cooking and wine. Spanish recipes and news.

http://www.donquijote.org/culture/spain/food/. Cultural aspects on Spanish food.

http://www.filewine.es/english/default.htm. An English version is available at this Spanish site. Includes a directory to wine by type and a glossary of Spanish terms.

http://www.foodculturemuseum.com/projects/archives/znewslettmay03v02.html. Food and Culture Museum (Barcelona) Web page.

http://www.gospain.org/cooking/. Spanish regional cooking.

http://www.marketuno.com/. Spanish products and recipes. Free resource for foreign buyers of Spanish food products.

http://www.softdoc.es/madrid_guide/eatingout/food_dictionary.html. Very useful food dictionary: Spanish food terms and their English equivalents.

http://www.spaintour.com/cooking.htm. Typical Spanish dishes and recipes.

http://www.xmission.com/~dderhak/recipes.html. Typical Spanish dishes and recipes, and historical and other information.

Bibliography

GENERAL REFERENCE WORKS

Contreras, Jesús. *Antropología de la alimentación*. Madrid: Eudema, 1993.

Corbeau, Jean-Pierre, and Jean-Pierre Poulain. *Penser l'alimentation: Entre imaginaire et rationalité*. Toulouse: Privat, 2002.

Davidson, Alan. *The Oxford Companion to Food*. Oxford: Oxford University Press, 1999.

De Garine, Igor, and Valerie De Garine, eds. *Drinking: Anthropological Approaches*. Oxford: Berghahn Books, 2001.

Flandrin, Jean-Louis, and Massimo Montanari, eds. *Food: A Culinary History*. New York, Columbia University Press, 1999.

Fortín, Jacques, ed. *L'Encyclopédie des aliments*. Paris: Fontaine, 1997.

Garrido, Antonio. "Acerca de la dieta familiar española del Barroco: Algunas pautas metodológicas." In *Antropología de la alimentación: Nuevos ensayos sobre la dieta mediterránea*, ed. González Turmo, Isabel Romero de Solís, and Pedro Romero de Solís. Seville: University of Seville & Fundación Machado, 1996.

Gracia, Mabel, ed. *Somos lo que comemos: Estudios de alimentación y cultura en España*. Barcelona: Ariel, 2002.

Medina, F. Xavier, ed. *La alimentación mediterránea: Historia, cultura, nutrición*. Barcelona: Icaria, 1996.

Montanari, Massimo. *El Hambre y la abundancia*. Barcelona: Crítica, 1993.

Poulain, Jean-Pierre. *Manger aujourd'hui: Attitudes, normes et pratiques*. Toulouse: Privat, 2002.

CHAPTER 1

Albala, Ken. *Food in Early Modern Europe*. Westport, CT: Greenwood Press, 2003.

Apicius. *De Re Coquinaria*. Milano: Bompiani, 2003.

Bolens, Lucie. *La cuisine andalouse: Un art de vivre XI-XIII siècles*. Paris: Albin Michel, 1990.

Castro, Teresa de. "L'émergence d'une identité alimentaire: Musulmans et chrétiens dans le Royaume de Grénade." In *Histoire et identités alimentaires en Europe*, ed. Martin Bruegel and Bruno Laurioux. Paris: IEHA / Hachette, 2002.

Chamorro, María Inés. *Gastronomía del Siglo de Oro español*. Barcelona: Herder, 2002.

Contreras, Jesús, ed. *Mercados del Mediterráneo*. Barcelona: Lunwerg, 2004. (English version inside.)

Defourneaux, Marcelin. *Daily Life in Spain in the Golden Age*. Stanford, CA: Stanford University Press, 1970.

Fàbrega, Jaume. *El llibre del porc*. Barcelona: La Magrana, 1996.

———. *La cuina catalana: Catalunya, Illes Balears, País Valencià, Andorra, Catalunya Nord, Franja de Ponent, l'Alguer*. Barcelona: L'Isard, 2001.

Fournier, Dominique. "Los alimentos revolucionarios: la llegada al Mediterráneo de los productos del Nuevo Mundo." In *Antropología de la alimentación: Ensayos sobre la dieta mediterránea*, ed. González Turmo, Isabel Romero de Solís, and Pedro Romero de Solís. Seville: Junta de Andalucía, 1993.

García Quesada, Alberto. *Antropología y alimentación: Aspectos socioculturales de los hábitos alimenticios en Canarias*. Santa Cruz de Tenerife: Dirección General de Salud Pública, 2001.

González Turmo, Isabel. "Spain: The Evolution of Habits and Consumption (1925–1997)." In *Rivista di Antropologia*. Supl. 76. Rome: Istituto Italiano di Autropologia, 1998.

Juan-Tresserras, Jordi. "Els orígens de l'alimentació mediterrània a la vessant nord-occidental de la Península Ibèrica." Ph.D. diss., University of Barcelona, 1997.

———. "La cerveza prehistórica: investigaciones arqueobotánicas y experimentales." In *Genó: Un poblado del Bronce final en el Bajo Segre*, ed. J. L. Maya, F. Cuesta, and J. López Cachero. Barcelona: Publicacions de la Universitat de Barcelona, 1998.

La alimentación en España, 2001. Madrid: Ministerio de Agricultura, Pesca y Alimentación, 2003.

Luján, Néstor, and Juan Perucho. *El libro de la cocina española: Gastronomía e historia*. Barcelona: Tusquets, 2003.

Marín, Manuela, and David Waines, eds. *La alimentación en las culturas islámicas*. Madrid: Agencia Española de Cooperación Internacional, 1994.

Martínez Llopis, Manuel. *Historia de la gastronomía española*. Huesca: la Val de Onsera, 1995.

Piera, Josep. "El oriente de al-Ándalus, una cocina de frontera." In *La alimentación mediterránea: Historia, cultura, nutrición*, ed. F. Xavier Medina. Barcelona: Icaria, 1996.

Portalatín, M. Jesús, and José L. García. *El hogar de las culturas*. Zaragoza: Diputación Provincial de Zaragoza, 1999.

Pujol-Puigvehí, Anna. "La alimentación en tierras catalanas en la antigüedad: su carácter mediterráneo." In *La alimentación mediterránea: Historia, cultura, nutrición*, ed. F. Xavier Medina. Barcelona: Icaria, 1996.

Riera, Antoni. "Jerarquía social y desigualdad alimentaria en el Mediterráneo noroccidental durante la Baja Edad Media. La cocina y la mesa de los estamentos populares." In *La alimentación mediterránea: Historia, cultura, nutrición*, ed. F. Xavier Medina. Barcelona: Icaria, 1996.

Rubiera, M. Jesús. "La dieta de Ibn Quzmân: Notas sobre la alimentación andalusí a través de su literatura." In *La alimentación en las culturas islámicas*, ed. Manuela Marín and David Waines. Madrid: Agencia Española de Cooperación Internacional, 1994.

Sánchez Araña, Vicente. *Cocina canaria*. León: Everest, 2002.

Santich, Barbara. *The Original Mediterranean Cuisine: Medieval Recipes for Today*. Devon, UK: Prospect Books, 1995.

Sentieri, Mauricio, and Guido N. Zazzu. *I semi dell'Eldorado: L'alimentazione in Europa dopo la scoperta d'América*. Bari: Dedalo, 1992.

Simón Palmer, M. del Carmen. *Libros antiguos de cultura alimentaria: Siglo XV–1900*. Córdoba: Imprenta provincial, 1994.

CHAPTER 2

Aguilera, César. *Historia de la alimentación mediterránea*. Madrid: Editorial Complutense, 1997.

Albala, Ken. *Food in Early Modern Europe*. Westport, CT: Greenwood Press, 2003.

Capel, José C. *Manual del pescado*. San Sebastián: R & B Editores, 1997.

Juan-Tresserras, Jordi. "La cerveza prehistórica: Investigaciones arqueobotánicas y experimentales." In *Genó: Un poblado del Bronce final en el Bajo Segre*, ed. J. L. Maya, F. Cuesta, and J. López Cachero. Barcelona: Publicacions de la Universitat de Barcelona, 1998.

Luján, Néstor. *Como piñones mondados: Cuento de cuentos de gastronomía*. Barcelona: Folio, 1994.

———. *El libro de la cocina española: Gastronomía e historia*. Barcelona: Tusquets, 2003.

Medina, F. Xavier. "Alimentación, dieta y comportamientos alimentarios en el contexto mediterráneo." In *La alimentación mediterránea: Historia, cultura, nutrición*, ed. F. Xavier Medina. Barcelona: Icaria, 1996.

Mestre, Rodrigo. *Guía de los embutidos de España*. Barcelona: Plaza & Janés, 1998.

———. *Guía de los platos tradicionales de España*. Barcelona: Plaza & Janés, 1999.

Millo, Lorenzo. *El banquete de la caza y los asados*. San Sebastián: R & B, 1996.
Piera, Josep. "El oriente de al-Ándalus, una cocina de frontera." In *La alimentación mediterránea: Historia, cultura, nutrición*, ed. F. Xavier Medina. Barcelona: Icaria, 1996.
———. *Els arrossos de casa i altres meravelles*. Barcelona: Empúries, 2000.

CHAPTER 3

Bernáldez, Andrés. *Memorias del Reinado de los Reyes Católicos*. Ed. Manuel Gómez and Juan de Mata. Madrid: Carriazo, 1962.
Gracia, Mabel. *La transformación de la cultura alimentaria: Cambios y permanencias en un contexto urbano (Barcelona, 1960–1990)*. Madrid: Ministerio de educación y Cultura, 1997.
Martínez Llopis, Manuel. *Historia de la gastronomía española*. Huesca: la Val de Onsera, 1995.
Medina, F. Xavier. *La Cocina en España: Anotaciones*. Barcelona: unpublished report, 1999.
———. "Mediterranean Food: The Return of Tradition." In *Rivista di Antropologia*. Supl. 76. Rome: 1998.
———. *Vascos en Barcelona: Etnicidad y migración vasca hacia Cataluña en siglo XX*. Vitoria-Gasteiz: Eusko Jaurlaritza/Gobierno Vasco, 2002.
Ramírez Goicoechea, Eugenia. *De jóvenes y sus identidades: Socioantropología de la etnicidad en Euskadi*. Madrid: CIS, 1991.
Redaction. "La Mitad de los Hogares de las Ciudades Españolas Tienen un Ordenador." Master-Net. http://www.masterdisseny.com/master-net/atrasadas/155.php3.
———. "Uso de Electrodomésticas en los Hogares Españoles." Electro-Imagen. http://www.electro-imagen.com/es/noticia/15.
Seseña, Natacha. *Cacharrería popular: La alfarería de basto en España*. Madrid: Alianza Editorial, 1997.

CHAPTER 4

Comas d'Argemir, Dolors. *Trabajo, género, cultura: La construcción de las desigualdades entre hombres y mujeres*. Barcelona: Icaria, 1995.
Díaz, Ismael. *Sabores de España*. Madrid: Pirámide, 1998.
Fundación Independiente. *La hora de Europa, la hora de España*. Madrid: Fundación Independiente, 2002.
Luján, Néstor, and Juan Perucho. *El libro de la cocina española: Gastronomía e historia*. Barcelona: Tusquets, 2003.
Roque, Maria-Àngels. "Unidad y diversidad de los estilos de vida." In *El espacio mediterráneo latino*, Dir. Maria-Àngels Roque. Barcelona: Icaria, 1999.
Vázquez Montalbán, Manuel. *Contra los gourmets*. Barcelona: Mondadori, 2000.

CHAPTER 5

Cantarero, Luis. "Gender and Drink in Aragon, Spain." In *Drinking: Anthropological Approaches*, ed. Igor De Garine, and Valerie De Garine. Oxford: Berghahn Books, 2001.

Díaz, Lorenzo. *Diez siglos de cocina en Madrid*. Barcelona: Folio, 1994.

Finkelstein, Joanne. "Dining Out: The Hyperreality of Appetite." In *Eating Culture*, ed. Ron Scapp, and Brian Seitz. Albany: The University of New York Press, 1998.

Gamella, Juan F. "Spain." In *International Handbook on Alcohol and Culture*, ed. D. B. Heath. Westport, CT: Greenwood Press, 1995.

González Turmo, Isabel. "L'Andalousie: Diète es styles de vie." In *Alimentation et nourritures autour de la Méditerranée*, ed. Martine Padilla, and Bénedicte Oberti. Paris: Karthala/CIHEAM, 2000.

———. *Sevilla: Banquetes, cartas, tapas y menús*. Seville: Ayuntamiento de Sevilla, 1996.

———. "The Pathways of Taste: The West Andalusian Case." In *Food Preferences and Taste: Continuity and Change*, ed. Helen Macbeth. Oxford: Berghahn Books, 1997.

Hartog, Adel P. den. "Technological Innovations and Eating Out as a Mass Phenomenon in Europe: A Preamble." In *Eating Out in Europe: Picnics, Gourmet Dinning and Snacks since the Late Eighteen Century*, ed. Marc Jacobs, and Peter Scholliers. Oxford, UK: Berg, 2003.

Jacobs, Marc, and Peter Scholliers, eds. *Eating Out in Europe: Picnics, Gourmet Dinning, and Snacks since the Late Eighteen Century*. Oxford, UK: Berg, 2003.

Luján, Néstor. *Veinte siglos de cocina en Barcelona*. Barcelona: Folio, 1993.

Medina, F. Xavier. *Vascos en Barcelona: Etnicidad y migración vasca hacia Cataluña en siglo XX*. Vitoria-Gasteiz: Eusko Jaurlaritza/Gobierno Vasco, 2002.

Millán, Amado. "Tapeo: An Identity Model of Public Drink and Food Consumption in Spain." In *Drinking: Anthropological Approaches*, ed. Igor De Garine, and Valerie De Garine. Oxford: Berghahn Books, 2001.

Warde, Alan, and Lydia Martens. *Eating Out: Social Differentiation, Consumption, and Pleasure*. Cambridge: Cambridge University Press, 2000.

CHAPTER 6

Ariño, Antoni. *Temes d'Etnografia valenciana IV: Festes, rituals i creences*. Valencia: Alfons el Magnànim, 1988.

Caro Baroja, Julio. *El estío festivo: Fiestas populares del verano*. Madrid: Taurus, 1984.

———. *La estación del amor: Fiestas populares de mayo a San Juan*. Madrid: Taurus, 1979.

Castro, Arachu. *Cultura y prácticas alimentarias en La Rioja*. Logroño: Gobierno de La Rioja, 1998.

Castro, Xavier. *Ayunos y yantares: Usos y costumbres en la historia de la alimentación*. Madrid: Nivola, 2001.

Fàbregas, Xavier. *De la cuina al menjador*. Barcelona: La Magrana, 1982.

Homobono, Ignacio. "Adaptando tradiciones y reconstituyendo identidades: La comensalidad festiva en el ámbito pesquero vasco-cantábrico." In *Somos lo que comemos: Estudios de alimentación y cultura en España*, ed. Mabel Gracia. Barcelona: Ariel, 2002.

Jacobs, Jerôme. *Fêtes et célébrations: Petite histoire de nos coutumes et traditions*. Paris: Librio, 2003.

Llopart, Dolors, et al. *Calendari de festes de Catalunya, Andorra i la Franja*. Barcelona: Alta-Fulla, 1989.

Tax, Susan. "Spanish Pork Products: *Olla* and Jam." In *The Anthropologist's Cookbook*, ed. Jessica Kuper. London: The Royal Anthropological Institute, 1977.

CHAPTER 7

Anuario Social de España 2004. Barcelona: Fundació La Caixa, 2004.

Aranceta, J., et al. "Documento de consenso: Obesidad y riesgo cardiovascular." *Clin. Invest. Arteriosc*. 15 (5) 2003.

Encuesta Nacional de Salud. Madrid, Ministerio de Sanidad, 2003.

Gracia, Mabel. *La transformación de la cultura alimentaria: Cambios y permanencias en un contexto urbano (Barcelona, 1960–1990)*. Madrid: Ministerio de educación y Cultura, 1997.

Grande Covián, Francisco. *La alimentación y la vida*. Madrid: Areté, 2000.

La alimentación en España, 2001. Madrid: Ministerio de Agricultura, Pesca y Alimentación, 2003.

Martínez, J. A., et al. "Variables Independently Associated with Self-Reported Obesity in the European Union." *Public Health Nutr*. 2 (1999).

Masana, Lluis. "Dieta mediterránea, colesterol e infarto de miocardio." In *La alimentación mediterránea: Historia, cultura, nutrición*, ed. F. Xavier Medina. Barcelona: Icaria, 1996.

Mataix, José. "Evolución de la dieta española en la segunda mitad del siglo XX." In *Antropología de la alimentación: Nuevos ensayos sobre la dieta mediterránea*, ed. Isabel González Turmo and Pedro Romero de Solís. Seville: University of Seville & Fundación Machado, 1996.

———. "La dieta mediterránea: dieta tradicional versus dieta recomendada." In *La alimentación mediterránea: Historia, cultura, nutrición*, ed. F. Xavier Medina. Barcelona: Icaria, 1996.

Panel de Consumo Alimentario 2003. Madrid: Ministerio de Agricultura, Ganadería y Pesca (avance inédito), 2004.

Plaza, I., et al. "Control de la colesterolemia en España, 2000. Un instrumento para la prevención cardiovascular." *Rev. Esp. Cardiol* 53, no. 6 (June 2000).

Rodríguez, F., F. Villar, and J. R. Banegas. "Epidemiología de las enfermedades cardiovasculares y de sus factores de riesgo en España." Sociedad Española de Arteriosclerosis, 2004. http://www.searteriosclerosis.org/aula_searterio sclerosis/tema1/epidemiologia.html.

Ros, Emili. "Dieta y enfermedades cardiovasculares: Recomendaciones de la Sociedad Española de Arteriosclerosis." In *La alimentación mediterránea: Historia, cultura, nutrición*, ed. F. Xavier Medina. Barcelona, Icaria, 1996.

Serra Majem, Lluís, and Joy Ngo de la Cruz, eds. *¿Qué es la dieta mediterránea?* Barcelona: Fundación para el Desarrollo de la Dieta Mediterránea, 2003.

Index

About the Author

F. XAVIER MEDINA is Senior Researcher in the Department of Mediterranean Cultures at the European Institute of the Mediterranean, Barcelona, Spain. He is also the president of the Spanish section of the International Commission on the Anthropology of Food and the general editor of the journal *Anthropology of Food*.

READINGS ON

NIGHT

THE GREENHAVEN PRESS
Literary Companion
TO WORLD LITERATURE

NIGHT

Wendy Mass, *Book Editor*

David L. Bender, *Publisher*

Bruno Leone, *Executive Editor*

Bonnie Szumski, *Series Editor*

Greenhaven Press, Inc., San Diego, CA

Every effort has been made to trace the owners of copy-
righted material. The articles in this volume may have
been edited for content, length, and/or reading level. The
titles have been changed to enhance the editorial purpose.
Those interested in locating the original source will find
the complete citation on the first page of each article.

Library of Congress Cataloging-in-Publication Data

Readings on Night / Wendy Mass, book editor.
        p.   cm. — (The Greenhaven Press literary
    companion to world literature.)
        Includes bibliographical references and index.
        ISBN 0-7377-0369-5 (pbk. : acid-free paper). —
    ISBN 0-7377-0370-9 (lib. : acid-free paper)
        1. Wiesel, Elie, 1928–   Un di òelò hoò geshòign.
    2. Wiesel, Elie, 1928–   . 3. Holocaust, Jewish (1939–
    1945)—Personal narratives—History and criticism.
    I. Mass, Wendy, 1967–   . II. Series.
    D804.196 .W547   2000
    940.53'18'092—dc21
                                                    99-055870
                                                         CIP

Cover photo: Corbis/Matthew Mendelsohn

"If we forget, we shall be forgotten. If we remember, then they will remember us."

—Elie Wiesel

CONTENTS

Chapter 5: The Legacy of *Night*

FOREWORD

*"'Tis the good reader that
makes the good book."*

Ralph Waldo Emerson

The story's bare facts are simple: The captain, an old and scarred seafarer, walks with a peg leg made of whale ivory. He relentlessly drives his crew to hunt the world's oceans for the great white whale that crippled him. After a long search, the ship encounters the whale and a fierce battle ensues. Finally the captain drives his harpoon into the whale, but the harpoon line catches the captain about the neck and drags him to his death.

A simple story, a straightforward plot—yet, since the 1851 publication of Herman Melville's *Moby-Dick*, readers and critics have found many meanings in the struggle between Captain Ahab and the whale. To some, the novel is a cautionary tale that depicts how Ahab's obsession with revenge leads to his insanity and death. Others believe that the whale represents the unknowable secrets of the universe and that Ahab is a tragic hero who dares to challenge fate by attempting to discover this knowledge. Perhaps Melville intended Ahab as a criticism of Americans' tendency to become involved in well-intentioned but irrational causes. Or did Melville model Ahab after himself, letting his fictional character express his anger at what he perceived as a cruel and distant god?

Although literary critics disagree over the meaning of *Moby-Dick*, readers do not need to choose one particular interpretation in order to gain an understanding of Melville's novel. Instead, by examining various analyses, they can gain numerous insights into the issues that lie under the surface of the basic plot. Studying the writings of literary critics can also aid readers in making their own assessments of *Moby-Dick* and other literary works and in developing analytical thinking skills.

The Greenhaven Literary Companion Series was created with these goals in mind. Designed for young adults, this unique anthology series provides an engaging and comprehensive introduction to literary analysis and criticism. The essays included in the Literary Companion Series are chosen for their accessibility to a young adult audience and are expertly edited in consideration of both the reading and comprehension levels of this audience. In addition, each essay is introduced by a concise summation that presents the contributing writer's main themes and insights. Every anthology in the Literary Companion Series contains a varied selection of critical essays that cover a wide time span and express diverse views. Wherever possible, primary sources are represented through excerpts from authors' notebooks, letters, and journals and through contemporary criticism.

Each title in the Literary Companion Series pays careful consideration to the historical context of the particular author or literary work. In-depth biographies and detailed chronologies reveal important aspects of authors' lives and emphasize the historical events and social milieu that influenced their writings. To facilitate further research, every anthology includes primary and secondary source bibliographies of articles and/or books selected for their suitability for young adults. These engaging features make the Greenhaven Literary Companion Series ideal for introducing students to literary analysis in the classroom or as a library resource for young adults researching the world's great authors and literature.

Exceptional in its focus on young adults, the Greenhaven Literary Companion Series strives to present literary criticism in a compelling and accessible format. Every title in the series is intended to spark readers' interest in leading American and world authors, to help them broaden their understanding of literature, and to encourage them to formulate their own analyses of the literary works that they read. It is the editors' hope that young adult readers will find these anthologies to be true companions in their study of literature.

INTRODUCTION

When Elie Wiesel's *Night* was first published in English in 1960, it sold only a few hundred copies a year. Today, at the beginning of the twenty-first century, it sells hundreds of thousands of copies each year and stands alongside Anne Frank's *Diary of a Young Girl* as a crucial Holocaust memoir. From the moment Wiesel picked up his pen to write *Night*, he has devoted his life to making sure people do not forget the Holocaust and its lessons. Students continue to study the causes and effects of the Holocaust in their history books, but by bringing *Night* into the classroom and presenting teenagers with a protagonist their own age, teachers dedicated to bringing the message closer to home hope to introduce new generations to the reality of the concentration camps.

One reason for *Night*'s continued success is its accessibility. Written from the viewpoint of a fifteen-year-old boy, Eliezer, the language is straightforward and easy to follow. At a little over a hundred pages, it is quickly read. The book does not set out to present every one of Eliezer's emotions or experiences in the camps. Rather, it focuses on a few days, a few events, a few conversations. The reader must fill in the blanks from the scenes they are presented with. Wiesel explains that what is left unsaid is as important as what is said.

In the essays presented in this book, a wide range of Holocaust scholars and educators explore distinct aspects of *Night* and its author. Some literary critics view *Night* solely as an autobiography, and have therefore focused their commentaries on aspects of the story itself. Others consider the author's technique from the perspective of literary criticism. Still others focus on *Night*'s place in the canon of Holocaust literature. This Literary Companion also includes a plot summary and character breakdown, along with a chronology of relevant events in Wiesel's life and of the Holocaust in general. Taken together—along with Wiesel's own words—the reader will be able to approach the study of *Night* from many angles as well as gain a full understanding of the power of Wiesel's memoir and the ability of one man's words to instill memory.

ELIE WIESEL: A BIOGRAPHY

In the nearly forty years of Elie Wiesel's writing life, he has written nearly as many books. This poor, shy boy from the Carpathian Mountains, Transylvania, became an adviser to presidents and prime ministers and queens, and a voice of memory for the whole world. One of America's most prolific writers and well respected lecturers, he is best known in literary and religious circles as the author of *Night*, his powerful 1958 Holocaust memoir. In the political arena, he is a messenger of peace, speaking out against human rights abuses wherever they occur. In addition to numerous literary and peace prizes, Wiesel is the recipient of nearly eighty honorary doctorates from prestigious universities around the world.

A CHILD IS BORN

Elie Wiesel was born to Shlomo and Sarah Wiesel on September 30, 1928, in Sighet, Transylvania, what was then and is now northern Romania. At the time of World War II the small mountain village belonged to Hungary. Shlomo Wiesel was a much-loved shopkeeper in Sighet, and was often called on to advise the townspeople. Elie didn't spend as much time with his father as he would have liked, since Shlomo was a busy and religious man, always involved with affairs of the town or synagogue. It was his mother, Sarah, whom Wiesel considered his closest ally. He also had two older sisters, Hilda and Bea, and one younger sister, named Tzipora. About his younger sister, Wiesel says, "We all loved her madly. My father treated her with a special tenderness, always had time for her. . . . He pampered her, spoiled her, as did we. Perhaps we sensed that time was short, that we had to shower her with all the love and all the joys and favors of which she would soon be deprived."[1]

By the time Wiesel was three years old, he was learning to read Hebrew and soon became immersed in religious training. The community of Sighet had a large population of Hasidic Jews whose faith and religious practice were all-important. A shy, sickly child, Wiesel loved studying the Torah and the Talmud, and his favorite activity was listening to his grandfather's Hasidic stories and songs. He often felt himself an outsider among the other students, and would give them small gifts in the hope of being liked and included. When Wiesel was twelve years old, he decided he wanted to study cabala, the Jewish teachings. However, Jewish tradition proclaims the task should be taken only by men over forty. Cabala is extremely taxing theologically and a certain amount of maturity is needed to process it. But Wiesel found a teacher anyway. Together with two other boys Wiesel dove headfirst into the world of mysticism.

HITLER'S THREAT

Even after the outbreak of World War II and Adolf Hitler's war against the Jews, most of Sighet was ignorant of the severity of the threat it faced. Anti-Semitism (blind hatred of Jews) had always been part of their lives, so they were used to it on a minor level. They did not realize that Hitler had put in motion his plan to exterminate the Jews of Europe. Wiesel's father was aware that some Jews were in danger, and was briefly involved in smuggling Jews out of Poland. Even though he was sent to jail for a few months for his actions, he still believed his family would be safe in Sighet.

The Nazi menace reached Sighet for the first time in 1942, when all the foreign Jews were rounded up and taken away by train. The handyman of the synagogue, Moshe, was among the deportees; after a period of fear and outrage, however, life returned to normal for the remaining townspeople. Until, that is, a very changed Moshe returned. He explained that the Jews had been forced to dig their own mass grave and were then shot and thrown into it. He himself was shot in the leg, but pretended to be dead until the German soldiers left. He made his way back to Sighet to warn everyone. Unfortunately, no one, not even his friend Wiesel, believed Moshe's story. They just couldn't believe human beings could be that evil. They were soon to learn otherwise.

In 1944 the German army invaded Sighet and forced the Jews to move into ghettos, fenced-off sections of town. They were made to wear a yellow star on their clothes, which would mark them as Jews. Wiesel's father told the family not to worry, and for a while, even in the ghetto, life ran smoothly. Suddenly, however, the Jews were told to prepare for deportation. A Christian maid, whom the Wiesels considered part of their family, offered to hide them from the soldiers. Wiesel's father refused, believing as long as they stayed together they would be all right. Wiesel and his family were herded into overcrowded cattle cars on the last convoy out of town. The train left Hungary and headed into Poland, where it finally reached its destination: Birkenau, the extermination section of the largest Nazi concentration camp, Auschwitz. The first sight that greeted Wiesel was a truckload of live babies and children being emptied into a huge fire. The shock and the screams and the smell of burning flesh was worse than any nightmare he could conjure. Wiesel's mother, sisters, and beloved grandmother were sent off in one direction, while he clung to his father's hand and lined up with the men. This was the last time he would ever see his mother and younger sister, Tzipora. The fifteen-year-old vowed at that moment that he would never forget the horrors that he witnessed that night.

A PRISONER OF DEATH

Years later he still can't think of that night without rage and despair. "In their barbarous madness they cast living Jewish children into specially tended furnaces. I see them now and I curse the killers, their accomplices, the indifferent spectators who knew and kept silent, and Creation itself, Creation and those who perverted and distorted it. I feel like screaming, howling like a madman so that the world, the world of murderers, might know it will never be forgiven."[2] Wiesel claims that when he gets to heaven he will stand before God and say, "Look! Look at the flames that burn and burn, hear the mute cries of Your children as they turn to dust and ashes."[3]

Stripped of their clothes and dignity, the prisoners were tattooed with an identification number on their forearms. From that point on, Wiesel was known to the SS guards only as A-7713. He and his father, spared the gas chamber, were sent a few miles away to a slave labor camp called Buna, where they worked in a warehouse sorting electrical supplies. Wiesel was later transferred to a heavy labor unit. Wiesel tried not to think about what had happened to the rest of his family and was grateful for his father's presence, company he had never had before. "I could cope thanks to my father. I would see him coming with his heavy gait, seeking a smile, and I would give it to him. He was my support and my oxygen, as I was his."[4]

Wiesel was constantly hungry, since the inmates were fed only black coffee in the morning and a crust of bread with watery soup at night. Death by starvation was an hourly occurrence. Every few weeks a "selection" was held, a process directed by Joseph Mengele, a notoriously cruel SS medical officer who decided who would be sent to the gas chambers and who was still fit to work. Wiesel tried to lay low and not draw any attention to himself. Any perceived infraction of the rules meant torture or death. Many times he didn't escape the guards' wrath and was beaten or whipped. His father was not spared this treatment either. Wiesel tried to remain religious in the camp, mostly to please his father. But he couldn't help wondering why God had deserted them. Later he wrote, "In a strange way I never stopped believing in God, but I stopped believing in God as always merciful, charitable and generous and kind and good and just."[5]

In January 1945 Wiesel had required surgery on his leg. While recovering in the camp hospital, he learned that the Russian army was approaching and that the prisoners were being transferred to a camp in Germany. He was given the option of staying behind in the hospital, but Wiesel was certain that the SS guards would kill the sick patients rather than let the Russians find them. He and his father decided to leave with the others. Wiesel later learned that the patients left behind were not killed but liberated by the Russian army a few days later.

Wiesel and his father joined twenty thousand other prisoners on a death march. They ran for forty-two miles as snow and icy winds whipped around them. The pain from Wiesel's swollen leg was excruciating, but with his father's help he forced himself to keep running. Anyone who slowed down was shot or trampled. Finally the prisoners were herded onto cattle cars and shipped to Buchenwald, a concentration camp in central Germany. It was now Wiesel's turn to help his father, who had become very ill with dysentery. He appealed to the doctors to help him, tried to get him to eat, and protected him fiercely from the other prisoners. His dedication earned him a severe beating from a guard and in the end he couldn't save his father. "I was sixteen years old when my father died. My father was dead and the pain was gone. I no longer felt anything. Someone had died inside me, and that someone was me."[6]

A few months later, in April 1945, Buchenwald was liberated by the American army. The war was over and the prisoners in the concentration camps were freed. Wiesel doesn't remember feeling joy; he was too empty and too hungry. He wound up in a makeshift army hospital set up nearby. The army doctors treated him for blood poisoning and he wavered for weeks between life and death.

FREEDOM

Wiesel was well cared for in the hospital and was soon well enough to leave Germany with the rest of the rescued children. A long ride in a luxurious train car brought them to France. At the station stops strangers offered hot food to the traumatized and still weak children. The young displaced survivors were housed and fed and treated with love and respect. Wiesel asked for, and received, prayer books and other religious material. It took a while before he could eat a meal without hiding some of it for later. He returned to his studies and played games with his new friends. One day a journalist came by and took a picture of Wiesel playing chess. By an amazing coincidence, his sister Hilda saw the picture in the newspaper in Paris and tracked him down. Each had assumed the other was dead. He learned that his other sister, Bea, had survived as well, and had returned to Sighet to look for him. They were reunited a few months later.

With the help of a tutor, Wiesel learned French. To make some money, he began holding Bible study classes and led a choir. He studied religion under a mysterious and brilliant teacher named Shushani, whom he now credits with making him the person and the Jew that he is today. Many of his friends went to Palestine (soon to become the State of Israel), but he wasn't ready to leave France and what was left of his family. Instead, he enrolled at the Sorbonne and lived the life of a very poor (and often deeply depressed) college student. While still in school, he became a journalist and finally felt useful. On May 14, 1948, Israel declared itself an independent Jewish state, and Wiesel received the news with tears of joy. He soon boarded a ship for his first visit to Israel and decided to become a foreign correspondent for Israeli newspapers.

A WRITER IS BORN

As a foreign correspondent, Wiesel traveled around the world and met fascinating people. In 1954, he interviewed the Catholic writer François Mauriac, who had received the Nobel Prize in literature in 1952. Mauriac's conversation focused on the suffering of Jesus on the cross, and finally an outraged Wiesel responded angrily that no one talks about the million Jewish children who suffered 6 million times worse only ten years ago. He tried to leave the apartment building but Mauriac reached out to him and begged to hear his story. As Wiesel told the barest outline of his experiences, the old man wept. Mauriac told him he must tell his story. He must speak out. Wiesel argued that he had vowed not to write for ten years, which he felt would be "long enough to see clearly. Long enough to learn to listen to the voices crying inside my own. Long enough to regain possession of my memory. Long enough to unite the language of man with the silence of the dead."[7]

The ten years were nearly up by that time, and Wiesel took Mauriac's advice not to wait any longer. He finally consented to write about his experiences at the hands of the Nazis, and once he allowed himself to put down the words, they just kept coming. The resulting memoir, *And the World Remained Silent*, written in Yiddish, was nearly eight hundred pages long. Shortened by almost seven-eighths, it was published in French in 1958 and in English in 1960, under the name *Night*. Mauriac provided the foreword to the memoir, which prompted the literary community to take notice of the slim volume by an unknown writer. Though very short, with frequent gaps between sections, Wiesel believes that was the only way he could truly tell the story: "Writing is not like painting where you add. It is not what you put on the canvas that the reader sees. Writing is more like a sculpture where you remove, you eliminate in order to make the work visible. Even those pages you remove somehow remain."[8]

At first people shied away from *Night*, in part because the subject matter is so disturbing and people did not want postwar reminders of wartime horrors. But eventually the book began to alter the way people looked at the Holocaust, and it became a crucial historical document. Today it is a staple of high school literature and history classes. It continues to receive high praise from politicians, theologians, fellow writers, and Holocaust scholars. *Night* also had the effect of spurring other Holocaust survivors to write their own eye-witness accounts of Nazi brutality. Wiesel encourages every survivor he meets to tell their story, and in fact, he will publish them himself. Influential talk show host and author Oprah Winfrey recently told Wiesel, "I read your book *Night*. I think I will never be the same again. I believe that every human being should read it, to somehow connect and experience what the world stood by in indifference and allowed to happen."[9]

WELCOME TO AMERICA

While in New York to cover a story in 1956, Wiesel was hit by a taxicab and spent a year recuperating. He published his first novel, *Dawn*, in 1961; his second novel, 1962's *The Accident*, is about a Holocaust survivor who is hit by a car. These two novels and almost all the rest to come dealt on some level with the Holocaust. Though not clearly autobiographical like *Night*, they are informed by Wiesel's experiences and unique insights.

He became an American citizen in 1963 (almost by default because his French visa had expired) and worked as a reporter for a newspaper in New York City. The following year Wiesel made his first trip back to his native Sighet, once again a part of Romania, and found that life went on as usual, and that nobody seemed to miss all those who had been killed. Strangers lived in his house, using his parents' old furniture. He wrote about his perceptions in his 1970 collection of essays, *One Generation After*. He also visited Russia and was shocked at the anti-Semitism that flourished there. The resulting book, *The Jews of Silence*, forced the world to wake up to their plight.

In 1969 he married Marion E. Rose, also a concentration camp survivor. Marion translated his books—always written in French—into English. Very much a team, she still translates his books today. In 1970 *A Beggar in Jerusalem* won Wiesel the prestigious French literary honor, the Prix Medicis. In 1972, Wiesel was thrilled to welcome their son Shlomo-Elisha (named after Wiesel's father) into the world.

A MAN OF PEACE

By the early 1970s, Wiesel was speaking out as well as writing about the horrors of war and hate and the Holocaust. In 1972 he began his teaching career at the City University of

New York, where he taught Jewish studies until 1976. Many of his students were children of survivors. Wiesel explained that they needed him to teach them Holocaust literature because their "parents are silent, and the children need to learn their truth, and live their life, and live their death."[10] He was then named Andrew W. Mellon Professor in the Humanities at Boston University, where he still teaches classes and lectures on philosophy and literature, rather than the Holocaust. A highly sought after and dedicated teacher, he will fly halfway around the world rather than miss a class. His lectures are always standing room only, and he never repeats a speech.

In 1979, Wiesel added "crusader for peace and justice" to his writing and teaching careers. Various activist groups were gaining attention by claiming that the Holocaust never happened. Wiesel refused to debate them, admitting that "I don't know how you react to all this. I can only tell you what one survivor feels—he is not sad, he is outraged."[11] Partly to counteract the outrageous lies, President Jimmy Carter created the Commission on the Holocaust, soon renamed the Holocaust Memorial Council. Wiesel was given the daunting task of chairing the commission, an honor that brought with it months of hard work, travel, and soul-searching. One of Wiesel's main tasks was to develop a museum in Washington, D.C., that would commemorate those lost in the Holocaust while serving as a reminder to mankind never to let it happen again. Wiesel led the commission on a trip to Europe and Russia to research and witness official memorials to the Holocaust, suggesting in some cases that local governments should do more to fulfill that duty. They also honored the memory of Swedish diplomat Raoul Wallenberg, a "Righteous Gentile" who saved thirty thousand Hungarian Jews by providing them with false papers and routes to safety.

The commission also initiated a new tradition. Each year there would be a Day of Remembrance. In his speech on the first commemoration, April 24, 1979, Wiesel told President Carter that "Memory may perhaps be our only answer, our only hope to save the world from ultimate punishment, a nuclear holocaust."[12]

In 1980, Wiesel traveled to Southeast Asia in a humanitarian effort to help starving Cambodian refugees. He went, he stated, because nobody came to help him when he was starving. He could not let victims' voices go unanswered.

The following year Wiesel was the honorary chairman of the World Gathering of Jewish Holocaust Survivors in Jerusalem. Thousands of survivors and their families came to share their stories and remember those lost.

MAKING A DIFFERENCE

In 1985, Wiesel made headline news when he confronted President Ronald Reagan at the White House. Wiesel was present to accept one of America's highest honors, the Congressional Medal of Achievement. But when he learned that President Reagan was about to embark on a trip to Germany that would include a visit to a cemetery in Bitburg where many SS soldiers are buried, he couldn't keep quiet. As he graciously accepted his medal he implored the president not to go, saying that his place is with the victims of the SS. The president insisted that his plans were inflexible and the trip took place. He also visited the site of the concentration camp Bergen-Belsen, and stressed that people must never forget the evils that took place during the Holocaust. Through this incident, Wiesel's name became even more well known as the issue was widely discussed in the media.

Wiesel's efforts to stir the moral consciousness of the world through his books, lectures, and deeds was recognized in 1986 when he was awarded the Nobel Peace Prize. As he received the award in Oslo, Norway, he summed up his life's mission:

> Do I have the right to represent the multitudes who have perished? Do I have the right to accept this great honor on their behalf? I do not. That would be presumptuous. No one may speak for the dead, no one may interpret their mutilated dreams and visions. . . . The world [knew what was happening in the concentration camps] and remained silent. And that is why I swore never to be silent whenever and wherever human beings endure suffering and humiliation. We must always take sides. Neutrality helps the oppressor, never the victim. Silence encourages the tormentor, never the tormented.[15]

With the money accompanying the Nobel award, Wiesel and his wife Marion created the Wiesel Foundation for Humanity. The foundation sponsors conferences and meetings around the world on various humanitarian topics geared toward education and opposition to hate and oppression. The proceeds from almost all of Wiesel's lecturing and publishing endeavors go to charitable pursuits.

New York City was proud of its new Nobel Prize winner,

and Wiesel was invited to throw the first ball of the Mets vs. Red Sox World Series at Shea Stadium. At his son's urging, Wiesel agreed. He recalls being scared that he would embarrass himself. Instead, he did a great job, and his picture appeared in *Sports Illustrated* with the caption, "For a man of peace, he threw a nasty palmball."[14]

Wiesel's next high honor came in 1992, in the form of the Congressional Medal of Freedom, presented to him by President George Bush. That same year Wiesel traveled to Bosnia, in the former Yugoslavia, to see firsthand the "ethnic cleansing" perpetrated against Bosnian Muslims by militant Serbs. He urged the newly elected Bill Clinton to help put an end to the atrocities, which seemed to him very similar to the Nazis' extermination of the Jews.

In 1993 Wiesel spoke passionately at the opening ceremony of the U.S. Holocaust Memorial Museum, a structure he had helped develop. President Clinton presided over the opening and from then on often consulted with Wiesel on matters of international ethics, and the two flew together to the funeral of Israeli prime minister Yitzhak Rabin in 1995.

That same year Wiesel published the first volume of his memoirs, *All Rivers Run to the Sea*. Constantly in demand, he travels the world lecturing and speaking out against inhumanity. At a lecture at the University of Pennsylvania, he posed a challenge to his rapt audience: "I fear that at some point in the year 2000, good, decent people among the gentiles, the very people we now call our friends, will say, 'You must let us forget what happened to your people in the 20th century. Our children cannot grow up with this knowledge.' And what will your answer be?"[15]

NOTES

1. Elie Wiesel, *Memoirs: All Rivers Run to the Sea*. New York: Alfred A. Knopf, 1995, p. 15.

2. Elie Wiesel, *Memoirs: All Rivers Run to the Sea*, p. 18.

3. Elie Wiesel, *Memoirs: All Rivers Run to the Sea*, p. 89.

4. Elie Wiesel, *Memoirs: All Rivers Run to the Sea*, p. 81.

5. Quoted in Jonathan Mahler, "A Master of 'And Yet': Elie Wiesel, a Prophet of Paradox," *Forward*, November 10, 1995.

6. Elie Wiesel, *Memoirs: All Rivers Run to the Sea*, p. 94.

7. Elie Wiesel, *A Jew Today*. New York: Random House, 1978, p. 15.

8. George Plimpton, ed., *Writers at Work*. New York: Penguin Books, 1988.

9. Quoted in Jonathan Mahler, "A Master of 'And Yet': Elie Wiesel, a Prophet of Paradox," *Forward,* November 10, 1995.

10. Elie Wiesel, *A Jew Today,* p. 40.

11. Elie Wiesel, *A Jew Today,* p. 46.

12. Irving Abrahamson, ed., *Against Silence: The Voice and Vision of Elie Wiesel.* New York: Holocaust Library, 1985, vol. 1, p. 35.

13. Elie Wiesel, "Wiesel Nobel Peace Prize Speech" in Historical Documents of 1986, Washington D.C.: *Congressional Quarterly,* Inc., 1987, pp. 1077-78.

14. Quoted in Yosef I. Abromowitz, "Is Elie Wiesel Happy?" *Moment,* February 28, 1994.

15. Quoted in Robert Leiter, "Wiesel: Judaism is not about catastrophe," *Jewish Exponent,* October 23, 1993.

CHARACTERS AND PLOT

CAST OF CHARACTERS

Eliezer: The main character of the story. A deeply pious teenage boy who barely survives internment in Auschwitz. He vows never to forget the atrocities against humanity that he witnessed.

Shlomo: Eliezer's father. A well-liked and highly respected storekeeper. He tries to take care of Eliezer in the camps, but eventually it is Eliezer who must take care of him. He dies of dysentery and abuse at the hand of a guard in Buchenwald.

Eliezer's Mother: She tries to keep her family's life moving as smoothly as possible in the ghetto. Eliezer assumes she was killed as soon as the convoy reached Birkenau, at Auschwitz.

Hilda and Bea: Eliezer's older sisters who helped their mother around the house and their father at his store. Eliezer is unaware of their fate once they reach the concentration camp and are separated.

Tzipora: Eliezer's younger sister who bravely prepares for deportation from her home. Comforted by her mother, she is led presumably to her death at Birkenau.

Moshe the Beadle: A handyman at the synagogue. A friend of Eliezer's who teaches him the mystical cabala, he is taken away by the Gestapo early in the war and returns to warn the town about the atrocities he witnessed. No one believes his stories.

Maria: A former housekeeper for the Wiesel family. A non-Jew, she is distraught by Jewish deportations and begs the Wiesels to hide at her house.

Madame Schachter: A distraught and hysterical woman on the train out of Sighet who screams about a horrible fire.

Akiba Drumer: An inmate who tries to keep the other prisoners' spirits up in the camps by singing Hebrew songs at night. He fails to escape one of the last "selections" and is killed. He asks his fellow prisoners to say the Kaddish, the Jewish prayer for the dead, for him after he goes.

Franek: The foreman at the warehouse where Eliezer and his father work. He quickly loses his initial compassion and forces Eliezer to give him the gold crown from his mouth.

Idek: A violent soldier in charge of Eliezer's unit. He whips Eliezer and beats his father.

Juliek: A friend of Eliezer's, and one of the musicians at Buna. He smuggles his violin with him on the final march, and the night before his death plays a beautiful tune.

Rabbi Eliahou: A beloved Polish rabbi whose son abandons him.

Yossi and Tibi: Brothers whose parents were killed. They befriend Eliezer when they work at the warehouse together.

Joseph Mengele: A cruel SS medical officer who oversees the "selections" and decides who lives and who dies.

PLOT SUMMARY

Night begins in 1941, two years after the outbreak of World War II, in the small town of Sighet, Transylvania, which was part of Hungary at the time. The main character, twelve-year-old Eliezer, is a happy, religiously devout Jewish boy studying the Torah (the Old Testament of the Bible) and Talmud, a collection of rabbinical teachings and commentaries. He loves his parents and three sisters dearly, and is looking forward to a life of study and prayer. A dose of teenage rebellion leads him to study the mystical teachings of the cabala with a poor handyman named Moshe the Beadle. Moshe teaches Eliezer to see things from many angles as they pore over the pages of the Zohar, a great mystical book of the cabala, together.

The next year, in 1942, the nonnative Jews of Sighet are deported under orders of the Nazis. The townspeople are sad to see them go, but don't worry about their safety. Eliezer is especially sad that Moshe was taken. A few months later, however, Moshe reappears. He has returned to say that everyone else in the transport had been killed, and that he escaped only by pretending to be dead. He came back to warn the others, but unfortunately, nobody, not even Eliezer, believes what they conclude is an absurd tale. Though the townspeople have heard reports of the war, they are optimistic that it will end soon and that they will be safe.

In the spring of 1944, however, German soldiers arrive in

Sighet. The Jews are soon forced to leave their homes and are moved into fenced-off sections of town called ghettos. Eliezer's family is lucky—their house is within the walls of the ghetto so they don't have to abandon their home. One night a man knocks on their sealed windows to warn them to leave town, but they can't open the window in time to receive his warning. One morning the Jews are told to wait outside in the hot sun until it is their turn to be shipped out. For the first time, they are treated cruelly and beaten. A non-Jewish housekeeper offers to hide Eliezer's family, but his father refuses, condemning the family to its fate.

During the long and disturbing train ride, a woman, Madame Schachter, continuously screams that there is a terrible fire. The others can't make her stop. When the train finally arrives at Auschwitz, a huge concentration camp in Poland, the deportees are shocked to see that there really is a fire. Eliezer watches in horror as young children are thrown to their deaths into the flames. The men are separated from the women; it is the last time Eliezer will ever see his mother and younger sister. He clings to his father for strength. His trust in God suddenly wavers for the first time in his life. How could God allow babies to be dumped in a fire? He vows never to forget the horrors he has witnessed that night.

Eliezer and his father pass the first "selection" and are allowed to live. They are forced to give up their clothes and don prison outfits. Instead of being called by name, an identification number is tattooed on each prisoner's arm. For a few weeks things are quiet. The prisoners eat tiny morsels of bread and soup and try to believe that their other family members are safe. Eventually, Eliezer and his father are led on a four-hour march to another camp called Buna, where, after they pass a medical exam, they are assigned light manual labor in a warehouse. The dentist keeps trying to take the gold crown from Eliezer's mouth, but Eliezer manages to hold onto it, knowing he might need it later as a bargaining tool.

The prisoners, always hungry and exhausted, try to keep out of the guards' way. Each day thousands are incinerated in the ovens only a few miles away at Auschwitz. Sometimes for no reason a guard will attack a prisoner, and one day Eliezer is beaten very badly. Another time it is his father who is beaten, and Eliezer can only stand and watch, knowing that if he protests his father will only suffer more. Soon Eliezer is forced to give up his gold crown, which isn't nearly as painful as the twenty-five lashes he receives when he accidentally walks in on a sexual encounter between a guard and a woman.

One day the Allies bomb the camp, but only one man who is trying to sneak extra food when the guards are away from their post, is killed. The SS often hang prisoners for one reason or another, but one day it is a child who is chosen. The prisoners are forced to watch as the life slowly drains from the "sad-eyed angel." If the inmates have any faith left in God, many lose it that day.

The Jewish holidays come and go, and Eliezer still can't accept God's silence. He refuses to fast on Yom Kippur and instead feels a heavy void where his love of God used to be. He is assigned to heavy manual labor and fears for his father back at the warehouse. Fortunately, they both pass the notorious Dr. Mengele's next "selection" and are not killed. But when it is time for the "selected ones" to be herded up, Eliezer's father's number is called. He gives a devastated Eliezer his knife and spoon before he is taken away. Somehow, he manages to convince the SS that he is still useful and is returned to the camp.

In the middle of an unbearably cold winter, Eliezer's foot becomes infected. He is admitted to the camp hospital, where he is shocked to recall that he used to sleep in a real bed with real sheets. A kind Jewish doctor performs surgery on Eliezer's foot and he is told to stay in the hospital for two weeks. But Eliezer is never given the chance to recuperate. The Russian army is approaching the camp, and the Germans have decided to move everyone to another camp, farther into German territory. Eliezer is given the choice to stay in the hospital (where his father could have joined him) or join the others for transfer. Fear that the sick prisoners will be killed by the SS guards leads the two to choose to leave the camp with the others. Had they stayed, they would have been freed by the Russians two days later.

In the pitch dark and icy cold, the prisoners are led on a seemingly endless running march. Anyone who falls behind the quick pace is instantly shot or trampled. The pain in Eliezer's foot is unbearable and he considers just giving up. His father convinces him to keep moving. When the prisoners are finally allowed to rest, many crowd into an abandoned factory shed where Eliezer and his father struggle to stay awake since they believe that if they fall sleep they may never wake up. At the end of the march, they are led into the town of Gleiwitz, and herded into barracks. Everyone—the living and the dead—are piled on top of each other. It is there that Eliezer hears the last tunes from his friend Juliek's violin.

After three days with no food or water, the prisoners are rounded up again in the snow. Eliezer saves his father from "selection" one last time, and the emaciated prisoners are shoved into roofless cattle wagons, a hundred to a wagon. Despair is great, and not many survive the trip. When the train arrives at the new concentration camp, Buchenwald, in Germany, only twelve prisoners are left alive in Eliezer's wagon. Once through the gates, Eliezer has to shout at his father to convince him not to curl up in the snow, for he will surely die there. The prisoners are finally brought to the barracks to sleep.

The next morning Eliezer searches for his father and finally finds him burning with fever. He has dysentery and is very weak. Eliezer gives him some soup and coffee and tries in vain to get medical help. The other prisoners steal his father's bread and Eliezer is furious. The guard suggests that Eliezer should take his father's portions, since he will die soon anyway, but Eliezer refuses. One night his father's screams of pain are cut off by a blow to his head by one of the guards. The next morning, to Eliezer's horror, his father is taken to the crematorium. The brief relief that Eliezer feels brings self-hatred.

For nearly three months Eliezer thinks of nothing but eating and sleeping. He no longer thinks about his family or anything else. The Germans are losing the war, and on April 5, 1945, they start evacuating the prisoners again, in an effort to stay one step ahead of the advancing Allied armies. The SS soldiers intend to blow up the camp before the Allies reach it. On April 10, a band of prisoners attack the SS and the guards flee. That evening, the American army liberates the twenty thousand prisoners that remain. Eliezer is among them. As he is about to eat the food his rescuers offer, Eliezer becomes seriously ill. When he is finally able to get out of his hospital bed, he looks at himself in a mirror for the first time since he left the ghetto in Sighet. A living corpse stares back at him.

CHAPTER 1

Major Themes

Loss of Innocence

Irving Halperin

Irving Halperin, an English and creative writing professor at San Francisco State University, establishes that *Night* is the story of one boy's loss of innocence. Before the concentration camp Eliezer had a concrete view of the world. He believed that if the Jews didn't cause any trouble they would be safe; after all, God would protect them. He thought he was living in a modern age where people looked out for each other. By the end of the book, he learned he was wrong on all counts.

Eliezer as a boy in Sighet, a small town in Transylvania, absorbed the religious beliefs of his teacher, Moché the beadle, at a Hasidic synagogue. Moché prescribed that one should pray to God for "the strength to ask Him the right questions."

> "Man raises himself toward God by the questions he asks Him," he [Moché] was fond of repeating. "That is the true dialogue. Man questions God and God answers. But we don't understand His answers. We can't understand them. Because they come from the depths of the soul, and they stay there until death. You will find the true answers, Eliezer, only within yourself!" (*Night*, 16)

Later, as a result of his experiences during the Holocaust, Eliezer would cease expecting to get answers to his questions; indeed, he would come to say that question and answer are not necessarily interrelated. Then what should men do—stop asking such questions? Not at all. The protagonists in the later novels, in *The Town Beyond the Wall* and *The Gates of the Forest,* contend that men must continue to pose them. But not to God, who, in the eyes of the Wieselean narrator, remained silent during the Holocaust. Rather, these questions must come out of the depths of men and be addressed to other men. For to be human, to exercise one's humanity, is to go on posing such questions, even in the face of the Absurd, of Nothingness.

Excerpted from *Messengers from the Dead: Literature of the Holocaust,* by Irving Halperin. Copyright ©1970 by the Westminster Press. Reprinted by permission of Westminster John Knox Press.

JUST LAY LOW

But such recognition for the protagonist was in the distant future. Meanwhile, in the beginning of *Night*, the boy Eliezer did not question Moché's teachings. He believed that as long as Jews studied and were pious no evil could touch them. The Germans proved he was mistaken when they occupied Sighet in the spring of 1944. In consequence, the first of Moché's teachings . . . to Eliezer was the notion that a Jew should live lowly, be self-effacing and inconspicuous. Certainly Moché was an "invisible" man. The narrator says of him: "Nobody ever felt embarrassed by him. Nobody ever felt encumbered by his presence. He was a past master in the art of making himself insignificant, of seeming invisible."

And yet remaining "invisible" did not help Moché; the Germans systematically disposed of him along with Sighet's entire Jewish population. In the beginning of the Occupation, Jews were ordered to wear yellow stars, then they were driven out of their homes and herded into ghettos. A "Jewish council" and Jewish police were imposed on them. Some of the populace desperately attempted to escape annihilation by stationing themselves in such places and at such tasks that would keep them out of sight. And they further deluded themselves by thinking: The Germans—after all, this was the twentieth century—would oppress them up to a certain point and no further. So the popular advice was: Just do what they tell you; they only kill those who put up resistance. But in the end, packs on their backs, the Jewish community was marched off to a transport center, jammed into cattle wagons, and sent off to concentration camps. Meekness, staying "invisible," had not worked. And it is as though Wiesel laments that here was another instance wherein the Jew contributed to his agelong fate as victim and "specialist" in suffering. Ought not the time come when the Jew will make history itself tremble—when, if need be, *he* will be the executioner? In sum, Eliezer learned from having undergone the Occupation and deportation, that it is useless to employ the disguises of the "invisible" Jew. And this recognition constituted the first major puncture of his heretofore innocent faith in the teachings of Moché.

DIDN'T GOD CARE?

[Fifteen-year-old Eliezer believed in God] before he came to Auschwitz. But there, in hell on earth, that faith was consumed in the flames that consumed children. There "God" was the official on the train ramp who separated life from death with a flick of a finger to the right or left. Yet some Jews continued to urge children to pray to God. "You must never lose faith," they said to Eliezer, "even when the sword hangs over your head. That's the teaching of our sages."

But could the sages have imagined the limitless depravity of the Nazis? Could they, in all their wisdom, have counseled a boy of fifteen on how to react to the mass burning of children? To see a child's head, arms, and legs go up in flame— that is an indisputable fact, a measurable phenomenon.

Did He care that children were being consumed by fire? This is the question raised by the narrator of *Night*. And if He does nothing to prevent the mass murder of children, Eliezer cries out: "Why should I bless His name?" This outcry is the sign of, as François Mauriac says in his foreword to the book, "the death of God in the soul of a child who suddenly discovers absolute evil." And this breakdown of religious faith calls forth Eliezer's resolve "never to forget."

> Never shall I forget that night, the first night in camp, which has turned my life into one long night, seven times cursed and seven times sealed. Never shall I forget that smoke. Never shall I forget the little faces of the children, whose bodies I saw turned into wreaths of smoke beneath a silent blue sky.
>
> Never shall I forget those flames which consumed my faith forever.
>
> Never shall I forget that nocturnal silence which deprived me, for all eternity, of the desire to live. Never shall I forget those moments which murdered my God and my soul and turned my dreams to dust. Never shall I forget these things, even if I am condemned to live as long as God Himself. Never.

So, too, on the eve of Rosh Hashanah, Eliezer, who until then had always been devoted to this holiday, thinks, bitterly:

> Why, but why should I bless him? In every fiber I rebelled. Because He has had thousands of children burned in His pits? Because He kept six crematories working night and day, on Sundays and feast days? Because in His great might He had created Auschwitz, Birkenau, Buna, and so many factories of death? How could I say to Him: "Blessed art Thou, Eternal, Master of the Universe, who chose us from among the races to be tortured day and night, to see our fathers, our mothers, our brothers, end in the crematory? Praised be Thy Holy Name, Thou Who hast chosen us to be butchered on Thine Altar?"

After Auschwitz, Eliezer could no longer speak of God's goodness or His ultimate purposes.

What is the immediate consequence of this loss of faith? Eliezer feels as though he were a lost soul condemned to wander in a haunted realm of darkness. Here the word "darkness" needs to be underscored, for it is a world at the poles from the one of "light" which Eliezer, as a student of the Cabbala and Talmud, inhabited in Sighet. By day the Talmud, and at night, by candlelight, he and his teacher Moché would study together, searching for "the revelation and mysteries of the cabbala." There was not only candlelight when they studied; the Talmud, the Zohar, the cabbalistic books themselves *were* light; they illuminated the nature of the "question" and suggested the answer; they seemed to draw Moché and Eliezer toward the shining realm of the eternal "where question and answer would become one."

But the light in *Night* is of brief duration; the atmosphere of the book is almost entirely that of blackness. The fires of Auschwitz consume the light, the religious faith, of Eliezer and leave him a "damned soul" wandering through a darkness where question and answer would *never* become one.

EVERY MAN FOR HIMSELF

What other kinds of disillusionment are experienced by Eliezer? I have already pointed out two—his realization that to be an "invisible" Jew did not protect one from the Nazis and, second, his turning away from God on witnessing the mass burning of children at Auschwitz. There was also his loss of faith in both the myth of twentieth-century civilized man and the tradition of the inviolable bonds between Jewish parents and children. Before coming to Auschwitz, Eliezer had believed that twentieth-century man was civilized. He had supposed that people would try to help one another in difficult times; certainly his father and teachers had taught him that every Jew is responsible for all other Jews. Until the gates of a concentration camp closed upon him he had no reason to doubt that the love between parents and children was characterized by sacrifice, selflessness, and utmost fealty.

But Auschwitz changed all that. There he was forced to look on while a young boy was tortured and then hanged—his death taking more than a half hour of "slow agony." There dozens of men fought and trampled one another for an extra ration of food. In one instance, he saw a son actually killing his elderly father over a portion of bread while other prisoners looked on indifferently. In Auschwitz the conduct of most prisoners was rarely selfless. Almost every man was out to save his own skin; and to do so he would steal, betray, buy life with the lives of others.

Eliezer's progressive disillusionment did not come about simply because of what he witnessed in Auschwitz; he did not only observe the breakdown of faith; he himself in part caused it to happen. Consider Eliezer's thoughts and conduct with respect to his father when both were concentration camp prisoners. Eliezer feels that his father is an encumbrance, an albatross, who jeopardizes his own chances for survival. The son himself is ailing, emaciated, and in attempting to look after the older man strains his own limited physical resources. Moreover, such efforts make him dangerously conspicuous—always a perilous condition for concentration camp prisoners. And yet he despises himself for not having lifted a hand when his elderly father was struck by a Kapo. He had looked on, thinking: "Yesterday I should have sunk my nails into the criminal's flesh. Have I changed so much, then?"

Eliezer's conflict of wanting to protect his father and, conversely, to be separated from him, is so desperate that when the father is on the verge of dying, the son feels ashamed to think: "If only I could get rid of this dead weight, so that I could use all my strength to struggle for my own survival, and only worry about myself." Again, when the dying man is struck with a truncheon by an officer, Eliezer, fearing to be beaten, stands still, like one paralyzed. Finally, when his father is taken off to the crematoria, the son cannot weep. Grief there is in him and yet he feels free of his burden. Thus another illusion is discarded by a boy who had been reared in a tradition that stresses loyalty and devotion to one's parents.

REVENGE OR RELEASE?

The death of his father leaves Eliezer in a state of numbness; he feels that nothing more can affect him. But there remains still another illusion he is to shed—the belief that on being liberated the prisoners would be capable of avenging themselves on the enemy. They had endured so much in order to live to the day of liberation. How often had the prisoners spoken to one another about what they would do to the Germans. And yet when Buchenwald is liberated, Eliezer observes with anger and disgust that his fellow prisoners are concerned only with bread and not revenge.

He has lost not only his father but also faith in God and humanity. Many of his previously untested beliefs in the staying powers of the "invisible" Jew, the unquestionable justice of God, the built-in restraints of twentieth-century civilization, and the enduring strength of familial bonds between Jewish parents and children have been peeled away. He will have to journey for a long time and through many lands before arriving at that point of retrospective clarity when he can even first frame the "right questions" concerning his season in hell. He will need to stand before some "false" gates before he can turn away from them. And yet, all through this time, he is to hold fast to the belief that his teacher Moché instilled in him: that there is an "orchard of truth," and that for entering the gate to this place every human being has his own key.

The Theme of Night

Ellen S. Fine

Ellen S. Fine is a French professor at The City University of New York and worked with Wiesel on the U.S. Holocaust Memorial Council. Fine contends that the title of Wiesel's book reflects the theme that the character experiences—a never-ending descent into the darkest of night. She demonstrates that Wiesel uses the motif of night as a metaphor for the horrors of the concentration camp and for the inner darkness that he must confront.

The theme of night pervades Elie Wiesel's memoir as suggested by the title itself, which encompasses the overall Holocaust landscape—[the concentration camp universe]—a world synonymous with methodical brutality and radical evil. The dark country presented to us is self-contained and self-structured, governed by its own criminal gods who have created laws based upon a death-dominated ideology. Wiesel uses the word night throughout his writing to denote this strange sphere, unreal and unimaginable in its otherworldliness. Wiesel notes, in *Harry James Cargas in Conversation with Elie Wiesel*, "Whenever I say 'night' I mean the Holocaust, that period. 'Night' has become a symbol of the Holocaust for obvious reasons. As we have said, a night has descended upon mankind, not only in Europe, but everywhere. Whoever was alive in those days has absorbed parts or fragments of that night. Night enveloped human destiny. Night is a symbol of that period, a frightening symbol. Whenever I try to speak of those nights, I simply say 'night.'" He speaks of that "kingdom of the night where one breathed only hate, contempt and self-disgust" in "A Plea for the Dead"; and in one of his speeches, refers to "the dark kingdom which . . . represented the other side of Sinai, the dark face of Sinai." "We were the children of night," he proclaims, "and we knew more about truth and the paths leading to it

Excerpted from *Legacy of Night*, by Ellen S. Fine. Copyright ©1982 by the State University of New York. Reprinted with permission from the author and SUNY Press.

than the wisest philosophers on earth."

Eliezer, the narrator of the book, is, in effect, a child of the night, who relates the journey from the friendly Jewish community tucked away in the mountains of Transylvania to Auschwitz—the frightening and foreign capital of the kingdom of night. During the course of the trip certain events take place which stand out in the narrator's memory and often occur during the nocturnal hours. The theme of night is linked to the passage of time in the account itself. Within the larger framework, more specific phases, characterized by the motifs of the *first* and *last* night, structure the descent into terror and madness, and point to the demarcations between the known and unknown.

Once Eliezer enters Auschwitz, he loses his sense of time and reality. Darkness envelops him and penetrates within: his spirit is shrouded, his God eclipsed, the blackness eternal. Pushed to his limits, the narrator experiences the *other* haunted and interminable night defined by French philosopher Maurice Blanchot as "the death that one does not find"; "the borders of which must not be crossed." The intermingling of particular nights with *Night*, the measuring of time alongside timelessness, corresponds to a style that interweaves a direct narration of events with subtle reflections upon the experience.

NIGHT'S SHADOWS ARE CAST

In 1941, when the narrative begins, Eliezer is a deeply Orthodox boy of twelve, living in the town of Sighet, situated on the Hungarian-Rumanian border. The word *night* is first mentioned with regard to his evening visits to the synagogue: "During the day I studied the Talmud, and at night I ran to the synagogue to weep over the destruction of the Temple" (*Night*, 14). While this nocturnal lamentation is part of a religious tradition, its prominent position in the text can be interpreted as a prediction of the bleak shadow cast upon Jewish communities throughout twentieth-century Europe.

Eliezer spends many of his evenings in the semidarkness of the synagogue where half-burned candles flicker as he converses with Moché, his chosen master of the Kabbala; they exchange ideas about the nature of God, man, mysticism, and faith. Night, here, exudes a poetic and pious atmosphere as the time for prayer, interrogation and dialogue within the context of the secure and the traditional. Indeed, the narrator's experience of benevolent night begins to change with Moché's expulsion from Sighet. Deported because he is a foreign Jew, Moché is sent to Poland, driven to a forest along with hundreds of other Jews, and shot in front of freshly dug pits. Wounded in the leg only, he rises from the mass grave and miraculously makes his way back to Sighet to recount what he calls "the story of my own death." "Jews, listen to me," he cries out. "It's all I ask of you, I don't want money or pity. Only listen to me" (17). No one in the *shtetl*, including Eliezer, believes his tale, and Moché is forced into silence, Wiesel's first example of the unheeded witness whose futile warnings predict the fate of the entire Jewish community. This occurs towards the end of 1942.

Without being explicit, Wiesel's narrative closely follows the historical events that led to the expulsion of the Hungarian Jews. The years 1942 and 1943 as rapidly described in the text were fairly normal for the Jews of Sighet. While anti-Jewish legislation was enacted and periods of calm alternated with those of turbulence, day still predominated over night. From 1938 to 1944, Hungarian prime ministers ranged from eager collaborators to those who collaborated reluctantly, resulting in cycles of despair and hope for the Jews who were unable to assess their situation realistically. In 1944 the Jewish community of Hungary was the only large group still intact. The circumstances changed drastically, however, in March, with the German takeover of the country and the installation of the pro-German Sztojay government, Adolph Eichmann, commander of the Special Action Unit *(Sondereinsatzkommando)*, came to Hungary to personally carry out one of the most concentrated and systematic destruction operations in Europe. In the spring of 1944, with the end of the war in sight, the Nazis deported and eventually wiped out 450,000 Jews, 70 percent of the Jews of Greater Hungary. The Jews from the Carpathian region and Transylvania were among the first to be ghettoized and then rounded up. Of the fifteen thousand Jews in Sighet's community alone, about fifty families survived.

The Germans were notorious for their methods of deceiving their victims by dispelling notions of fear and creating the illusion of normality as they went about setting the machinery of extermination in motion. Eliezer speaks of life's returning to normal, even after the Nazis forced the Jews of Sighet into two ghettos fenced off from the rest of the population by barbed wire. At least, he remarks, Jews were living among their brothers and the atmosphere was somewhat peaceful. This deceptively secure setting was soon to be shattered.

FIRST AND LAST NIGHTS

"Night fell," says the narrator, describing an evening gathering of friends in the courtyard of his family's house in the large ghetto. A group of about twenty was listening attentively to tales told by his father, when suddenly a Jewish policeman entered and interrupted his father's story, summoning him to an emergency session of the Jewish council. "The good story he had been in the middle of telling us was to remain unfinished," Eliezer notes (22). . . .

Suspended in the midst of its natural flow, the father's story is a metaphor for Jewish life and lives abruptly brought to a standstill in the middle of the night. When the father returns at midnight from the council meeting, he announces news of the deportation to be held the following day.

From this point on, time is defined by the first and last night. Eliezer refers to "our last night at home," spent in the large ghetto after watching the first transport of victims parade through the streets under the blazing sun, the infernal counterpart to night. Then, there is the last evening in the small ghetto, where Eliezer, his parents, and three sisters observe the traditional Sabbath meal: "We were, we felt, gathered for the last time round the family table. I spent the night turning over thoughts and memories in my mind, unable to find sleep" (31).

Expelled from the small ghetto, Eliezer and his family, along with other members of the community, are thrown into cattle cars where they endure three long nights. Day is left far behind. The theme of night corresponds here to the reduction of space. Whereas the gentle gloom of the synagogue provided the framework for a boundless exploration of sacred doctrines, the ghetto period—in its progression from larger to smaller—serves as a transitional space, leading to the nailed-up doors of the cattle wagons, which plunge the prisoners into the confinement and extreme darkness of a night without limits.

The night of the cattle wagons is hallucinatory. Madame Schächter, a woman of fifty, who along with her ten-year-old son had been deported separately from her husband and two elder sons, starts to go mad. On the third and last night in the train, she screams out as if possessed by an evil spirit, conjuring up vivid images of fire and a furnace. Some of the men peer through the barred train window to see what Madame Schacter is pointing to, but all they can glimpse is blackness. Night is both within and without, surrounding the mad prophet who continuously cries out, as if to predict the end of the world, but who is forcefully silenced by those around her who do not want to believe in the foreboding signs. At the terminus, Birkenau–Auschwitz, Madame Schacter gives one last howl: "Jews, look! Look through the window! Flames! Look!" (36). As the train stops, the victims, in disbelief, observe red flames gushing out of the chimney into the black sky. . . .

A NEVER-ENDING NIGHT

When Eliezer sees the vivid flames leaping out of a ditch where little children are being burned alive, he pinches his face in order to know if he is awake or dreaming in this nightmarish atmosphere of "Hell *made immanent.*" The young boy watches babies thrown into the smouldering pits and people all around murmuring *Kaddish* (the Jewish prayer for the dead) for themselves—the living dead—as they slowly move in a kind of *danse macabre.* They give the eerie impression that they are participating in their own funeral. For a moment, the narrator contemplates throwing himself on the barbed wire, but the instinct for survival prevails. As he enters the Holocaust kingdom on that first night he recites a ritualistic incantation, which marks his initiation into one long and never-ending night and commits him to remember it always:

> Never shall I forget that night, the first night in camp, which has turned my life into one long night, seven times cursed and seven times sealed. Never shall I forget that smoke. Never shall I forget the little faces of the children, whose bodies I saw turned into wreaths of smoke beneath a silent blue sky.
>
> Never shall I forget those flames which consumed my faith forever.
>
> Never shall I forget that nocturnal silence which deprived me, for all eternity, to the desire to live. Never shall I forget those moments which murdered my God and my soul and turned my dreams to dust. Never shall I forget these things, even if I am condemned to live as long as God Himself. Never.

This invocation summarizes the principal themes of Wiesel's first book, joining the theme of night to those of fire, silence, and the death of children, of God, and of the self. The moment of arrival designates the end of the reality-oriented structure of "outer" night, and the shift to "inner" night, in which time is suspended. As dawn breaks Eliezer observes: "So much had happened within such a few hours that I had lost all sense of time. When had we left our houses? And the ghetto? And the train? Was it only a week? One night—*one single night?* . . . Surely it was a dream" (46).

Indeed, like a dream sequence, the events of the camp journey have been accelerated and condensed into a short interval. "One of the most astonishing things," says Wiesel, "was that we lost all sense not only of time in the French meaning of the word, of *durée*, but even in the concept of years. . . . The ten-year-old boy and the sixty-year-old man not only looked alike, felt alike and lived alike, but walked alike. There was a certain 'levelling.'" This levelling process seems to occur in one night, a notion often repeated by the author:

> In a single night, a single hour, one acquires knowledge and grows up. The child finds himself an old man. From one day to the next, familiar structures and concepts vanish, only to reappear in different forms. One gets used to the new order in spite of everything.

The concept of time that governs life in normal conditions thus changes radically in the concentrationary universe. But even more important than time is the highly organized and methodological procedure that deprives an individual of his humanness and transforms him into a thing while still alive. The *défaite du moi*, the "dissolution of the self," is the worst kind of living death and is a recurring theme in Holocaust literature.

After one single night in Auschwitz, Eliezer is turned into a subhuman, identified only by an anonymous number. . . . His spirit is arrested in the confines of night: the empire of darkness has taken possession of his inner being. For the boy of fifteen, history has stopped.

THE VERY LAST NIGHT

Although time is essentially abolished in the kingdom of death, the narrator nevertheless continues to structure outer

reality in the account itself by noting the nights that mark
the principal stages of the trip. After three weeks in Auschwitz, he and his father are sent in a work transport to Buna,
where they spend several weeks. The Germans finally evac-
uate the camp as Russian troops approach. Before the long
cold voyage to Buchenwald, Eliezer meditates on the motif
of *the last night:*

> The last night in Buna. Yet another last night. The last night
> at home, the last night in the ghetto, the last night in the train,
> and, now, the last night in Buna. How much longer were our
> lives to be dragged out from one 'last night' to another? [89]

The march from Buna to Buchenwald takes place in
blackness, amid glacial winds and falling snow. The boy realizes that the night he is leaving will be replaced by one
even more unfathomable on the other side; the *invisible darkness* of the tomb. As the procession winds its way through the
thick snow, numerous corpses are strewn upon its trail. After several days without food or water, the remaining prisoners are thrown into open cattle cars and transported to
Buchenwald. For the starved skeletons who speed through
the frozen landscape, "days were like nights and the nights
left the dregs of their darkness in our souls" (105). Suddenly,
on the last day of this seemingly endless journey, a fierce cry
rises up from among the inert bodies of the entire convoy—a
collective death rattle that seems to emanate from beyond the
grave. This shared song of death when no hope is left is a
protest to the world which has abandoned them. A brutal expression of the agony of those who have reached their limits,
this massive convulsion *is* the primeval language of night.
Finally, late in the evening, twelve survivors out of the hundred who started out reach Buchenwald.

The last night—and the most significant—is January 28,
1945. Eliezer's father, sick with dysentery, his head bloody
from the blows of an SS guard, lies curled up miserably on
his bunk bed. When his son awakens the next day, he realizes that his father has been carted away before dawn—perhaps still alive. It is the finality of this moment that virtually
ends the narrative, plunging Eliezer into a realm where no
light penetrates and where, on some level, the *child of night*
remains for the rest of his life.

Initiation and Journey Motifs

Ted L. Estess

In order to best relay the story of Eliezer's experiences during the Holocaust, Ted L. Estess, author of the book *Elie Wiesel* and professor of religion and literature at the University of Houston, contends that Wiesel sets the story within the framework of two common themes—the Initiation and the Journey. Since the topic is so horrendous, Wiesel must find ways to tell it so that the horror is truly felt by the reader. By using these straightforward and established storytelling motifs, the reader better understands the main character's experiences.

Night tells what Eliezer underwent from the end of 1941 to April, 1945. To give form to the events Wiesel employs two familiar framing devices: those of a story or initiation and a story of journey. Inside these loose frames, Wiesel arranges the vignettes so that the story reads like a simple chronicle of Eliezer's experience. In order not to violate the experience he is relating, Wiesel refrains from imposing too severe an order on what was essentially an eruption of disorder in his world.

As an initiation story, the narrative explores the way in which a boy in his early teens goes through difficult trials to discover something new about himself, his people, and the world in which he is to live. Early in the story, the narrator suggests the importance of "initiation." The initiation to which he refers is conducted by Moché, Eliezer's teacher in the mysteries of the Kabbala and other secret matters of Jewish thought. Given the multitude of possible starting points for the story, it is crucial that Wiesel chose to open with Moché. The opening suggests that Wiesel wants us to read the story in the light of this picture of Eliezer as a religious seeker. What happens subsequently largely takes its mean-

Excerpted from *Elie Wiesel*, by Ted L. Estess. Copyright ©1980 by The Frederick Ungar Publishing Co. Reprinted by permission of Continuum International.

ing from the contrast between the experience of the Holocaust and Eliezer's early religious intensity.

This opening accentuates the initiation motif as well. The initiation to which the narrator refers involves a religious master and an earnest seeker. The master presumably knows something that the disciple does not; he is in touch with a hidden truth that can be discerned only after a long quest. Moché introduces Eliezer to the *Zohar*, the Book of Splendor, a mystical commentary on the first books of the Bible. As a Kabbalist, Moché is concerned with directing his student's soul toward the long, arduous ascent of the ladder of mystical enlightenment to a final disclosure of and union with the Eternal God. With the war, everything changes for the boy, but the change occurs downward toward darkness and nothingness. His initiation ends in despair and chaos, not hope and order; in isolation and horror, not in a community sustained by joy.

Under the tutelage of Moché, Eliezer had set out on a path leading to life. Instead, he enters into death, which takes over his existence. Death is everywhere in the camps: in the chimneys and fences, in the faces of the executioners, and in the eyes of the prisoners. Death floats in the clouds as the smoke from the chimneys slowly rises day after day. "Around me," Eliezer says, "everything was dancing a dance of death. It made my head reel. I was walking in a cemetery, among stiffened corpses, logs of wood." Silently but perceptibly, death enters the soul of Eliezer, and although he escapes physical death, he comes to belong more to the dead than to the living. At the end of the narrative, Eliezer looks at himself: "From the depths of the mirror, a corpse gazed back at me. The look in his eyes, as they stared into mine, has never left me."

THE LONG JOURNEY

The motif of initiation in *Night* is closely associated with the motif of journey. Before the Holocaust, Eliezer had set out on a spiritual journey whose destination was union with God. He had hoped that Moché would draw him "into eternity," away from the vicissitudes of bodily existence in time. Again, Eliezer's expectations are radically reversed, for he is forced into the worst of physical journeys. It begins with the ride in the cattle train to Auschwitz. After three weeks there, he walks to Buna, where he remains until January, 1945. During that time, the prisoners are marched to work outside the camp every day. In January, 1945, there is a savage march in the snow to Gleiwitz, followed closely by a ten-day ride in an open cattle car to Buchenwald. All the while, the young boy increasingly becomes obsessed with physical survival. Instead of a disclosure of divine mystery at the end of this journey, there is the death of God and a revelation of absolute evil at the heart of things. Instead of being transported out of the body and into the bliss of eternity, Eliezer moves steadily into degradation in an agonized physical world. . . .

THE STUDY OF KABBALAH

Eliezer's father didn't want him to study Kabbalah (also spelled Kabbala or Cabala or cabbala) until he was older. In The Essential Kabbalah: The Heart of Jewish Mysticism, *professor Daniel C. Matt explains why.*

Traditionally, restrictions have been placed on the study of Kabbalah. Some kabbalists insisted that anyone seeking entrance to the orchard must be at least forty years old, though [the great 16th century kabbalist] Moses Cordovero stipulated twenty years. Other requirements included high moral standards, prior rabbinic learning, being married, and mental and emotional stability. The point is not to keep people away from Kabbalah, but to protect them. Mystical teachings are enticing, powerful, and potentially dangerous. The spiritual seeker soon discovers that he or she is not exploring something "up there," but rather the beyond that lies within. Letting go of traditional notions of God and self can be both liberating and terrifying. In the words of Isaac of Akko, "Strive to see supernal light, for I have brought you into a vast ocean. Be careful! Strive to see, yet escape drowning."

Daniel C. Matt, *The Essential Kabbalah: The Heart of Jewish Mysticism.* New Jersey: Castle Books, 1997, p. 17.

The change in his journey from a spiritual odyssey to a physical one is accompanied by a shift in Eliezer's stance on religious matters. At the beginning of the story, Eliezer takes the mysteries of the Kabbala to be the key to what is ultimately real. Later he speaks of "cabbalistic dreams." Earlier the holy days were the grandest days; later he views Yom Kippur as a "mirage." Eliezer radically questions religious beliefs, in part because he fears that the beliefs themselves contribute to the prisoners' destruction. Some victims submit willingly to the executioner because they see submission almost as a religious obligation.

But Eliezer's journey has spiritual dimensions as well. His spirit moves downward in an ever narrowing spiral. The first and last words of the English version of the book reflect one dimension of the contracting movement of the whole. The English version opens with the word "they" and ends with the word "me." "They" refers to the Jewish community in which Eliezer had lived. That community and the town of which it was a part linked him to the cosmos and to all of history. Its rituals and holy days imbued the passing of time with order and majesty. The world of that community was rich in stories, memories, and hopes for time and eternity.

Eliezer's movement into the night represents a gradual and seemingly inevitable contraction of this earlier world as one after another of its elements are stripped away. First the larger world of the town contracts into a ghetto, and then, it is left behind. Along the way, the religious community is destroyed, God absents Himself, the family is shattered. With the death of Eliezer's father, the spiraling down into the narrowing chasm is complete, and Eliezer is left "terribly alone in a world without God and without man." The journey is at its end.

The Theme of Silence

Simon P. Sibelman

*Simon P. Sibelman, author of Silence in the Novels of
Elie Wiesel begins his exploration on this theme with
Night. He outlines how Wiesel first developed the notion of the Holocaust as a journey into ever deeper
layers of silence. In Night, the prisoners quickly learn
that any behavior other than silence will lead to their
deaths. The silence of God, the inactivity of the world
around them, and the stifling of their loved one's
voices lead to a complete loss of self. Sibelman shows
how Wiesel accomplishes this by weaving the sparse
page layouts and the quick pacing of the sentences
with the arc of the main character's tragic story.*

Night is a testimony, a true story that mercilessly projects
the reader into Hitler's inferno. Eugene Heimler suggests
that "you can only create from something which is negative," and it does seem that Wiesel has used the evil of the
Holocaust as the generative material for a work that recounts the deportation and destruction of a single Hungarian Jewish community and details the loss of the witness's
identity, who is reduced to a physical and spiritual cadaver
at the novel's end. As shall be demonstrated, this text is written in ever more negative layers of silence.

In *Night*, silence combines with sparse, tautly concise
prose in which the naked horrors of the concentration camp
infrequently appear, and from which hysteria and disingen-
uous sentimentality are banished. If the Holocaust as
macro- /micro-experience reflecting on the human condition cannot be properly expressed, then one must shroud in
silence those unspeakable elements. Wiesel has stated that
uttering the ineffable is almost impossible. His idea elicits a
paradox common to Holocaust literature. The survivor must
bear witness to what has been; yet aspects of that reality

cannot be told. Despite this, the author/survivor must strive to achieve what he or she can. Wiesel's acceptance of the need to speak, in spite of the imposed silence of Auschwitz and of the impotence of words to describe the event, highlights his personal quest for a sense of truth.

In *Night*, one is faced with silence in its most negative forms. It exists firmly as the novel's core. In referring to silence, I am not alluding to the high frequency of the word silence itself, but to those other structural features . . . described and employed by Wiesel to evoke silence, notably the white spaces and long pauses. Within the space of this slim volume, Wiesel interrupts the text with such blank spaces eighty-two times. Elsewhere, the author himself emphasizes the importance such bits of white space signify when he writes: ". . . in the universe Auschwitz, everything is mystery. . . . White spaces themselves have their importance." Clear evidence of this abounds in this true story.

The theme of silence found in *Night*, however, extends far beyond such textual elements of words and blanks. If this testimony represents the absolute negative pole attainable by silence, we must undertake to seek out its cancerous growth within other elements as they are drawn into the vortex of the evil. The primary level at which one discovers this negative silence is the utter destruction of the self. "Silence in its primal aspect, is a consequence of terror, of a dissolution of self and world that, once known, can never be fully dispelled." This loss of identity effectively silences the image that constitutes human essence. [As writer Victor Frankl explains], "One literally became a number: dead or alive that was unimportant; the life of a number was completely irrelevant." This destruction extends beyond simple identity as it seeks to silence the unique world of childhood and innocence. One must therefore seek to trace the evolution of the antithesis of all human values, in general, and the Jewish ethos, in particular, an action that is achieved by a painful silencing of words by words as readers are conducted into the chaos of silent, destructive negativity. Proceeding a step beyond, one must subsequently seek the ultimate denial of God, humanity, and the word in order to arrive at the heart of the Holocaust.

The first element of life that must be silenced is time. Time lies at the heart of existence, a principle particularly true in Jewish thought and teachings. Abraham Joshua Heschel notes that "Judaism is a religion of time aiming at the sancti-fication of time." So it is that at the beginning of *Night*, time meticulously and meaningfully guides the young protagonist through life, through his studies and prayers. Time is repre-sented as a creative force, a bridge linking man to eternity.

The first incursion of night into the harmonious passage of time is the deportation and subsequent return of Moshe the Beadle. The destructive silence of the Jewish tragedy has taken its toll. . . . "He closed his eyes, as though to escape time" (*Night*, 17). More importantly, this silencing of time brings with it other startling transformations. . . . "Moshe had changed. There was no longer any joy in his eyes. He no longer sang. He no longer talked to me of God or the cab-bala." As time is silenced, creativity ceases, and negative si-lence descends over life.

Moshe's return not only marks the initial transformation of time, but it evokes a curious response from the Jewish community of Sighet. Moshe (whose name is Moses), the prophet who has seen the advancing night, is viewed as be-ing a madman. The Jews would prefer to purchase his si-lence, to erase his message. Ironically, Moshe's purchased mutism only permits the Jews of Sighet to resume life be-hind a protective facade of silence that descends. But this brief contact with the night has unquestionably altered life. Though the Allied broadcasts offer a degree of hope, Wiesel underlies the text with a bitter irony: The utter silence of the Allies concerning the fate of Europe's Jewish population.

Though metamorphosing, time persists in its existence. With its natural passage the Nazis arrive. The course which would lead to Birkenau has been set into motion. Ghettos were established where life sought to maintain a degree of normalcy. Stories, part of the fabric of Jewish life, continued to be told. But, in the middle of things, the good stories being told are silenced and will remain forever unfinished. Words have lost their positive creative powers. The only remaining significant communication becomes nonverbal. Whereas time had previously stimulated creativity, it now stifles the word/Word. Time comes to represent a negative force, and even the "ongoing tale" is tainted by it.

Religious traditions whose foundations rest on the posi-tive nature of time are effectively altered. . . . "We had the traditional Friday evening meal. We said the customary grace for the bread and wine and swallowed our food without a word." The traditional Jewish Sabbath meal, which inaugurates the day of rest, is a time of joy and song. The table is literally considered an altar to God around which special Sabbath songs, *zmirot*, are sung. Family and friends join together in peace and speak of God, the Sabbath, and the joys of life. These elements are pointedly absent. . . .

Wiesel's use of the Sabbath in this context is essential, for if the silencing of time is to be absolute, the element of *kdusha* (holiness), which first appears in the Bible with reference to time—"And God blessed the seventh day and made it holy" (Genesis 2:3)—must be removed. Holiness is lodged in time, most notably on one particular day: the Sabbath. . . . As the final blow, therefore, the Sabbath, replete with its holiness, is silenced. . . . "Saturday, the day of rest, was chosen for our expulsion." The synagogue where Sabbath prayers had previously been offered is transformed into a scene of desecration. . . .

> The synagogue was like a huge station. . . . The altar was broken, the hangings torn down, the walls bare. There were so many of us that we could scarcely breathe. We spent a horrible twenty-four hours there. There were men downstairs; women on the first floor. It was Saturday; it was as though we had come to attend the service. Since no one could go out, people were relieving themselves in a corner.

Not only has the Sabbath been stilled, but with this act of unholiness, universal *menuhah* (rest; repose) has been destroyed. In the ensuing timeless silent void, there is no place for the Jews of Sighet.

The final rupture of time occurs with the arrival of the deported Jews at Birkenau-Auschwitz. After a seemingly endless night in the stinking confines of the cattle cars, time ceases to exist as they enter the kingdom of night where all the imagined horrors of two millennia of Christian iconography become real.

> Not far from us, flames were leaping up from the ditch, gigantic flames. They were burning something. A lorry drew up at the pit and delivered its load—little children. Babies! Yes, I saw it—saw it with my own eyes . . . those children in the flames.

Such a vision cannot be real; it cannot exist within a normal temporal framework. . . ."I pinched my face. Was I still alive? Was I awake?" Moral time, creative time, that dimension in which humanity exists and in which it discovers traces of the living God has been abrogated. . . . "I had lost all sense of time. . . . Surely it was a dream." The coup de grace is finally dealt by the camp code of hairlessness. All vestiges of age disappear as young and old are reduced to naked, hairless beings. With the erasure of time, little remains of the protagonist.

This argument has merely attempted to point to the silencing of time within the Wieselian universe. In *Night*, time ceases to have a creative dimension and enters the realm of pure negativism. As Wiesel's work evolves, time will remain fragmented as he passes from the world of the living to the domain of the dead. This particular feature produces a unique literary structure that will facilitate the blending of the past, present, and future, and will reinforce the notion of the instantaneous multiplicity of various levels of perception and significance. . . .

As time is closely related to our understanding of reality, its silencing must therefore effect the existence and perception of truth. As previously noted, when Moshe the Beadle returned from his deportation and sought to warn the Jews of Sighet about the existence of the concentration camp, no one would believe him. His vision of truth could not be accommodated within a traditional temporal framework. This attitude is strengthened when, during the journey to Auschwitz, Moshe's words are echoed and even intensified in the frightening prophetic ravings of Mme. Schächter.

Within the timeless world of the sealed cattle cars that serve as the bridge between Sighet and Auschwitz, between life and death, the journey becomes a metonymy of existence in the concentration camp. In this environment, Mme. Schächter's voice painfully reiterates the horrific reality Moshe's had announced earlier, and which their current journey represents. The others react to her much as they had to Moshe: They attempt to silence her. Nothing, however, is capable of stifling her violent, prophetic outbursts. . . .

Eliezer has come to exist within a timeless void from which truth has been either exiled or deformed. In this silent wasteland, he will suffer the destruction of his own beliefs in a just and true God, as well as in the goodness of fellow human beings. Wiesel accomplishes this annihilation of Eliezer's essence within the space of seventeen pages as the devouring black flame of the concentration camp rapidly erases the being who had existed. Within the text, silence becomes the method by which Eliezer is reduced to a cipher.

This silence is evoked by several techniques. Sparse dialogue couples with terse, journalistic language, and long pauses to create a taut, fearful atmosphere. The word *silence* and its synonyms do not recur frequently, a choice that saves them from becoming meaningless clichés. Wiesel does, however, strike upon another technique: Punctuation. The use of punctuation accentuates the rapid respiration of the text and creates a feeling of impending doom. The text progresses haltingly, tripping and failing on its descent to hell.

Another striking feature is the absolute lack of gruesome detail, or even the mention of death. For the reader, these elements exist, but only in the meta-silence that Wiesel imposes and which forms the background of the story. The language of the concentration camp is one which cannot be expressed in common terms. . . . Wiesel does relegate certain realities of the concentration camp to silence. And yet, unexpressed elements do eventually rise from the depths to extinguish the voices of the living.

[Scholar] Roland Barthes believes that the voice is the symbolic substance of human life. As a symbol of life, the voice has no rightful place in the kingdom of death and is therefore methodically silenced. First, the protagonist's father's voice is stilled, then Eliezer's. Gradually, language itself is silenced. Life as it has been perceived ceases to exist.

With time and creative language silenced, the spirit of the concentration camp proceeds to invade Eliezer's soul and crushes his spiritual identity. One of the most painful acts is the demolition of the protagonist's view of God. The young talmudic student deeply believed in God, and had always nurtured the notion of the unique convenantal relationship between the Jews and God. Man would supplicate; God would respond. To those faced with the reality of Auschwitz, God reveals Himself as an impotent entity who has been robbed of His attributes of justice and mercy by the Angel of Death. For Wiesel, the God of the yeshiva student has abdicated His Throne.

The pious Jew prays three times daily. During the morning prayers, psalms are chanted to the Creator of the Universe. Within the horrific kingdom of night such psalms would prove to be ironically blasphemous or utterly senseless. So it is that Wiesel composes a new psalm, one which reflects the negativity of Auschwitz and the eclipse of God. . . . This striking text similarly signifies the protagonist's utter disillusionment with God. Former beliefs possess no validity. Eliezer has found that his God is lost amid the negative silence of the concentration camp. And God's own silence amid such incarnate evil indicts and condemns Him. Yet despite such a challenge to his beliefs, Eliezer never rejects the existence of God. The silence of Auschwitz has submitted the omnipotent God of Eliezer's youth to the test of truth, only to find Him wanting.

Not only is God called to the bar in this silence; the very notion of humanity, the enlightened being to which Mauriac makes reference in his Preface to the novel, is likewise examined and found to be wanting. The vision of the human race has radically altered. On "planet Auschwitz," human moral responsibilities are silenced and deformed into indifference. Humankind blindly and mutely accepts the events of the Holocaust. Human guilt is first evidenced while the Jews of Sighet are still in their ghetto. The "others" in the town indifferently accept matters, and eventually witness the deportation of their Jewish neighbors. Their silence condemns them and, by extension, all humanity. . . . The very fact that the Jewish population could so easily be deported destroys Eliezer's innocent illusions about human goodness and justice. Thus, for the protagonist, the corrosive, negative mentality of the concentration camp philosophy, that of every person for himself/herself and every person being your enemy, evolves and assumes primacy. The view of humanity, created in the image of God, is shattered and banished. The last shreds of respectful human dignity fall away under the cries of camp guards. The ultimate silencing blow to human identity occurs when Eliezer is stripped of his name and thereafter becomes A-7713.

By the conclusion of this third episode, the silent backdrop of Auschwitz has annihilated the voices of the pre-Holocaust world. The remainder of the narrative merely serves to supplement this initial silencing. The voice that is bound up with life and in life is strangled and muted. Only the chaotic, destructive silence of the evil remains.

Each of the various episodes comprising the story of *Night* reflects the omnipresent scenic silence of Auschwitz. Wiesel's use of the morphological, syntactic, and semantic aspects of silence permit the novel to descend into the depths of depraved negativity. And the principal question raised by the theme of silence emerges as: Where was God?

This becomes the central issue about which silence and all other themes come to revolve.

In the opening episodes, Eliezer had been transported from the light of learning and truth to the blackness of the void as experienced at Auschwitz. Prayer and praise were cut off before a silent God. The only force to which one could respond, the only source of potency, were the Nazis. . . . Each step, every example, emphasizes the absence of the divine and the presence of evil. Akiba Drumer, another character whose faith is shattered, poses this most serious question: "Where is God?" Those three words, like the four opening notes of Beethoven's Fifth Symphony, pound out the single most urgent question against which Eliezer and all humanity must struggle. Where was God? At the public hanging of a young boy that obsessive question arises from the meta-silence before uneasily dissolving again into it:

> "Where is God now?"
> And I heard a voice within me answer him:
> "Where is He? Here He is—He is hanging here on this
>   gallows. . . ."

This particular scene reflects the final silencing of the young protagonist's faith and hopes in the God of his youth. The powerful God of his religious studies possesses no meaning in Auschwitz. How could one maintain belief in the majesty and justice of God in the face of such debasement and depravity? The overwhelming silence of God generates a spiritual revolt within Eliezer, so that on Rosh Hashana, he refuses to pray or to bless God's Name. God stands in the dock, accused by Eliezer of silent indifference. This rebellion casts the protagonist into the depths of a void where he is painfully alone in a world whence God has been exiled. This bitter estrangement culminates ten days later on Yom Kippur when Eliezer abandons the obligatory fast and stresses: "I no longer accepted God's silence."

As Eliezer no longer possesses faith in God, he must seek strength and life elsewhere. In the context of traditional Jewish life, such a source of comfort and renewal can be found within the family. Yet the family unit Eliezer had known was forever ruptured upon his arrival in the concentration camp when his mother and sisters had been marched off to the gas chambers. His only hope lies in his father whose hand he tightly holds. . . .

But his father's voice, that had come to signify life, is gradually silenced. Without his voice, Eliezer's father effectively no longer exists in this world. The child assumes the role of father, the father the child. And yet, even as his father weakens, even as their relationship together is gradually silenced—a relationship that represents the last vestige of Eliezer's Jewishness—the protagonist refuses to abandon his father. . . . Unable to cry when his father dies, Eliezer has but one thought: Free at last! Death has silenced his only link with the past, with the family, with tradition.

The path that Eliezer has trod with his father is now his alone. His father, his God, his world, are dead. This is his inheritance. "In *Night* I wanted to show the end, the finality of the event. Everything came to an end—man, history, literature, religion, God. There was nothing left." So it is that the protagonist has been swallowed by the silent void of Auschwitz. . . . "From the depths of the mirror, a corpse gazed back at me.". . . Eliezer will always exist in a realm of ghosts. The cadaverous gaze in the mirror at Buchenwald reflects the paralyzed, mute victim perfectly.

CHAPTER 2

The Art of *Night*

READINGS ON
NIGHT

More Questions than Answers

Benj Mahle

Benj Mahle, an English teacher at Frank B. Kellogg Junior High in Rochester, Minnesota, was initially frustrated at not being able to answer the questions Night *raised about the Holocaust. How could the Germans have done it? Why didn't the Jews listen to warnings? Mahle deduced that Wiesel knows there are no easy answers to the events that took place, and purposefully left many things open for interpretation. He believes that it is in the very questioning itself that one begins to feel the anguish that the prisoners experienced; and that trying to find the answers to the past will bring hope for the future.*

In teaching *Night*, Elie Wiesel's puissant and often poetic account of his Holocaust experiences, I used to feel a gnawing inadequacy when my ninth grade students would ask questions for which I had no satisfactory responses. "Why," they'd ask, "did the Jews of Sighet not believe Moche the Beadle when he described to them the details of the pogrom he had miraculously survived?" Or, "How could the Nazis dump a truck load of babies into a burning pit, and feel nothing? How could a son attack and kill his own father for a mouthful of bread? How could anyone survive a forty mile march through the freezing night with only snow to eat?" Only recently have I become comfortable with answering "I don't know" or "I'm not sure" when they confront me with questions like those.

This change results from my latest rereading of *Night* wherein I've concluded that Elie Wiesel intended his account to be ambiguous, that he hoped to raise more questions than he would answer.

For example, consider his treatment of the theme of reli-

Excerpted from "The Power of Ambiguity: Elie Wiesel's *Night*," by Benj Mahle, *English Journal*, vol. 74, no. 6, October 1985. Copyright ©1985 by the National Council of Teachers of English. Reprinted with permission.

gious faith. In chapter three, the young Elie—heretofore a profound believer—first experiences the atrocities of the Auschwitz camp. Subsequently he declares, "Never shall I forget those flames which consumed my faith forever." *Consumed* suggests total destruction. Yet there are subtle suggestions that at least a flicker of faith remains. For as he details the horrors being perpetrated by men, he consistently contrasts these with benign, even appealing images of nature. Since we frequently perceive nature as a reflection of God, is it not possible to interpret these images as evidence of God's concern? In this passage Elie is being moved to a new camp (the italics are mine):

> Ten gypsies had come and joined our supervisor. Whips and truncheons cracked around me. My feet were running without my being aware of it. I tried to hide from the blows behind the others. *The spring sunshine . . .*

Later,

> The gypsies stopped near another barracks. They were replaced by SS, who surrounded us. Revolvers, machine guns, police dogs. The march had lasted half an hour. Looking around me I noticed that the barbed wires were behind us. We had left camp.

> *It was a beautiful April day, the fragrance of spring was in the air. The sun was setting in the west.*

> But we had been marching for only a few moments when we saw the barbed wire of another camp. An iron door with the inscription over it: "Work is Liberty"—Auschwitz.

These references to the natural beauty of this day may give support to the notion that God is offering hope. On the other hand, perhaps the author is sarcastically suggesting that God merely deigned to ease their suffering by allowing that it should be done in pleasant weather. Consider another passage from chapter three—Elie's moving and deeply poetic description of his first night in camp:

> Never shall I forget that night, the first night in camp, which has turned my life into one long night, seven times cursed and seven times sealed. Never shall I forget that smoke. Never shall I forget the little faces of the children, whose bodies I saw turned into wreaths of smoke beneath a *silent blue sky.*

Few things in nature stir in us more hope for a fine day that blue skies. Yet I wonder if the contrast here is supposed to provide a suggestion of hope? Is it instead a quiet condemnation of God's apparent silence, represented by the

A POEM ABOUT TEACHING *NIGHT*

Thomas E. Thorton, an English teacher in New York, struggles over using Night *to teach his young students about the Holocaust. He expresses his anguish in a poem published in* English Journal.

On Wiesel's *Night*
I cannot teach this book. Instead,
I drop copies on their desks,
like bombs on sleeping towns,
and let them read. So do I, again.
The stench rises from the page
and chokes my throat.
The ghosts of burning babies
haunt my eyes.
And that bouncing baton,
that pointer of Death,
stabs me in the heart
as it sends his mother
to the blackening sky.
Nothing is destroyed
the laws of science say,
only changed.
The millions transformed into
precious smoke ride the wind
to fill our lungs and hearts
with their cries.

No, I cannot teach this book.
I simply want the words
to burn their comfortable souls
and leave them scarred for life.
                    Thomas E. Thorton
                    East Greenbrush, New York

Thomas E. Thorton, "On Wiesel's *Night*", *English Journal*, vol. 79, no. 2, February 1990, p. 87.

tranquility of nature at a moment when it would seem right that a sudden tempest should douse the flames or the earth should open up and swallow the murderers? Elie Wiesel consistently provides readers with details rather than explanations. And I believe his purpose in providing these contrasting images is appropriately ambiguous.

In the first pages of his book, the author states that his teacher, Moche the Beadle, believed that "every question possessed a power that did not lie in the answer." The questions posed by my students during their reading of *Night* evince a power that has moved many of them to seek more information. Ultimately, in attempting to find their own answers, these students experience shock and revulsion that in the entire history of the human race such questions should ever have needed to be asked. Their curiosity and the complexity of the issues forces them to experience the power of these questions with their hearts as well as their heads.

So, I no longer feel frustration when I don't satisfy the curiosities of my students during their study of *Night* and the Holocaust. For I've concluded that what is important is *not* that all these questions should be answered; what is important is that all of us should continue to ask them. I believe it was to this end that Elie Wiesel created a *poetic* account of awful beauty, ambiguity, and power. He must have sensed that as long as we question the events of the Holocaust, our memory of it—and our outrage—will be an eternal flame within each of us.

Facing the Horror
of History

Lea Hamaoui

Lea Hamaoui, a professor at Baruch College in Brook-
lyn, acknowledges how difficult it is for any writer to
truly capture the essence of history. This is particularly evident in the case of the Holocaust, when readers want to believe that such horrors didn't really take
place. She explores the methods Wiesel uses in *Night*
to lure the reader so deeply into the story that by the
end of it the horror is undeniably real.

To render historical horror is to render, by definition, that
which exceeds rendering; it projects pain for which there is
no solace, no larger consolation, no redemptive possibility. . . .
The young Eliezer staring into the mirror upon his liberation
from Buchenwald has gained knowledge, but this knowledge
in no way justifies the sufferings that preceded it. It is not a
sign of positive spiritual development. Nor is it linked to
restorative changes in the moral and political realm. *Night* is
not about a moral political order violated and restored, but
about the shattering of the idea of such an order. . . .

Night proceeds from experience that is not universal. It
does not expand from kernels of the familiar but from the
unfamiliar, from data in historical reality. The deaths of
Eliezer's father, of Akiva Drummer, of Juliek the violinist
and of Meir Katz are different because, after all of the pain,
there is nothing to be extracted by way of compensation.
They are not symbolic but very real, and we experience not
a purging of feelings tapped but the fear of the unpredictable
in life to which we, like the Jews of *Night,* are subject.

If symbol is something that stands in place of something
else, the historical narrative does not stand in place of our
experience, but alongside it. We experience historical narrative much the way we experience a neighbor's report of his

Excerpted from "Historical Horror and the Shape of *Night*," by Lea Hamaoui, in *Elie
Wiesel: Between Memory and Hope,* edited by Carol Rittner (New York: New York University Press, 1990). Reprinted by permission of Carol Rittner.

or her visit to a place we have not ourselves visited. The report is informational—it is "adjacent" to our experience, neither interpretive nor metaphorical nor symbolic. It is "other" than our experience but also part of the same historical matrix within which we experience the flow of our own lives. *Night* threatens and disturbs in a way that symbolic narrative does not.

Night is Wiesel's attempt to bring word of the death camps back to humanity in such a form that his message, unlike that of Moshe the Beadle to Eliezer and to the Jews of Sighet, will not be rejected. The word I wish to stress here is *form*. The work, which is eyewitness account, is also much more than eyewitness account. In its rhetorical and aesthetic design, *Night* is shaped by the problematic of historical horror and by the resistances, both psychic and formal, to the knowledge Wiesel would convey.

When the narrator, Eliezer, sees a truck filled with children who are dumped into a fiery ditch, he cannot believe what he has seen: "I pinched my face. Was I alive? Was I awake? I could not believe it. How could it be possible for them to burn people, children, and for the world to keep silent? No, none of this could be true. It was a nightmare."

Eliezer cannot believe what is before his eyes. His disbelief seems to numb him physically—he pinches his face to ascertain that the medium of that vision, his body, is alive, perceiving, present. So fundamental is the horror to which he is an eyewitness that seeing comes at the expense of his bodily awareness of himself as a vital and perceiving entity. What Eliezer witnesses contradicts psychic underpinnings of existence so thoroughly that his very awareness brings with it feelings of deadness.

It is precisely this moment, this confrontation with data that negates the human impulses and ideas that structure our lives, with which Wiesel is concerned. We cannot know that which we cannot know. In order to bring the fact of Auschwitz to us, Wiesel must deal with the inherent difficulty of assimilating the truth he would portray.

His method is simple, brilliant and depends upon a series of repetitions in which what is at stake is a breakdown of critical illusions. At this level, the experience of the reader reading the narrative is structurally parallel to his experience of life, at least as Karl Popper describes it. Life, in Popper's view, resembles the experience of a blind person who runs into an obstacle and thereby experiences its existence. Through the falsification of our assumptions we actually make contact with "reality." The refutation of our errors is the positive experience we gain from reality.

THROUGH ROSE-COLORED GLASSES

Eliezer's tale is the story of a series of shattered expectations, his and our own. The repetition of this "disappointment," of optimism proven hollow and warnings rejected, becomes the crucial aesthetic fact or condition within which we then experience the narrator's account of his experiences in Auschwitz, in Buna, in Gleiwitz, and in Buchenwald. In this way we come to experience the account of the death camps as an account cleansed of past illusion, pristine in its terrible truth.

The quest for this truth is established at the outset of the narrative in the figure of Moshe the Beadle. Eliezer is devoted to his studies of Talmud. His decision to study Kabbalah with Moshe focuses the narrative on the problematic of reality and imbues it with the spiritual longings of this quest.

> There are a thousand and one gates leading into the orchard of mystical truth. Every human being has his own gate . . .

> And Moshe the Beadle, the poor barefoot of Sighet, talked to me for long hours of the revelations and mysteries of the cabbala. It was with him that my initiation began. We would read together, ten times over, the same page of the Zohar. Not to learn it by heart, but to extract the divine essence from it.

> And throughout those evenings a conviction grew in me that Moshe the Beadle would draw me with him into eternity, into that time where question and answer would become one.

The book, which begins with Eliezer's search for a teacher of mystical knowledge and ends with Eliezer's contemplating his image in a mirror after his liberation from Buchenwald, proposes a search for ultimate knowledge in terms that are traditional, while the knowledge it offers consists of data that is historical, radical, and subversive.

If directionality of the narrative is established early, a counter-direction makes itself felt very quickly. Following Eliezer's dream of a formal harmony, eternity and oneness toward which Moshe would take him, Eliezer's initiation into the "real" begins:

Then one day they expelled all the foreign Jews from Sighet. And Moshe the Beadle was a foreigner.

Crammed into cattle trains by Hungarian police, they wept bitterly. We stood on the platform and wept too.

Moshe is shot but escapes from a mass grave in one of the Galician forests of Poland near Kolomaye and returns to Sighet in order to warn the Jews there. He describes children used as targets for machine guns and the fate of a neighbor, Malka, and of Tobias the tailor.

From this point onward in the narrative, a powerful counter-direction of flight away from truth, knowledge, reality, and history is set into motion. Moshe is not believed, not even by his disciple, Eliezer. The Jews of Sighet resist the news Moshe has brought them:

I wanted to come back to Sighet to tell you the story of my death . . . And see how it is, no one will listen to me . . .

And we, the Jews of Sighet, were waiting for better days, which would not be long in coming now.

Yes, we even doubted that he [Hitler] wanted to exterminate us.

Was he going to wipe out a whole people? Could he exterminate a population scattered throughout so many countries? So many millions! What method could he use? And in the middle of the twentieth century?

RESISTING THE NEW REALITY

Optimism persists with the arrival of the Germans. After Sighet is divided into a big and little ghetto, Wiesel writes, "little by little life returned to normal. The barbed wire which fenced us in did not cause us any real fear."

While the narrative presses simultaneously toward and away from the "real," the real events befalling the Jews of Sighet are perceived as unreal:

On everyone's back was a pack. . . . Here came the Rabbi, his back bent, his face shaved, his pack on his back. His mere presence among the deportees added a touch of unreality to the scene. It was like a page torn from some story book, from some historical novel about the captivity of Babylon or the Spanish Inquisition.

The intensity of the resistance peaks in the boxcar in which, Eliezer and his family are taken to the death camp. Madame Schächter, distraught by the separation from her pious husband and two older sons, has visions of fire: "Jews, listen to me! I can see a fire! There are huge flames! It is a furnace!" Her words prey on nerves, fan fears, dispel illusion: "We felt that an abyss was about to open beneath our bodies." She is gagged and beaten. As her cries are silenced the chimneys of Auschwitz come into view:

> We had forgotten the existence of Madame Schächter. Suddenly we heard terrible screams: Jews, look! Look through the window! Flames! Look!
>
> And as the train stopped, we saw this time that flames were gushing out of a tall chimney into the black sky.

The movement toward and away from the knowledge of historical horror that Moshe the Beadle brings back from the mass grave and the violence that erupts when precious illusions are disturbed, shapes the narrative of *Night*. The portrait and analysis of the resistances to knowing help situate the reader in relation to the historical narrative and imbue the narrative with the felt historicity of the world outside the book. Eliezer's rejection of the knowledge that Moshe brings back, literally, from the grave, predicts our own rejection of that knowledge. His failure to believe the witness prepares the reader for the reception of Eliezer's own story of his experience in Auschwitz by first examining the defenses that Eliezer, and, thereby, implicitly, the reader, would bring to descriptions of Auschwitz. The rejection of Moshe strips the reader of his own deafness in advance of the arrival at Auschwitz.

EYES WIDE OPEN

Once stripped of his defenses, the reader moves from a fortified, to an open, undefended position vis-à-vis the impact of the narrative. Because the lines between narrative art and life have been erased, Wiesel brings the reader into an existential relationship to the historical experience recounted in *Night*. By virtue of that relationship, the reader is transformed into a witness. The act of witnessing is ongoing for most of the narrative, a narrative that is rife with horror and with the formal dissonances that historically experienced horror must inflict upon language.

Human extremity challenges all formal representation of it. It brings the world of language and the world outside language into the uncomfortable position of two adjacent notes

THE BURDEN OF THE DEAD

In Confronting the Holocaust: The Impact of Elie Wiesel, *English professor and author Lawrence L. Langer contemplates the burden that the dead continue to bestow upon Wiesel and on all of us.*

The compelling fact is that the millions of people [murdered in the Holocaust] are *not* gone, they haunt the writer with a ghostly persistence that casts a shadow on the imagination and leaves a disfiguring scar on the characters who populate his literary world. The imagination contending with the Holocaust is never free to create an independent reality; it is circumscribed by the literal event, by the history of the horror, by the sheer mass of anonymous dead who impose a special responsibility on the writer's talent. That burden is one feature of the altered consciousness that our age requires of us. The spirit of tragedy cannot absorb these dead; neither time nor history will silence their wail. . . . They present us with the dismal image of men dying for nothing.

This is a bizarre challenge for a reader nurtured on life, hope, and the future. . . . We all know the final lines from Elie Wiesel's first, and still one of his finest works, *Night:* "From the depths of the mirror, a corpse gazed back at me. The look in his eyes, as they stared back into mine, has never left me." Multiply that corpse a hundred, a thousand, a millionfold, and we will understand more clearly what is implied when we are told [by Holo-

on a piano keyboard that are simultaneously pressed and held. The sounds they produce jar the ear. In a work of historical horror, language and life, expression and experience are perceived as separate opaque structures, each of which is inadequate to encompass the abyss that separates them.

The most powerful passages in *Night* are those that mark Eliezer's arrival in Auschwitz. The family is separated. Eliezer and his father go through a selection and manage to stay together. Eliezer watches a truck drop living children into a ditch full of flames. He and his father conclude that this is to be Eliezer's fate as well. Eliezer decides he will run into an electrified wire fence and electrocute himself rather than face an excruciating death in the flaming ditch.

The moment is extraordinary and extreme beyond the wildest of human imaginings. Hearing his fellow Jews murmur the Kaddish, a formula of praise of the Almighty that is the traditional prayer for the dead, Eliezer revolts: "For the caust scholar Alvin Rosenfeld] that because of the Holocaust, "the imagination has come to one of its periodic endings and stands at the threshold of new and more difficult beginnings."

The burden of the dead, of *such* dead, which the Holocaust has bequeathed to us and which is present on nearly every page Elie Wiesel has written, was anticipated before the invention of the extermination camp. In an essay unpretentiously called "Thoughts for the Times on War and Death," published in 1915 shortly after the outbreak of World War I, Sigmund Freud recognized how a conflict of such dimensions would disfigure conventional assumptions about dying. We "cannot maintain our former attitude towards death," Freud insisted, "and we have not yet discovered a new one." Thirty years later the Holocaust confirmed Freud's intuition, for he had also argued that until men found a way of absorbing into their cultural assumptions the phenomenon of mass dying for no justifiable reason, they would continue to live psychologically beyond their means. One of the main problems of the Holocaust writer is to find a secure place, somewhere between memory and imagination, for all those corpses who, like the ghost of Hamlet's father, cry out against the injustice of their end, but for whom no act of vengeance or ritual of remembrance exists sufficient to bring them to a peaceful place of rest.

Alvin H. Rosenfeld and Irving Greenberg, eds., "The Divided Voice," in *Confronting the Holocaust: The Impact of Elie Wiesel,* Bloomington: Indiana University Press, 1978.

first time, I felt revolt rise up in me. Why should I bless His name? The Eternal Lord of the Universe, the All-Powerful and Terrible, was silent. What had I to thank Him for?" The Jews continue their march and Eliezer begins to count the steps before he will jump at the wire:

> Ten steps still. Eight. Seven. We marched slowly on, as though following a hearse at our own funeral . . . There it was now, right in front of us, the pit and its flames. I gathered all that was left of my strength, so that I could break from the ranks and throw myself upon the barbed wire. In the depths of my heart, I bade farewell to my father, to the whole universe.

And the words of the Kaddish, hallowed by centuries and disavowed only moments before, words of praise and of affirmation of divine oneness, spring unbidden to his lips: "and in spite of myself, the words formed themselves and issued in a whisper from my lips: *Yitgadal veyitkadach shme raba* . . . May His name be blessed and magnified." Eliezer does not run to the wire. The entire group turns left and enters a barracks.

The question of formal dissonance in *Night is* revealing. The narrative that would represent historical horror works, finally, against the grain of the reader and of the psychic structures that demand the acknowledgments, resolutions, closure, equivalence, and balances. . . .

The words of the Kaddish in *Night* do not express the horror to which Eliezer is a witness. They flow from an inner necessity and do not reflect but deflect that horror. They project the sacredness of life in the face of its most wrenching desecration. They affirm life at the necessary price of disaffirming the surrounding reality. The world of experience and the world of language could not, at this moment, be further apart. Experience is entirely beyond words. Words are utterly inadequate to convey experience.

NEVER FORGET

The dissonance makes itself felt stylistically as well. Eliezer sums up his response to these first shattering hours of his arrival at Auschwitz in the most famous passages of *Night* and, perhaps, of all of Wiesel's writing: "Never shall I forget that night, the first night in camp, which has turned my life into one long night, seven times cursed and seven times sealed." The passage takes the form of an oath never to forget this night of his arrival. The oath, the recourse to metaphorical language ("which has turned my life into one long night"), the reference to curses and phraseology ("seven times cursed") echo the biblical language in which Eliezer was so steeped. He continues: "Never shall I forget that smoke. Never shall I forget the little faces of the children, whose bodies I saw turned into wreaths of smoke beneath a silent blue sky." The oath is an oath of protest, the "silent blue sky," an accusation: "Never shall I forget those flames which consumed my faith forever." Here and in the sentences that follow, Wiesel uses the rhythms, the verbal energy, imagery, and conventions of the Bible to challenge, accuse, and deny God:

> Never shall I forget that nocturnal silence which deprived me, for all eternity, of the desire to live. Never shall I forget those moments which murdered my God and my soul and turned my dreams to dust. Never shall I forget these things, even if I am condemned to live as long as God Himself. Never.

The elaborate oath of remembrance recalls the stern biblical admonitions of remembrance. The negative formulation of the oath and the incremental repetition of the word "never" register defiance and anger even as the eight repetitions circumscribing the passage give it rhythmic structure and ceremonial shape. Ironically, these repetitions seem to implicate mystical notions of God's covenant with the Jews, a covenant associated with the number eight because the ceremony of entrance into the covenant by way of circumcision takes place on the eighth day after birth. The passage uses the poetry and language of faith to affirm a shattering of faith.

The passage is a tour de force of contradiction, paradox, and formal dissonances that are not reconciled, but juxtaposed and held up for inspection. In a sparely written, tightly constructed narrative, it is the only extended poetic moment. It is a climactic moment, and, strangely, for a work that privileges a world outside words altogether, a rhetorical moment: a moment constructed out of words and the special effects and properties of their combinations, a moment that hovers above the abyss of human extremity in uncertain relationship to it.

Like the taste of bread to a man who has not eaten, the effect of so poetic a passage lies in what preceded it. Extremity fills words with special and different meanings. Eliezer reacts to the words of one particular SS officer: "But his clipped words made us tremble. Here the word 'furnace' was not a word empty of meaning; it floated on the air, mingling with the smoke. It was perhaps the only word which did have any real meaning here."

THE REAL NIGHT

Wiesel's narrative changes our conventional sense of the word "night" in the course of our reading. Night, which as a metaphor for evil always projects, however subliminally, the larger rhythm and structure within which the damages of evil are mitigated, comes to stand for another possibility altogether. The word comes to be filled with the historical flames and data for which there are no metaphors, no ameliorating or sublimating structures. It acquires the almost-tactile feel of the existential, opaque world that is the world of the narrative and also the world in which we live.

Perhaps the finest tribute to *Night* is to be found in the

prologue of Terrence Des Pres's book on poetry and politics, *Praises and Dispraises.* Des Pres is speaking of Czeslaw Milosz and of other poets who have lived through extremity and writes: "If we should wonder why their voices are valued so highly, it's that they are acquainted with the night, the nightmare spectacle of politics especially." Des Pres uses the word "night" and the reader immediately understands it in exactly Wiesel's revised sense of it.

To be acquainted with the night, in this sense, and to bring that knowledge to a readership is to bring the world we live in into sharper focus. The necessary job of making a better world cannot possibly begin from anywhere else.

Christian Imagery

Michael Brown

Michael Brown, a professor of humanities and language studies in Toronto, fears that the Christian symbolism Wiesel incorporates into *Night* might be misinterpreted. It may lead the reader to believe that Wiesel is turning his back on Judaism, as in fact some Jews did following the Holocaust. Through close analysis of *Night* and Wiesel's intentions, he asserts that Wiesel's motives may have been to show not only how difficult it is for Jews to keep their faith after the Holocaust, but also that since Christianity was the main faith of those who committed the acts of atrocity in the first place, it ought to be difficult being Christian as well.

However much one might regret it, few can fail to sympathize with, and even to participate in, the theological questioning which the Holocaust has sparked. The survivors—and, in a sense, we are all survivors—need ways of understanding. Yet the explanations which past generations have offered for Jewish suffering do not satisfy. Some Jews have been relatively unaffected, but others have lost their belief in God entirely and not regained it. Still others see the Holocaust as the symbol of God's ultimate rejection of Judaism and have become Christian. Rabbi Elisha ben Abuyah, the Talmud relates, foreswore belief in God after witnessing the death of only one innocent child. One cannot but understand if faith breaks after having witnessed the death of six million innocent men, women and children. . . .

The conversion of Jews to Christianity as a response to the Holocaust seems all the more ignoble in the light of the traditional Christian explanation of Jewish suffering. Christians have understood that suffering to be divine punishment for the Jews' twofold sin, first, of failing to recognize the divinity and Messiahship of Jesus and then, according to

Excerpted from "On Crucifying the Jews," by Michael Brown, *Judaism*, vol. 27, no. 4, Fall 1978. Reprinted with permission from the American Jewish Congress.

the classical reading of history, of causing his death. The sins of the Jewish parents are to be visited upon their children: Jews for all time are punished for the blindness and cruelty of their ancestors. Their permanent downcast state serves as witness to the truth of Christianity. . . .

Some Christians still adhere to the traditional doctrine regarding Jewish suffering and understand the Holocaust as one more manifestation of the wrath of God being visited upon the Jews for their 2000-years-ago sin. One can appreciate the desire of theological conservatives to see all events fitting into classical doctrine. Still, to an outsider, such an explanation seems unacceptable on its own terms. What kind of God would require the degradation, torture, and death of a million Jewish children in the twentieth century as atonement for the shortsightedness of their ancestors two millennia ago? How can anyone believe in such a deity?

Indeed, how can one account for the attraction of Jews to such a belief, especially since Christianity is the faith system, at least nominally, of the perpetrators of the Holocaust? Not surprisingly, many Jews respond with a special measure of distaste when faced with Holocaust survivors who have embraced Christianity. Incomprehension and discomfort are no less acute in confronting works of literature and art which use Christian myth and symbol to interpret the Holocaust.

In fact, Jewish writers who employ Christian terminology to write about the Holocaust have generally evoked dumbfounded consternation from Jewish critics. Elie Wiesel's *Night* . . . is one of the most widely read works of Holocaust literature, . . . yet the obvious Christian elements in these works have been ignored by critics who are either too embarrassed or are just uncomprehending. . . .

PLACING BLAME

Classical Judaism understood the destruction of the Temple, the subsequent exile, and most other tribulations of the Jews as punishment for their failure to achieve *tikkun olam bemalkhut shaddai,* the construction in Palestine of the ideal society revealed to them at Sinai and later by God himself, the society which was to serve as a model for the entire world. . . .

One might, of course, look upon the state of Israel as the rebirth of the "saving remnant." But it is hard to imagine that Judaism, which could not countenance the sacrifice of one man, Isaac, as a testimonial to faith, would consider six million human sacrifices, all of them unwilling, an appropriate means of bringing about the restoration of Jewish sovereignty.

But even if classical Judaism offers no acceptable mythological frame for interpreting the Holocaust, the use of Christian mythology should be out of bounds to Jews. The Cross is not a universal symbol of suffering; it is a very particular Christian mode of understanding experience. Judaism has different myths from Christianity and different values, although it shares a good many with it, especially those which originated in the Hebrew Bible. Jews cannot see Jewish experience—or any experience—in Christian terms and remain authentic Jews. To be themselves, Jews must express themselves in Jewish symbolic language, or, at the very least, in neutral language. When they opt for other symbols and myths, they can easily be seen to be rejecting Judaism and, indeed, may be doing so. This is especially the case with regard to Christian myth and symbol, because of the tension and competition which have almost always characterized the Christian-Jewish relationship.

Is it then the case that [Elie Wiesel has] . . . sold out? Is their faith so broken that they have become closet Christians and now create entirely outside of the Jewish framework? The motivations of artists are not easily fathomed and the artists themselves are unlikely to be of assistance. Plato accused poets of not understanding their own poetry. In part, he was right. Robert Frost used to say that his job was to create poetry, while that of the readers was to understand it. But, while artists may be of little help in explaining their own works, the works themselves can sometimes be illuminating with regard to their creators. And, in fact, *Night*, . . . and especially the way in which Christian imagery is used in [it does] . . . yield some clues about the writer's motivation. . . .

CRUCIFYING THE INNOCENT

This book, Wiesel's first and, to this reader, his most powerful work to date, is autobiographical, although apparently fictionalized to some extent. It is the tale of the journey from the sunny, imperturbable tranquility of a Transylvanian town into the nightmare of the concentration camps. It is the story of a father and his son, of their relationship which, alone, preserves the humanity of both and their will to live, and of the ultimate destruction of both humanity and the will to live by the Nazis' deliberate process of dehumanization.

In many ways *Night* is a very Jewish book. Its main characters, except for the Nazis and their collaborators, are all identifiably and positively Jewish. The narrator, Wiesel, is an aspiring young cabbalist when the book opens, and his father is one of the pillars of the Sighet Jewish establishment. When the Jews of Sighet are deported, the narrator sees the deportation in terms of the exile of the Jews to Babylon or, later, from Spain.

It is no surprise that in the hell of Birkenau many of the characters in the book—rabbis and laymen, including the narrator—lose their faith. God seems absent. In response, some people become defiant, although even their defiance is Jewish. (Wiesel, for instance, eats on Yom Kippur.) Others simply surrender their lives. Death becomes commonplace at Birkenau.

Two deaths, however, are not ordinary, and the narrator treats them rather differently from the others. The first is that of his friend, Akiba Drumer; and here there is introduced the Christian theme. Drumer bears the name of a great Jewish sage, a contemporary of Elisha ben Abuyah. Rabbi Akiba, however, kept faith in adversity. He sacrificed his life rather than obey the Roman prohibition against teaching Torah in Palestine. He died teaching others how to live by Torah, how to build the ideal world. Unlike his namesake of Roman times, Akiba Drumer, in his trials, loses faith in God. He cannot "see a proof of God in this Calvary." Like Jesus, in the Gospels of Matthew and Mark, Drumer predicts the hour of his own death and then dies, wondering, in the words of the Psalmist, why God has abandoned him.

The other extraordinary death is that of a beautiful child, a servant of one of the *kapos*. The narrator refers to the child, as do the other inmates, as "the little servant, the sad-eyed angel." In retribution for the sabotage activities of his boss, "the sad-eyed angel" is put to death, one of three people hanged together on a gallows. That there are three (two adults and one innocent child between them) suggests the Gospels' portrait of an innocent Jesus crucified together with two robbers, one on either side. The similarity with Jesus does not end there. Death does not come immediately to "the sad-eyed angel" when he is hanged, as it did not to Jesus. Suspended from the gallows, he dies slowly before the eyes of the unwilling onlookers. Then someone asks:

Where is God now?

The narrator responds to a voice within himself and answers:

Where is He? Here He is—He is hanging here on this gallows. . . .

In what is probably the climactic scene of *Night*, God dies on the gallows, just as Christians understand God to have done in the person of Jesus almost 2000 years ago.

Wiesel does not write of God rising. In François Mauriac's introduction to *Night*, however, an introduction to which Wiesel seems not to object, the Christian myth is completed. With unintended irony Mauriac asserts that, in modern Israel, "the Jewish nation has been resurrected from among its thousands of dead [millions!]," and that Wiesel himself physically resembles "that other Israeli, his brother, . . . the Crucified, whose Cross has conquered the world.". . .

NO GLORY HERE

Since [Wiesel] . . . lived through the Holocaust in Hitler's Europe, . . . [he is], in fact, portraying [his] own [life] and experiences in Christian terms. The question remains: how is one to understand a Jew's having done so? . . .

In the opinion of this writer, . . . those who evince embarrassment at the Christian imagery of [*Night*], . . . fail altogether to grasp the significance of the work that they seek to interpret. To be sure, . . . Wiesel, . . . uses a Christian mythological frame and not a Jewish one. That, in itself, however, does not constitute evidence of wavering in the direction of a commitment to Christianity. Neither do the comments or behavior of the artist, which, as noted earlier, must always be taken with a grain of salt. . . .

Wiesel's non-Jews are not the focus of his book, and there are not many of them in it. He never identifies his gentiles as Christian, although they must be presumed to be at least nominally so, since they are Germans, Poles, and other Europeans. These Christians almost all serve as *kapos*, concentration camp authorities, Gestapo agents, or Hungarian or Roumanian police.

A few of them show some small degree of kindness to their Jewish victims. Most, however, as might be expected from what we know all too well about the camps, are brutish and brutal. They treat the Jews like animals; they are themselves predators and scavengers. There is not a single idealized or even admirable Christian in the book. Once, at a particularly difficult moment, the narrator hears a kind word from a young girl working in the camp. After the war he meets that same girl by accident in Paris. They reminisce. Finally, he summons the courage to ask; and, indeed, she turns out to be a Jew. The one kind non-prisoner with whom he had come in contact during all those long months was not a gentile, after all, but a Jew with Aryan papers. . . .

What emerges . . . , then, is, on the one hand, an approach to the Holocaust through Christian symbols and imagery, and, on the other hand, a portrait of Christians and their world as cruel and bestial. In that bestial society, the Jews suffer the fate of Jesus. They are crucified. It is the Christians who crucify them. . . . Jesus represents an ideal for human life and death; but his only true followers are Jews. They are the ones who live and die like him. If the Church has traditionally thought of itself as the true Israel, Wiesel, . . . seems to believe that the Jews are the true Christians. And, ironically, the Christians in their works behave like the Jews as the Gospels portray them. . . .

Shattering the Myths

Can it be that Christian imagery is the most compelling way of understanding the suffering of the Jews? Can it be that Christian symbols and mythology, those of the faith system of the perpetrators of the Holocaust, suggest the highest ideal of behavior for human beings? Especially in light of the fate of Europe's Jews, would not the central Jewish ideal of *tikkun olam,* striving to perfect the world of men, be a more desirable goal for all men and, certainly, a more seemly one for Jews? . . .

Night is testimony that Wiesel's beliefs were shattered, at least for a time. Perhaps, too, Jewish symbols do seem to these artists inadequate or inappropriate for interpreting their experiences and those of the other Jews of Hitler's Europe. It may be that, in the eyes of Wiesel, . . . *tikkun olam* is an anachronism, and Christ-like death is the only possibility in a world which has been conquered by the Cross.

None of this, however, is the point of the [book], which does not really portray Jewish experience or Jewish belief. . . . For the most part, [it] attempts to interpret Christianity. [It] depicts the Christian world. [It is] heavily ironic and very biting. Wiesel . . . portrays a Holocaust kingdom in which Judaism cannot even begin to work at *tikkun olam,* its vision of a just and orderly society. Jews can only die. Their only decision is how to die. . . .

It is the nominal and the committed Christians, who prevent the achievement of the Jewish vision, and who do so, at least in part, by acting according to their own religious mythology and doctrine, supposedly suffused with love and mercy. . . .

In allowing the crucifixion of the Jews, however, Christians were destroying themselves as well. . . . "the sad-eyed angel" on the gallows, stands for both love and justice denied. [He is] Jesus as Christians have claimed to understand him. In the Holocaust, the followers of Jesus destroyed those Jews and, thus, their own central myth as well. . . .

There can be no question, of course, that the Christian imagery in [*Night*] . . . is intentional. It is too obvious to be otherwise. [Wiesel] . . . uses Christian symbols to interpret the Holocaust, viewing the destruction of the Jews as a modern version of the passion [of Jesus in Christianity]. . . .

[*Night*] asserts that the Holocaust was, at root, a Christian phenomenon and not a Jewish one, that foremost it raises theological questions for Christianity. . . . The Holocaust calls into question not the possibility of remaining Jewish, but rather, the possibility of remaining Christian.

How Wiesel Tells the Story That Can Never Be Told

Colin Davis

Elie Wiesel has often stated that the true story of the Holocaust can never be told. In *Night*, then, he struggles with the need to tell an impossible story. Colin Davis, the author of *Elie Wiesel's Secretive Texts*, suggests that the way Wiesel tried to overcome this dilemma was by utilizing very specific strategies. He wrote the story in the past tense, tightly organized his material, and by showing the reader how communication and language broke down in the camps, he prepared the reader to understand that "words will always fall short of truth."

Critics have implied that *Night* should be *read*, but not *interpreted*. [Holocaust scholars] Robert McAfee Brown and Ted Estess, for example, both preface their commentaries on *Night* with disarming remarks on the inappropriateness of critical analysis: "Of all Wiesel's works, [*Night*] is the one that most cries out not to be touched, interpreted, synthesized. It must be encountered at first hand." "One is reluctant to apply the usual conventions of literary analysis to the book, for by doing so one runs the risk of blunting the impact of its testimony by too quickly speaking of secondary matters. Against the horror of the story, literary considerations seem somehow beside the point."

Some readers have nevertheless insisted that *Night* should be read as a literary text. Denis Boak describes it as "a highly conscious literary artifact," and Zsuzsanna Ozsvath and Martha Satz argue that "the power of [*Night*] as a document of the Holocaust owes much of its intensity to its literary quality.". . .

RELYING ON LITERARY DEVICES

Night does not offer unmediated, uninterpreted realities. Events are filtered through the eyes of a narrator, Eliezer, whose primary function is to seize their meaning as he organizes them into a coherent narrative. He exhibits considerable control in his organization of material. The nine short chapters divide the text into manageable units that can be summarized as follows:

Chapter 1. In Sighet. Buildup to deportation.
Chapter 2. In train. Arrival in Birkenau.
Chapter 3. First experiences of Auschwitz. Transfer to Buna.
Chapter 4. Life in Buna. Hangings.
Chapter 5. Selections. Evacuation of camp.
Chapter 6. Evacuation through snow. Arrival in Gleiwitz.
Chapter 7. In train to Buchenwald.
Chapter 8. Death of father.
Chapter 9. Liberation of Buchenwald.

Throughout *Night* Wiesel uses the past historic tense as part of a retrospective narrative. He is "telling a story" in a way that becomes more problematic in his later, more formally sophisticated fiction, with its changing narrative voices, shifting time scales, and unstable tense systems. In *Night* the past historic gives the narrator retrospective command over his material. This allows him to organize and underline its significance, as well as to calculate and control its effect on the reader. Since this narrative mastery is important to the central tension of *Night*, it is worth briefly describing some of the means by which it is achieved.

Direct comment. The narrator interrupts his description of events and comments directly; for example, while life for the Jews in the ghetto is still relatively tolerable, the narrator shows the wisdom of hindsight:

It was neither the German nor the Jew who reigned over the ghetto: it was illusion.

Reader's knowledge of history. Much of *Night* is written a terse, telegraphic style. Eliezer avoids commentary or planation when the reader's knowledge of history c expected to fill in gaps. The use of place names prc clear example:

But we arrived at a station. Those who were near
dows told us the name of the station:
  - Auschwitz.
No one had ever heard that name.

In front of us, those flames. In the air, that sr

It must have been midnight. We had arrived. At Birkenau.

Warning and premonition. The Jews of Sighet are constantly being warned of what will happen to them. Moché recounts the atrocities of the Nazis, but is not believed. In the train to Auschwitz Mme Schachter has a premonitory vision ("- A fire! I can see a fire! I can see a fire!"), but she is bound, gagged, and beaten up by the other Jews. Later, the Jews are told what will happen to them:

> Sons of dogs, do you understand nothing then? You're going to be burned! Burned to a cinder! Turned to ashes!

Eliezer's direct comments also have a premonitory function:

> From that moment everything happened with great speed. The chase toward death had begun.

Retrospective viewpoint. Related to the latter point is the way in which the narrator can explain what he did not know at the time of the events being described due to knowledge acquired in the period between experiencing and describing. He uses phrases like "Later we were to learn," "I learned later," "I learned after the war," "Many years later."

Repetition of themes. One of the central concerns of *Night* is Eliezer's relationship with his father and his ambiguous sense of guilt and liberation when his father dies. Eliezer's feeling that he has betrayed his father is reflected in other father-son relationships that he compulsively describes. Bela Katz, seconded to the *Sonder-Kommando,* places his own father's body into the furnace at Birkenau; the narrator refers to a child who beats his father; during the long march from Buna to Gleiwitz, Rabi Eliahou is left behind by his son, who has run on ahead, Eliezer believes, "in order to free himself from a burden that could reduce his own chances of survival"; and on the train to Buchenwald, a man murders his own father for the sake of a piece of bread.

Preparation of effects. Eliezer introduces striking or unexpected details that seem out of place at first, but that reinforce the impact of what comes later. After the first execution that he witnesses, Eliezer seems unmoved: "I remember that that evening I found the soup excellent . . ."; later, the cruel execution of a young boy is interpreted as reflecting the 'eath of God, and Eliezer picks up his words from the previ-is page: "That evening, the soup had the taste of corpse." In na the treatment of the children seems to indicate a more nane attitude than we had been led to expect:

> Our convoy contained several children of ten, twelve years of age. The officer took an interest in them and ordered that some food be brought for them.

A page later, a more sinister explanation for the officer's interest is suggested as a new character is introduced:

> Our block leader was a German . . . Like the head of the camp, he liked children. Immediately after our arrival he had had some bread, soup and margarine brought for them (in reality, this affection was not disinterested: children here were the object, amongst homosexuals, of a real trade, as I was to learn later).

Through these devices, the narrator filters, interprets, and assimilates the experience of the Holocaust. Wiesel adopts a form and techniques that seem to confirm the Jewish expectation of the meaning of history and the interpretability of experience.

DENYING HIS OWN TRUTH

The essential problem of *Night* derives from the tension between the formal coherence and retrospective authority of the narrative, and the subject-matter of the work. Wiesel has always emphasized that the Holocaust can be neither understood nor described; it is a unique event without precedent, parallel, analogy, or meaning. This results in a problem of communication, and the survivors' predicament is particularly acute. They must, and cannot, recount the experience of the death camps: "Impossible to speak of it, impossible not to speak of it" (*A Jew*). *Night*, then, is written in the knowledge of its own inevitable failure: the survivor must tell his story, but will never communicate the truth of his experience; what is kept silent is more true than what is said, words distort and betray, the Holocaust cannot be understood or described, the constraints of reality ensure that the story will always fall short of truth. As Wiesel writes in *A Jew*, "In order to be realistic, the stories recounted less than the truth."

The failure of narration to command belief is reflected at the very beginning of *Night* in the incredulous reaction encountered by Moché the Beadle. Moché is disbelieved, his story dismissed as imagination or madness, utterly contrary to reality. Finally, he chooses silence rather than futile narrative. Later, Eliezer meets with a similar reaction when he goes to warn a friend of his father's about the liquidation of the ghetto: "- What are you talking about? . . . Have you gone mad?" Eliezer is reduced to silence: "My throat was dry and the words were choked there, paralysing my lips. I couldn't say another word to him"; and paradoxically it is this silence that convinces the father's friend: "Then he understood." In its opening pages the text describes an anxiety about its own status and its communicative capabilities. The messenger is unwelcome and his story disbelieved or dismissed. The narrative process itself is interrupted. Eliezer's father is recounting a story when he is called away to be told of the deportation of the Jews: "The good story that he was telling us would remain unfinished." The father's "good story" is unfinished and supplanted by the less pleasant story that the son will now recount.

The failure of narrative represented at the beginning of *Night* by these incidents is reflected in the writing of the text as a whole. The retrospective stance of the narrator and the control he exhibits over the presentation of his material put him in a privileged position of authority and understanding; at the same time, what he describes is the destruction of all points of certainty, resulting in the collapse of the interpretative authority that his stance as narrator seems to arrogate. *Night* is above all a narrative of loss; in the course of the text, family, community, religious certainty, paternal authority, and the narrator's identity are corroded or destroyed. The theme of loss also has consequences for the validity of the narrative. The narrator constantly expresses the desperate hope that what he is witnessing is not real; thereby he draws attention to the desire to deny the truth of his own experience, to subvert the credibility of his own narrative:

> Wasn't all that a nightmare? An unimaginable nightmare? . . .
> No, all that could not be true. A nightmare . . . It was surely a
> dream.

This does not mean that narrated events did not take place; but it does disclose a reluctance within the testimony itself to accept the validity of experience. While *Night* never discredits the authority of its narrator, significant aspects of the text seem to resist acknowledging what Eliezer nevertheless knows to be true. . . . The narrator of *Night* seeks to deny the evidence of his senses. The witness simultaneously suggests "this is true" and "this cannot be true."

When Words Fail

This tension is compounded by a mistrust of language, which, Wiesel has suggested, was corrupted by the Holocaust: "The absolute perversion of language dates from that period."

> If our language is corrupted it is because, at that time, language itself was denatured. Innocent and beautiful words designated the most abject crimes . . . The first crime committed by the Nazis was against language.

This corruption of language is reflected in the course of *Night*. The book begins in a world of confident speech: Moché the Beadle teaches Eliezer the mysteries of the Kabbalah; the father gives paternal advice; Eliezer narrates his childhood. However, the precariousness of this confidence in language is signaled by Moché's story of Nazi atrocities, which is true but discredited and disbelieved, and the father's never-finished anecdote. The rest of the text, and indeed all Wiesel's texts, fall under the shadow of these failed narratives. In Auschwitz language itself is devalued and stripped of its conventional meanings. Only one word retains its significance:

> The word "chimney" was not a word empty of sense here: it floated in the air, mixed with the smoke. It was perhaps the only word here that had a real meaning.

The degradation of language is shown most clearly in the use of direct speech in the course of *Night*. The advice and teaching of Eliezer's father and Moché are supplanted by the curt imperatives of the concentration camp guards: "Everyone get out! Leave everything in the wagon! Quickly!"; "-Men to the left! Women to the right!" The dialogue between Eliezer and his father acquires a surreal, futile quality as the son repeats the father's imperatives—now devoid of all imperative force—and begins to usurp his father's authority:

> - Don't let yourself be carried off by sleep, Eliezer. It is dangerous to fall asleep in the snow. You can fall asleep for good. Come, my little one, come. Get up.

Get up? How could I? How could I get out from this good covering? I heard the words of my father, but their meaning seemed empty to me, as if he had asked me to carry the whole hangar in my arms . . .

> - Come, my son, come . . .
> - Come, father, let us get back to the hangar . . .
> He did not reply. He was not looking at the dead.
> - Come, father. It's better over there . . .
> - There's nothing to fear, my little one. Sleep, you can sleep. I will stay awake.
> - First you, father. Sleep.
> He refused.

As *Night* unfolds the father's speech indicates most dramatically the decay of linguistic authority and the sources of traditional authority in general. Initially, the father is presented as a well-respected figure: "The Jewish community of Sighet held him in the highest consideration; he was often consulted on public affairs and even on private matters." In particular, his authority is reflected in his command of language:

> My father told anecdotes to them and explained his opinion on the situation. He was a good storyteller.

Eliezer first disregards his father's authority (he begins to study the Kabbalah despite his father's warnings), and then in his narrative, undermines the validity of his father's views. This is done gently in the early stages of the text; Eliezer's father sees little to worry about in the decree ordering Jews to wear the yellow star:

> - The yellow star? So what? You don't die of that . . .
> (Poor father! What did you die of, then?) . . .

As this loss of authority is taking place, the father's speech undergoes a decline from command to incoherence. His first speech in the book underlines his assurance and confidence with language:

> - You are too young for that. It's only when you are thirty, according to Maimonides, that you have the right to explore the perilous world of mysticism. First you must study the basic texts that you are capable of understanding.

This contrasts starkly with the unfinished sentences of his final speeches:

> - Eliezer . . . I must tell you where to find the gold and silver that I buried . . . In the cellar . . . You know . . . I'm wasting away . . . Why do you behave so badly toward me, my son . . . Water . . . My son, water . . . I'm wasting away . . . My guts . . .

The fundamental double bind at the core of Wiesel's writing lies in the fact that he must and cannot write about the Holocaust. His experiences during the war are at the source of his urge to narrate and to bear witness; at the same time, those experiences corrode the foundations of his narrative art as they undermine faith in mankind, God, self, and language. *Night* is a work sustained by its own impossibility: the need to tell the truth about something that entails a crisis of belief in truth. The tension of *Night* lies in its simultaneous assertion that what it narrates is true and that it cannot be true; such events cannot be perpetrated or seen or described. The narrator wants to believe he is mistaken at the very moment when he claims to be most brutally honest. So *Night,* despite its apparent simplicity, is a deeply paradoxical work: a first-person narrative that recounts the destruction of identity, a testimony in which the narrator wants most urgently to undermine his own credibility, a coherent account of the collapse of coherence, an attempt to describe what the author of the text insists cannot be described.

Wiesel's Literary Techniques

Mildred L. Culp

Author Mildred L. Culp analyzes the major literary
techniques that Wiesel employs in writing *Night*.
Rather than merely telling his story as a straight
autobiographical memoir, Culp points out Wiesel's
use of comic irony, narrative viewpoint, symbolism,
and imagery. She believes it is the use of these techniques that allows *Night* to rise above straight autobiography and into the realm of art.

Night tells the compelling story of the Holocaust as only art
can. It is at once historical and beyond history. A memorial
to the dead, it is a living reminder of the need to reflect upon
history for the insights it bequeathes the present. But it is
told in the form of a story, which suggests to the reader that
Wiesel values art for its ability to find ultimate meaning. To
personalize that story, he juxtaposes the Holocaust with a
child's recollection of his experiences and creates "a curious
blend of beauty and suffering." The author's use of the first-
person narrative makes his material even more immediate.
This technique of memoir also transforms history into an organizing principle for form. The "I" organizes the form of
Night and, finally, becomes its form.

Wiesel is in dialogue first with the "I" creating the memoir and then with the events of history that lead to a theology. The second dialogue proves more interesting than the
first, but too many critics alight on it only briefly and bypass
formal considerations. If Wiesel's "message" were intended
to be expressed without the aid of metaphor, the author
would have exchanged the memoir for an essay or for historical analysis. The autobiographical writing suggests that
Wiesel believed his self-actualization could be communi-
cated best through the medium of art. Therefore, it is formal

Excerpted from "Wiesel's Memoir and God Outside Auschwitz," by Mildred L. Culp,
Explorations in Ethnic Studies, vol. 4, no. 1, January 1981. Reprinted by permission of
the National Association for Ethnic Studies, Inc.

considerations to which we must turn.

Wiesel uses the tools of the consummate artist. Evidence of his technique appears throughout the narrative in comic incongruity, irony, temporal changes, symbolism, and imagery.

THE IRONY OF COMEDY

Comic scenes are created to magnify the tragic quality of the story. As if to underscore the seriousness of his subject, the writer refers to the wish of the Jews of Sighet that Passover end, "so that we should not have to play this comedy any longer." Passover, therefore, has turned into a religious celebration that is completely out of place. Later, after Eliezer is permitted to keep his pair of new mudcoated shoes, he thanks God for "having created mud in his infinite and wonderful universe." Under normal conditions, God is not usually exalted for the mud of the earth, and the universe of *Night* is not "wonderful."

In a world where comedy is incongruous, brutality transforms human beings. Just before the liberating Russian army arrives, for example, the prisoners dress in layers for the evacuation. Wiesel comments, "Poor mountebanks, wider than they were tall, more dead than alive; poor clowns, their ghostlike faces emerging from piles of prison clothes. Buffoons!" This scene is a reminder of the early incident in which the thinnest prisoner swims in his uniform, and the heaviest one is barely covered. But the reader does not laugh at this comedy, because the writer is recounting the life of suffering in a world where reasonable expectations are confounded and where human responsibility has been abandoned. The boy's world is dreamlike and must be shared through the story-telling impulse: "it was like a page torn from some story book."

If the reader misses the significance of the incongruity, Wiesel adopts irony as a stylistic device to communicate the irrationality of the concentration camp experience. The Jews of Sighet, crammed into a box car travelling to Auschwitz in the spring of 1944, have never heard the name of their destination. In fact, the group is so oblivious to its fate that it believes what it is told: "There was a labor camp. Conditions were good. Families would not be split up. . . . We gave thanks to God." The ultimate irony, thanking God at Auschwitz. Every sentence is clipped and matter-of-fact. Wiesel's genius is clear in his ability to keep the reader as aware of the deception in the "facts" as the Jews are taken in by them.

Irony strikes the reader once again on Yom Kippur, when the starving Jews debate whether they should fast. Some of the prisoners believe that challenging the danger inherent in observing the holiday under the circumstances of the concentration camp would impress God as devout. In this incident "the absurd [emerges as] the breakdown of the accustomed order in God's world, the dissolution of a long established relationship between man and God."

HINDSIGHT IS 20-20

A third narrative device involves changing the shape of the dimension of time. *Night* itself denies temporality the character it usually assumes by repeating history and creating a perspective which shows the author within history and outside of it simultaneously. For the Jews, though, the present alone has meaning, because it is the abnormality, the very brutality of that present with which they must contend in order to survive. From this standpoint, the future and past lose their meaning. This is particularly noticeable in Eliezer's repeated comments about the inactive memories of the prisoners, and the reader's perception that the boy wonders only occasionally what happened to his mother and Tzipora, his little sister.

More particularly, however, the narrator leaps out of his story by presenting an analogous incident which occurred after the camp experience but reinforces its universal qualities. First the author establishes the dreamlike nature of the world by disclosing that Eliezer's senses are blurred when he arrives at Buchenwald. The transtemporal qualities of the Holocaust are disclosed in three specific incidents. The first occurs when Eliezer's father expresses minimal concern for having to wear the yellow star: "The yellow star? Oh, well, what of it? You don't die of it." Wiesel's aside, "(Poor Father! Of what then did you die?)" comes from the present but speaks of oppression against the Jews throughout history.

The second scene is Eliezer's beating by Idek. The child's blood runs and a French girl, who is passing as Aryan and does not speak with other prisoners, tries to comfort him. Although Eliezer is uncertain of the girl's background, the act reinforces his sense of her Jewishness. Wiesel then moves directly to his chance meeting with her on the Metro in Paris many years after the war. The significance of the meeting reflects that "the solidarity of Jewish people is based on the simplest and most courageous of human acts: the communication of one Jew to another that he is a Jew, and thus shares his identity." When the woman affirms their common heritage, the writer attests to the transtemporal dimension of the affirmation.

ART WAS *NOT* WIESEL'S GOAL

Author and book reviewer Robert Kanigel asserts in his book Vintage Reading *that Wiesel did not set out to create great literary art when he wrote* Night. *Rather, getting across the emotions of the young boy was what mattered.*

On the seventh day of Passover, the leaders of the Jewish community are arrested. "From that moment, everything happened very quickly. The race toward death had begun."

The race toward death had begun.

More artful writers might have avoided such language. Show, don't tell, says good writing practice. Don't destroy hard-won immediacy with flights of melodrama. This is not the only time Wiesel evinces such a superficial lack of literary polish.

Yet, peculiarly, what might otherwise be a defect here enhances the author's credibility. It is as if *Night* had been not so much "composed" as plucked whole from a ravaged heart. His is no mere pretty rendering, Wiesel seems to tell us. The horrors he experienced fall beyond the rules and restraints of "art." Giving vent to his grief, anger and despair comes first. He must throw in his lot with his town and his people, not with the worldwide community of literati.

Robert Kanigel, *Vintage Reading: From Plato to Bradbury.* Baltimore: Bancroft Press, 1998, p. 239.

A more arresting episode occurs during deportation as the Russian front closes. When a German workman throws a piece of bread into the wagon, a boy, like a ravenous wolf, kills his father over the food. And then he is killed by the other men.

But the author demonstrates that the significance of the incident is not isolated to the Holocaust, because he shifts to an experience in Aden some years later. In this particular scene some passengers on a pleasure boat are amused by the reactions of "natives," to whom they are throwing coins. When Wiesel sees two children on the verge of killing each other over some money, he asks a wealthy Parisienne to stop tossing coins overboard. She responds indifferently that she enjoys giving "to . . . charity." Each of these events illustrates Wiesel's perception that the experience and meaning behind the Holocaust are not confined to the concentration camp alone.

SYMBOLISM AND IMAGERY SPEAK VOLUMES

Wiesel's command of symbolism permeates his book. The symbols suggest death, evil, and insight. Each assumes a significance beyond itself and keys the reader into the main theme of the memoir, which is the opening of Eliezer's—and the reader's—eyes to God's dissociation from the events of Auschwitz. Indeed, the symbols in *Night* come to suggest that when humanity assumes responsibility for the Jews or any other group of people, God faces the death of God's creation and therefore moves outside of it.

Death imagery pervades the personal record, and symbols of life are transformed into symbols of death. Before leaving Sighet, for example, the townspeople are shadows whose lives are being drained. They are the goods of the market place, a commodity whose humanity is denied by the events of the Holocaust. In fact, the faded portraits symbolize the Jews of Sighet whose value has disappeared. Thereafter, the Jews are "dried-up trees, dried-up bodies, numbers, cattle or merchandise, rags, starved stomach[s]." Depersonalized and dehumanized, they are closest to death when, like the narrator's father struck down by dysentery, they become ghosts.

Even religious symbols hint of death. Altogether, these reflect the Jews' very real concern for their once vital faith. The world of Sighet becomes "an open tomb" leading to death. In such a place there are numerous travesties made upon Judaism. Hitler's agents choose the Sabbath to deport the Jews and the synagogue to detain them. This synagogue the deportees must profane by relieving themselves in it. Then at Birkenau, someone faced with the prospect of dying in the crematorium begins to recite the Kaddish. Wiesel observes poignantly, "I do not know if it has ever happened before, in the long history of the Jews, that people have recited the prayer for the dead for themselves."

Wiesel's imagery is most effective when it illuminates the omnipresence of evil through images and symbols of darkness and light. As in most literature, night stands for evil or death, but here light is distorted to mean the same. Fiery stars foreshadow the crematory ovens. Eliezer asks if his experience is not a nightmare and comes to realize that a series of nights, one "last night" after another, will introduce him to evil. Here he describes the first:

> Never shall I forget that night, the first night in camp, which has turned my life into one long night, seven times cursed and seven times sealed. Never shall I forget that smoke. Never shall I forget the little faces of the children, whose bodies I saw turned into wreaths of smoke beneath a silent blue sky. Never shall I forget those flames which consumed my faith forever. . . . Never shall I forget those moments which murdered my God and my soul and turned my dreams to dust . . . even if I am condemned to live as long as God Himself. Never.

This passage in *Night* incorporates many of the important images used by Wiesel and provides insight into his theology. It shows how the prisoners' days are converted into nights which darken their souls, but that God exists. It makes the light of the furnace satanic, because the furnace stands as a mockery of the candles lighted on the anniversary deaths of loved ones. In fact, the word "furnace" is meaningful as a reflection of the atrocity inflicted upon the Jews. As one theologian has observed, "A fire lit by men with the purpose of consuming men strikes at the very heart of creation," because this is a world overseen by humanity—not God.

THE WINDOWS OF THE SOUL

Eyes, Wiesel's most frequently used symbol, direct the reader to the Nazi *Weltanschauung*. In one moving scene, while a little boy called "a sad-eyed angel" is dying an agonizing death symbolic of the cosmic tragedy Wiesel recounts, the prisoners are forced to march in front of him and look directly into his eyes. Theologically, this is one of the must crucial sections of the memoir. Many readers have concluded that the incident symbolizes the death of God, when actually a close reading of *Night* suggests the slow destruction of a tortured child with refined and beautiful features as an act of humanity. When Eliezer says his own eyes are open to a world without God or humanity, he is speaking of Hitler's world. He remains above the bestiality of that world only through the act of reflecting upon it.

The concept of vision is abstracted by three prophets, Moche the Beadle and Madame Schachter, who are the seers capable of providing advance warning to the Jews, and Akiba Drumer, who appears to be a false prophet. The first two are victimized for their appearance of insanity. Moche is cast out; Madame Schachter, labeled insane. The mystic who has cabbalistic dreams of the deliverance of the Jews finds a verse in the Bible which may be interpreted to mean that his people will be saved within two weeks. Then the selection determines his fate. Wiesel's message is clear: medieval Jewish mysticism is irrelevant in the concentration camp, because the God of this tradition is not operative there.

Wiesel even enlists the aid of his reader's eyes when his characters may be unable to comprehend the significance of certain relationships. The orphaned Czech brothers who "lived, body and soul, for each other" are virtually inseparable. A rabbi and his son struggle to maintain eye contact. In particular, Eliezer's relationship with his father establishes a new covenant, and the two remain within the sight of each other whenever possible. All of these reflect the author's perception of "the crucial" importance of human relationships in the camps, which lend stability by affirming the importance of the human community in an inhumane world. They also show that God's covenant with God's people is still very much alive.

CHAPTER 3

Relationships

READINGS ON
NIGHT

The Holocaust Poisoned Eliezer's Relationships

Ted L. Estess

According to Ted L. Estess, author of the book *Elie Wiesel* and professor of religion and literature at the University of Houston, Eliezer's primary relationships were destroyed by the Holocaust. Estess claims that the relationships between Eliezer and God, the bond between him and his father, and his own understanding of himself were gradually destroyed by life in the concentration camp. Estess sees this as one of the most important points that Wiesel has to make, and believes it lays the foundation for Wiesel's later books.

Above all, [in *Night*] Wiesel is concerned with relationships. In speaking of the meaning of the Holocaust, he emphasizes this: "Something happened a generation ago, to the world, to man. Something happened to God. Certainly something happened to the relations between man and God, man and man, man and himself."

Night records how the Holocaust poisoned and nearly destroyed all primary relationships in Eliezer's life. His relationship to himself—and by this is meant his understanding of himself—is called into question on the first night at Auschwitz. He says:

> The student of the Talmud, the child I was, had been consumed in the flames. There remained only a shape that looked like me. A dark flame had entered into my soul and devoured it.

Eliezer's sense of himself as a pious Jewish youth jars with his situation in the death camp: nothing in his previous identity could prepare him for this confrontation with absolute evil. Faced with this discrepancy between his situa-

Excerpted from *Elie Wiesel*, by Ted L. Estess. Copyright ©1980 by The Frederick Ungar Publishing Co. Reprinted by permission of Continuum International.

tion and his understanding of himself, Eliezer no longer knows who he is or what he has to do.

ELIEZER BEGINS TO LOSE GOD

His relationship to God is similarly disrupted. Immediately, Job-like, Eliezer begins to question the justice of God. How could God allow good people to suffer so? In accord with the pattern of reversals, Eliezer reverses the place of man and God. When, for example, the Jews assemble to pray on Rosh Hashanah, he comments: "This day I had ceased to plead. I was no longer capable of lamentation. On the contrary, I felt very strong. I was the accuser, God the accused." In much Jewish theology of suffering, God places the Jews on trial either as punishment for sin or as a way of further purifying the chosen people for their redemptive task. In *Night,* the relationship between God and man is first questioned and then reversed: God becomes the guilty one who has transgressed and who deserves to be on trial. God, not man, has broken His promises and betrayed His people.

While his relationships to himself and to God are crucial for Eliezer, his relationship to his father is important as well. Through much of his time in the death camps this relationship remains the single tie to his life in Sighet. Just as Eliezer's relationship with God is the center of the religious dimension of the story, his relationship with his father is the center of the psychological quandary. To Wiesel, the two relationships are intrinsically connected, but they are not reducible to each other. They are distinct, each with its own integrity and its own significance. Both add focus to Eliezer's identity, so that the loss of either is psychically disturbing, and the loss of both altogether devastating.

THE SON AND THE FATHER

The tenacity with which Eliezer clings to his father reflects an effort to draw back from the abyss that opens up with the loss of all human ties. The relationship functions as a touchstone to which Eliezer (and the entire narrative) returns again and again. He measures what is happening within himself in terms of what is happening in his relationship with his father. If he can sustain his unconditional commitment to his father, then something might abide in a world in which all is changing. Since anything can suddenly be taken away from the inmates of the death camps, Eliezer makes

only one thing necessary to him: absolute fidelity to his father. God has broken His promises to His people; Eliezer, in
contrast, determines ever more resolutely not to violate his
covenant with his father.

Eliezer's struggle to maintain decency in his principal relationships finally focuses on this question: Will he betray
his father and choose his own life at his father's expense?
Eliezer watches one young man kill his father for a piece of
bread; he sees another, Rabbi Eliahou's son, run off and
leave his father in the snow. Gathering the last particles of
outrage he possesses, Eliezer prays to a God whom he no
longer trusts: "My God, Lord of the Universe, give me
strength never to do what Rabbi Eliahou's son has done."

After the long journey to Buchenwald, Eliezer's complex
relationship to his father reaches its culmination. Seeing
that Eliezer's struggle to keep his father alive is depleting his
meager energy, the head of the block counsels him:

> Listen to me, boy. Don't forget that you're in a concentration
> camp. Here, every man has to fight for himself and not think of
> anyone else. Even of his father. Here, there are no fathers, no
> brothers, no friends. Everyone lives and dies for himself alone.

In response, Eliezer reflects: "He was right, I thought in the
most secret region of my heart, but I dared not admit it."
Eliezer continues to struggle against what he considers to be
the final debasement of his humanity: to choose himself
over his father. But when his father dies, Eliezer makes this
disturbing admission:

> And, in the depths of my being, in the recesses of my weak-
> ened conscience, could I have searched it, I might perhaps
> have found something like—free at last!

ELIEZER IS COMPLETELY ALONE

With this event the concentration camp has worked its
horror completely in the boy's soul. In his view, he is guilty
of having acquiesced in his father's death. The reader is
likely to pity Eliezer, but Eliezer asks for no sympathy. In
disclosing his feelings, Eliezer simply confesses the extent
to which the Holocaust has corrupted the primary relationships of life. In stripping away a person's past, in push-
ing him to the limits of his physical endurance, in revers-
ing all the expectations he had of man and God—in all
these ways life in the camps forced the victim to choose
himself without regard for the other. "At that moment,"

Eliezer sadly admits, "what did the others matter!". . .

An initial shock takes over Eliezer's soul when he sees that the Germans and his fellow Hungarians can be monstrous in their relationships to the Jews; a more unsettling disclosure is that God Himself can betray His people; but the final and perhaps most devastating shock arises from the disclosure that Eliezer himself is capable of disregard for his own father. The insight that no relationship is immune to the eruption of evil: this is what the experience of the Holocaust discloses to Wiesel. . . .

During his final months in the camps, the scope of Eliezer's world shrinks. He comments:

> I have nothing to say of my life during this period. It no longer mattered. After my father's death, nothing could touch me any more. . . . I had but one desire—to eat. I no longer thought of my father or of my mother.

Night reminds us that there are some simple and ordinary elements of human existence—food, trust, conversation, and, as a context for all things, human relationships—without which the spirit withers. Deprived of these things, the self can hardly expect to find significance in life.

Fathers and Sons

Ellen S. Fine

Ellen S. Fine, a professor at The City University of
New York and special adviser to the chairman of the
U.S. Holocaust Memorial Council, demonstrates how
for much of *Night* the strong bond between Eliezer
and his father (and other father-son pairs) is the
only thing that keeps them both alive in the concentration camp. Eventually the atrocities the pair were
forced to endure couldn't keep resentment and guilt
out of the relationship. Despite the son's ambivalent
feelings and thoughts of abandoning his dying
father, the Nazi's attempt to destroy the bonds
between them ultimately does not succeed.

If the nocturnal forces of death envelop and endure, miraculously, from within the depths of the Holocaust universe
surges the will to survive. Father and son struggle to remain
human, acting as lifelines for each other. They fight to keep
alive by mutual care and manage to create a strong bond between them in the most extreme of circumstances. Yet competition for survival causes a conflict between self-interest
and concern for the other. Close ties break down in the kingdom of Night and even the solidarity built up between
Eliezer and his father is undermined by feelings of anger
and ambivalence brought about by Nazi techniques specifically designed to destroy human relationships.

"A residue of humanism persists illogically enough in our
world, where there is a 'void' at the center of things," Wylie
Sypher observes, in *Loss of the Self in Modern Literature and
Art*. For a child of fifteen entering the perverse world of the
concentration camp, the "residue of humanism" is the presence of his father. Separated from his mother and three sisters upon their arrival at Birkenau, Eliezer becomes obsessed with the need to hold on tightly to his father's hand,
the only object of life in a universe where every moment

holds the possibility of death. "My hand shifted on my father's arm. I had one thought—not to lose him. Not to be left alone." Warned by an anonymous prisoner to lie about their ages, the fifteen-year-old boy and the fifty-year-old man instantly become eighteen and forty, and are thus able to follow Dr. Mengele's wand to the left-hand column (life) instead of the right-hand one (crematoria).

The fear of being torn apart from his last family link haunts the narrator throughout the book. During the "levelling" process, as he is being stripped bare of all possessions, he is fixated on one thought—to be with his father. Later, when the boy is recovering from a foot operation in the Buna hospital and finds out that the camp is about to be evacuated, he runs outside into the deep snow, a shoe in his hand because his foot is still swollen, and frantically searches for his father: "As for me, I was not thinking about death, but I did not want to be separated from my father. We had already suffered so much together; this was not the time to be separated." Upon arrival in Buchenwald after the long torturous convoy in the open wagons, Eliezer is again haunted by the familiar fear and fiercely clutches his father's hand.

This obsession to hold on to the father has been interpreted by the French scholar André Neher as juvenile. He feels that "Elie remains a small, dependent child in spite of the overabundant maturity resulting from his experience." However, if the gesture of grasping the hand is somewhat childlike, and the son's vow never to be severed from his father has a desperate tone, the primary relationship between father and son appears to be more an interdependency based upon mutual support in the midst of surrounding evil. Father and son, joined together in front of the sacrificial altar, recall the Biblical story of Abraham and Isaac (the *Akeda*), described by Wiesel in *Messengers of God* with the emphasis on commitment in a world threatened by destruction: "And the father and son remained united. Together they reached the top of the mountain; together they erected the altar; together they prepared the wood and the fire." Wiesel cites a text from the Midrash in which the Biblical pair are envisaged as "victims together," bound by their communal offering.

Until the last pages of *Night*, reciprocal devotion sustains both Eliezer and his father and is linked to the recurring Wieselean theme of rescue—saving the life of another human being and thereby saving one's own. The narrator reports several instances during which his father's presence stops him from dying. When Eliezer files past the fiery pits on the first hallucinatory night in Auschwitz, he has thoughts of suicide. He is deterred from killing himself by the voice of his father who tells him that humanity no longer cares about their fate, and that at this time in history everything is permitted. The father's voice, though sad and choked, represents a life force, which combats the all-encompassing blackness.

During the long march from Buna to Gleiwitz, the prisoners are forced to gallop through the snow, and Eliezer, pained by his throbbing foot, is again drawn to death as an escape from suffering. Once more the paternal presence helps him to resist the appeal of death. Because he feels that his father needs him, the son does not have the right to succumb. His will to survive is ultimately linked to the existence of his father:

> Death wrapped itself around me till I was stifled. It stuck to me. I felt that I could touch it. The idea of dying, of no longer being, began to fascinate me. Not to exist any longer. Not to feel the horrible pains in my foot. . . . My father's presence was the only thing that stopped me . . . I had no right to let myself die. What would he do without me? I was his only support.

After seventy kilometers of running, as morning approaches, the survivors are allowed to rest. The narrator sinks into the soft snow, but his father persuades him to go into the ruins of a nearby brick factory, since to sleep in the snow means to freeze to death. The open shed, too, is crusted with a thick cold carpet enticing its weary victims, and Eliezer awakes to the frozen hand of his father patting his cheeks. A voice "damp with tears and snow" advises the boy not to be overcome by sleep. Eliezer and his father decide to watch over each other: they exchange vows of protection, which bind them together in revolt against the death that is silently transforming their sleeping comrades into stiffened corpses.

Later on, when the men pile on top of each other in the barracks of Gleiwitz, Eliezer struggles to rid himself of an unknown assassin slowly suffocating him with the massiveness of his weight. When he finally liberates himself and swallows a mouthful of air, the boy's first words are to his father whose presence is acknowledged by the sound of his voice, "a distant voice, which seemed to come from another world." The voice once again is a lifeline, a reassurance against death. Yet the otherworldliness of the father's speech suggests that he is beginning to lose hold of his vital forces; eternal night beckons to him.

The last time the father rescues the son is in the open cattle car shuttling the victims from Gleiwitz to Buchenwald. On the third night of the trip, the narrator suddenly wakes up: somebody is trying to strangle him. He musters enough strength to cry out the one word synonymous with survival—"Father!" Too weak to throw off the attacker, his father calls upon Meir Katz, an old friend from his hometown, who frees Eliezer. The father thus saves his son's life through a surrogate, one of the most robust in the group, but one who dies before the men reach Buchenwald and whose abandoned corpse is left on the train.

During the various phases of the nocturnal journey the other side of the rescue motif is also apparent: the son carefully watches over his father and at times delivers the latter from death. These brief moments of solidarity disrupt the machinery of destruction and prove to be examples of human resistance in the face of the inhuman. When Eliezer's father is selected for the gas chamber in Gleiwitz, the youth runs after him, creating enough confusion to finally reunite father and son in the right-hand column, this time the column of life. Shortly after this episode, Eliezer saves his father's life in the convoy to Buchenwald. Lying inert in the train, his father is taken for dead by the men who are throwing out the corpses. Eliezer desperately slaps his father's nearly lifeless face in an attempt to revive him and succeeds in making him move his eyelids slightly, a vital sign that he is still alive. The men leave him alone.

Upon arrival at the camp, the father reaches the breaking point. He sinks to the ground, resigned to dying. Eliezer is filled with rage at his father's passivity, and realizes he must now take charge. "I found my father weeping like a child," he says when later he finds him stretched across his bunk, crying bitterly after being beaten by the other inmates for not properly taking care of his bodily needs. The boy feeds his helpless father and brings him water. We see here the reversal of roles: the transformation of the once-powerful paternal authority into a weak, fearful child and that of the de-

pendent child into an adult. By assuming responsibility for
the sick old man, the son becomes a kind of father figure, il-
lustrating Wiesel's contention that in the inverted world of
the concentration camp, old men metamorphosed into children and children into old men in one never-ending night.

The reversal of roles in *Night* has been viewed by André
Neher as "an anti-*Akeda*: not a father leading his son to be
sacrificed, but a son guiding, dragging, carrying to the altar
an old man who no longer has the strength to continue."
Wiesel's text, he observes, is "a re-writing of the *Akeda* under the opaque light of Auschwitz. It is no longer a narrative
invented by the imagination of a poet or philosopher. It is the
reality of Auschwitz." This reality offers a sharp contrast to
the Biblical event. Whereas in the Bible God saves Isaac
from being sacrificed by sending a ram to replace him, He
does not intervene to save the father at the altar of Auschwitz. God allows the father to be consumed by Holocaust
flames and the son is forced to recognize the inevitable—
that he is impotent in the face of death's conquest and God's
injustice. He must slowly watch his father acquiesce to
death. Symbol of reason, strength, and humanity, the father
finally collapses under the barbaric tactics of the Nazi op-
pressor to which Eliezer is a silent witness.

If the theme of father-son is characterized, in general, by
the reciprocal support necessary for survival in extremity,
the sanctity of the relationship is nevertheless violated by
the camp conditions. In contrast to the son's need to protect
and be protected by his father, there appears the opposing
motif: the abandonment of the father. The Nazi technique of
attempting to eradicate all family ties and creating a state of
mind in which men view each other as enemies or
strangers—what can be called the *concentration camp philosophy*—is demonstrated in *Night* through a series of incidents showing the competition for survival between fathers
and sons.

Bela Katz, the son of a merchant from Eliezer's hometown and a member of the *Sonderkommando* [the squad of
prisoners required to take the bodies out of the gas chambers and put them in the crematoria] in Birkenau, is forced
to shove the body of his own father into the crematory
oven. A *pipel* [young prisoners of about age thirteen
granted power over the others in exchange for "favors" bestowed upon the S.S.] in Buna beats his father because his

father does not make his bed properly. A third instance, and the one the narrator constantly uses as a measure of his own behavior, is the deterioration of relations between Rabbi Eliahou and his son. Shunted from camp to camp for three years, the boy and his father have always managed to stay together. But after the seventy-kilometer march from Buna to Gleiwitz they are separated. The Rabbi reaches the shed and looks for his son. He tells Eliezer that in the obscurity of the night his son did not notice him fall to the rear of the column. However, Eliezer remembers seeing the youth run past the staggering old man and is horrified by this clear example of abandonment:

> A terrible thought loomed up in my mind: he had wanted to get rid of his father! He had felt that his father was growing weak, he had believed that the end was near and had sought this separation in order to get rid of the burden, to free himself from an encumbrance which could lessen his own chances of survival.

Eliezer prays to God to give him the strength never to do what Rabbi Eliahou's son has done.

Perhaps the most devastating example of the breakdown of human bonds occurs in the cattle cars going to Buchenwald during the final phase of the journey. Some workers amuse themselves by throwing pieces of bread into the open wagons and watching the starved men kill each other for a crumb. Eliezer sees an old man about to eat a bit of bread he was lucky enough to snatch from the crowd. Just as he brings the bread to his mouth, someone throws himself on top of him and beats him up. The old man cries out: "Meir, Meir, my boy! Don't you recognize me? I'm your father . . . you're hurting me . . . you're killing your father! I've got some bread . . . for you too . . . for you too . . ." The son grabs the bread from his father's fist; the father collapses, murmurs something and then dies. As the son begins to devour the bread two men hurl themselves upon him and others join them. The young narrator is witness to the entire event: "When they withdrew, next to me were two corpses, side by side, the father and the son. I was fifteen years old."

Having witnessed fathers beaten, abandoned, and killed, the author, through his narrator, has chosen to represent the *son's betrayal of the father* and has omitted situations in which the father mistreats the son. As Terrence Des Pres has pointed out in *The Survivor*, the principle of jungle rule in the camps is frequently belied by examples of human solidarity. Wiesel elects to record the acts of care and decency performed by his father. By not being critical of the paternal figure in a world too often governed by viciousness, the author protects his father's image and honors his memory. This unconscious process of selection reveals the subjective aspect of the eyewitness account and of the survivor's perceptions. The focus upon the abuses of the sons is perhaps a projection of the author-narrator's own feeling of guilt; he identifies with them at the same time that he condemns them for having let their fathers perish. Despite Eliezer's efforts to save his father's life throughout the camp experience, the boy is critical of his own reprehensible behavior, and ultimately takes the blame for his father's death upon himself.

From the first day, the son helplessly witnesses the debasement of his father. When Eliezer's father is seized with colic and politely asks the *Kapo* where the lavatories are, he is dealt such a heavy blow that he crawls back to his place on all fours like an animal. Instead of defending his father's honor by striking the *Kapo*, Eliezer remains paralyzed, afraid to speak out. This fear makes him aware that his values are changing:

> I did not move. What had happened to me? My father had just been struck, before my very eyes, and I had not flickered an eyelid. I had looked on and said nothing. Yesterday, I should have sunk my nails into the criminal's flesh. Had I changed so much, then? So quickly? Now remorse began to gnaw at me. I thought only: I shall never forgive them for that.

This feeling of impotence is repeated in Buna when Idek, the *Kapo*, in a fit of madness beats Eliezer's father with an iron bar. The son's reaction is not simply that of a passive onlooker; he is furious at his father:

> I had watched the whole scene without moving. I kept quiet. In fact I was thinking of how to get farther away so that I would not be hit myself. What is more, any anger I felt at that moment was directed not against the Kapo, but against my father. I was angry with him, for not knowing how to avoid Idek's outbreak. That is what concentration camp life had made of me.

At the end of the narrative, when an SS guard strikes the sick father on the head with his bludgeon, Eliezer again looks on without moving, terrified of being beaten himself.

We see here the brutal effect of concentration camp life upon an individual psyche. Rage against the aggressor has been displaced onto the victim, and concern for the other has regressed into a preoccupation with self-survival, reduced to primitive and instinctual bodily needs. Eliezer is condemned to the role of the impotent witness, incapable of crying out, of seeking revenge, or, finally, of saving his father's life. Although he has fantasies of destroying his father's assassins, he can only behold his bloody face in despair. He is unable to respond to his father's last summons for help—an utterance of his name, "Eliezer."

Yet more than the sense of complicity, after the father dies the son feels ambivalent and even somewhat liberated. Earlier in the text, his mixed emotions surface during an alert in Buchenwald, when Eliezer, separated from his father, does not bother to look for him. The next day he sets out but with highly conflicting feelings:

> Don't let me find him! If only I could get rid of this dead weight, so that I could use all my strength to struggle for my own survival, and only worry about myself. Immediately I felt ashamed of myself, ashamed forever.

Eliezer's desire to rid himself of his oppressive burden, to lose his dependent father in the crowd, makes him recall with horror Rabbi Eliahou's son during the evacuation from Buna. When the narrator finally locates the feverish and trembling old man lying on a plank outside, he frantically claws his way through the crowd to get him some coffee. Later, he halfheartedly offers his dying father what is left of his own soup. While his deeds demonstrate care and devotion, his thoughts are of withdrawal and abandonment. Actions and intentionality, behavior and fantasies, do not correspond. The fifteen-year-old judges himself guilty: "No better than Rabbi Eliahou's son had I withstood the test."

The head of the block tells Eliezer that it is too late to save his old father and that instead he should be eating his father's ration. In his innermost recesses, Eliezer believes that the *Kapo* is right, but is torn by shame and runs to find more soup for his father. We see here the clashing principles for survival that dominated the death camp universe. On one hand, the rule of eat or be eaten, devour or be devoured prevailed. In the struggle of all against all, the *Kapo* teaches Eliezer, "every man has to fight for himself and not think of anyone else. Even of his father. Here, there are no fathers, no brothers, no friends. Everyone lives and dies for himself alone." And yet on the other hand, a *Kapo* tells the prisoners:

"We are all brothers, and we are all suffering the same fate. The same smoke floats above all our heads. Help one another. It is the only way to survive.". . .

The ambivalent feelings of the fifteen-year-old with regard to his father and food are intensified after his father dies:

> I did not weep, and it pained me that I could not weep. But I had no more tears. And in the depths of my being, in the recesses of my weakened conscience, could I have searched it, I might perhaps have found something like—free at last.

The relief soon turns into a deep sense of guilt, for having failed to save his father, for having survived in his place, and for having thoughts of being liberated by his death. The protector has been transformed into a betrayer. Unconsciously, the youth may even feel that he has acted out a son's worst Oedipal fear: he has psychically become "his father's murderer."

The survival guilt that Eliezer painfully endures culminates with the face in the mirror at the end of the narrative. Several days after the liberation of Buchenwald by American soldiers, and after a severe bout of food poisoning during which the boy almost dies, he looks at himself in the mirror for the first time since the ghetto. A stranger—a child of Night—peers at him, and the text concludes with the dark image of death itself: "From the depths of the mirror, a corpse gazed back at me. The look in his eyes, as they stared into mine, has never left me." The distinction made between *his* eyes and *mine,* conveying the notion of the fragmented self, is stressed in the original French: "Son regard dans mes yeux ne me quitte plus" ("His look in my eyes no longer leaves me"). The staring corpse is a permanent reminder of the "dead" self, that part of the narrator which was engulfed by the black smoke of Auschwitz and which will plague him for the rest of his life.

The cadaverous reflection in the mirror also suggests the son's identification with his dead father, to whom he remains attached. According to Robert Jay Lifton, survival guilt is related to "the process of identification—the survivor's tendency to incorporate within himself an image of the dead, and then to think, feel and act as he imagines they would." At the end of the night, Eliezer incorporates his father into his own psyche and projects this image onto the mirror as his double. The haunting specter with its penetrating glance serves to keep the paternal presence alive and is the son's means of defending himself against his loss. The mirror image epitomizes Eliezer's state of mourning and his desire to join his father, whose death is experienced as a death of the self. "When my father died, I died," Wiesel reveals. "That means that one 'I' in me died. . . . At least, something in me died."

CHAPTER 4

Literary Interpretation

READINGS ON
NIGHT

Night as Wiesel's Anti-Exodus

Lawrence S. Cunningham

The story of the Exodus from Egypt describes how three thousand years ago God led the Hebrews out of Egypt, fed them, and guided them to safety. Lawrence S. Cunningham, professor of religion at Florida State University, Tallahassee, and author of *The Sacred Quest* and *Christian Spirituality*, clearly illustrates that *Night* is the story of the "anti-Exodus." By comparing the focal points of both stories, he shows that the joys and victories of the Exodus mirror the horrors and death of the concentration camps. Cunningham believes Wiesel used this framework to tell his story to emphasize how the Jews felt abandoned by God.

The natural order of Wiesel's life was the God-intoxicated milieu of the Hungarian town of Sighet. This particular town was, like his own early life, insulated, timeless, unchanging. The events that began to unfold in 1943–1944 provided the immediate context out of which the natural order of Hungarian Judaism was changed and inverted into the death-dominated life of the camps. What has been largely overlooked is that Wiesel, writing some years after these events, frames the story of that inversion in terms of the oldest "biography" of his own people: the story of the Exodus. The life-giving biblical myth of election, liberation, covenant and promise becomes the vehicle for telling the story of the unnatural order of death-domination. It is as if Wiesel, either consciously or unconsciously, felt constrained to write a near parody of the Exodus story in order to give reality and urgency to the story that he feels is his vocation to tell and tell again.

The village of Sighet was a settled one. There was a rural rhythm, a sense of God's worship being done; a feeling of

Excerpted from "Elie Wiesel's Anti-Exodus," by Lawrence S. Cunningham, *America*, vol. 130, no. 16, April 27, 1974. Reprinted with permission from the author.

fraternity; and a longing for the Messiah. This village, as Wiesel remembers it and describes it, was a happy and secure place. An angel came to that village and told the people to pack up and flee, for death would come to them. The angel was Moshe the Beadle, a simple man who sought God in the mysteries of the cabala and who had seen, further to the west, the face of evil in the form of execution squads who shot Jews before open ditches. Unlike the angel of Passover, this messenger was thought to be crazy; nobody listened.

But Moshe had, in fact, been right. The orders came for the Jews to pack their possessions in haste and get ready to leave. There was a rumor among some that they would be sent to work in brick factories to the west. In this particular form of the Exodus, a people were to go out to make bricks as slaves, not to leave behind such an enforced work. But even that was to prove an optimistic rumor. The people left in haste, but they left in cattle cars for the west. During the train journey there was to be another mad visionary, Madame Schacter, who cried out to her fear-crazed companions: "Jews, listen to me! I can see a fire! There are huge flames! It is a furnace!" But she was insane, and her insanity was exacerbated by hunger, thirst, crowding and the stench of many humans in a small railroad car. Only when the train stopped at Birkenau, the reception depot for Auschwitz, did people look into the sky and see the guides that Madame Schacter had seen in her lunatic visions: a tall chimney that belched forth both smoke and flame. These flames did not, however, guide the chosen people. These flames signified something obscenely different: "Never shall I forget that smoke. Never shall I forget the little faces of the children, whose bodies I saw turned into wreaths of smoke beneath a silent blue sky. Never shall I forget those flames which consumed my faith forever."

A DIFFERENT KIND OF DESERT

When this new "going out" of the Jews was completed, the final destination was the desert. But it was not the biblical desert, where people wandered with a purpose. Here there was no manna sent from heaven to be found as the dew on plants in the morning. Nor was there to be a rain of quail to eat. In this desert the food that was sent "tasted of corpses." Nor was a brazen serpent fashioned and raised up in order for men to look on it and feel the venom of serpents disappear from their veins. In this desert there were other instruments erected and men were told to bare their heads and look on these new instruments: gallows in the courtyards where men were ordered to look up at children hung for camp infractions. And venom coursed through the hearts of the spectators to spew out in their thoughts: Where is God? Where is He? Where is God now?

That question becomes the central one for the inhabitants of the camps, and it is the central question of *Night.* The Jews of old were told to flee the fleshpots of Egypt in order to find God in the desert. They were His people just as He was their God. But in the new covenant of the anti-Exodus, people come into the desert not to be forged into a people, but to have their peoplehood exterminated. To be chosen in the camp meant to be chosen for the ovens. In an obscene use of the biblical vocabulary, election and "being chosen" meant to be marked for death.

Thus, the ancient dialogue between God and men now turned into a long and progressive silence in which the desert experience of Auschwitz and Buchenwald obscured and muted the presence of God. God became for the people of the desert someone to be accused and screamed at, not Someone who guided them into the wilderness in order to receive their prayer and their worship. The unfolding of this death becomes clearer in the novel if careful attention is paid to the parallel that Wiesel sets up between the death of his father and the death of his God. . . .

GOD NEVER SHOWED UP

When one studies the trajectory of Wiesel's relationship to his father in Auschwitz and Buchenwald, one is struck with the parallel trajectory of his fundamentally ambivalent relationship with the God of the Covenant, the God of Abraham, Isaac and Jacob. It is as though his own father was the icon of God. At the beginning of the experience in the camp, there was an unquestioned and unambivalent sense of the worship of God (Why do I pray? Why do I breathe!). The question of survival, an increasingly important question even to the point where it became *the* question, puts a strain on this intimate sense of obligation to God: to fast on Yom Kippur was to take a step closer to death since in the camp every day was a fast; to accuse oneself of fault on the Day of Atonement seemed to reverse the natural order of existence since it was the inmate who was grievously and unjustly offended. Slowly but inexorably there is a psychic transformation. One does not call for repentance or forgiveness, not even on Yom Kippur; especially not on that day. By some mad reversal that day becomes a special time to hurl an accusation. In short, to affirm the ancient covenant and its attendant responsibility is to hasten one's physical and psychical death. It is to hasten the day of "chosenness"—the day when Doctor Mengele will point his finger of election.

It is at this level that the whole drama of the Exodus becomes totally and completely reversed. The whole dynamic of the Exodus story is based on the idea of a people who must go out in order to worship their God in freedom and security. But the new Exodus ends in what Wiesel calls "the Kingdom of the Night." In the Bible God has found his people before they go to find Him. In the New Exodus, the people not only had found God but served Him; they went out only to lose Him. In the biblical experience the people are constituted and elected as a people by their fidelity to God. In this Exodus they are to find that their future means peoplelessness (forgive the neologism but how else can it be said?), framed in terms of a final solution.

In his recent work, *The Seduction of the Spirit,* Harvey Cox has emphasized the crucial importance of telling stories as a fundamental part of "being religious." Elie Wiesel has told his story within the subtle framework of an earlier story so that from this powerful mix of thanatography and liberation myth people may be forced to see the grim visage of postmodern man: the possible death of history; the dying of persons, peoples and comfortable divinities. God may not be dead for Elie Wiesel; there may be even a possibility of a new Exodus. Be that as it may, *Night* insists that the old order has been overturned and the form of the question has been radically changed. God may still live, but if He does, He has much to answer for.

Death Replaced Life as the Measure of Existence

Lawrence L. Langer

Out of the great body of Holocaust literature, Lawrence L. Langer, the Alumnae Chair Professor of English at Simmons College in Boston, claims that *Night* best shows the way that death became the measure of existence for the prisoners of the concentration camps. By focusing on this theme, Wiesel changes the consciousness of the reader so that they realize that life after the Holocaust can never be the same. Once Eliezer witnesses the murder of the innocent children, everything he thought he knew about life was proven wrong. As he watched people die all around him, he faced the realization that his life would now be measured only by the fact that he was not dead yet. The constant death chipped away at his soul—every time a prisoner died, a part of the others died with them. By the time of Eliezer's release, he was fully dead inside.

Most of the autobiographies concerned with the Holocaust numb the consciousness without enlarging it and providing it with a fresh or unique perception of the nature of reality, chiefly because the enormity of the atrocities they recount finally forces the reader to lose his orientation altogether and to feel as though he were wandering in a wilderness of evil totally divorced from any time and place he has ever known—a reality not latent in, but external to, his own experience. The most impressive exception to this general rule is a work that has already become a classic in our time, . . . Elie Wiesel's *Night*.

A reader confronted with this slim volume himself becomes an initiate into death, into the dark world of human

Excerpted from *The Holocaust and the Literary Imagination*, by Lawrence L. Langer. Copyright ©1975 by Yale University. Reprinted by permission of Yale University Press.

suffering and moral chaos we call the Holocaust; and by the end he is persuaded that he inhabits a kind of negative universe . . . a final rejection of love, of family, of the past, of order, of "normality.". . . Wiesel's *Night* is the terminus a quo for any investigation of the implications of the Holocaust, no matter what the terminus ad quem; on its final page a world lies dead at our feet, a world we have come to know as our own as well as Wiesel's, and whatever civilization may be rebuilt from its ruins, the silhouette of its visage will never look the same.

Night conveys in gradual detail the principle that . . . death has replaced life as the measure of our existence, and the vision of human potentiality nurtured by centuries of Christian and humanistic optimism has been so completely effaced by the events of the Holocaust that the future stretches gloomily down an endless vista into futility. The bleakness of the prospect sounds melodramatic but actually testifies to the reluctance of the human spirit to release the moorings that have lashed it to hope and to accept the consequences of total abandonment. Disappointed in a second coming, man has suffered a second going, a second fall and expulsion, not from grace this time but from humanity itself; and indeed, as we shall see in one of the most moving episodes in his harrowing book, Wiesel introduces a kind of second crucifixion, consecrating man not to immortality but to fruitless torture and ignominious death. Yet one is never permitted to forget what is being sacrificed, what price, unwillingly, the human creature has had to pay for the Holocaust, what heritage it has bequeathed to a humanity not yet fully aware of the terms of the will.

NIGHT VS. THE DIARY OF ANNE FRANK

Works like *Night* furnish illumination for this inheritance, an illumination all the more necessary (especially if one is to go on to explore the literature succeeding it) when we consider how unprepared the human mind is to confront the visions it reveals. . . .

Anne Frank's *Diary* was written in the innocence (and the "ignorance") of youth, but its conclusions form the point of departure for Wiesel's *Night* and most authors in the tradition of atrocity; indeed, their work constitutes a sequel to hers and ultimately challenges the principle that for her was both premise and epitaph—"In spite of everything, I still think people are good at heart"—a conception of character which dies hard, but dies pitilessly, in *Night* and in literature of atrocity in general. . . .

Yet Elie Wiesel recognized, as Anne Frank could not, that the values she celebrated might form an indispensable core for creating a magnetic field to attract fragments of atrocity, so that a permanent tension could be established between the two "forces"—a similar tension exists in some of the dreams we examined—a kind of polarity between memory and truth, nostalgia and a landscape of horror eerily highlighted by the pale reflection from vacant moral spaces. The literary effect is that memory ceases to offer consolation but itself becomes an affliction, intensifying the torment of the sufferer. Or rather, the usual content of memory is replaced by the harsh events of life in the concentration camp, until the past loses the hard edge of reality and the victim finds that both past and future, memory and hope—the "luxuries" of normal existence—are abruptly absorbed by an eternal and terrifying present, a present whose abnormality suddenly becomes routine. At this moment, life becomes too much for man and death assumes the throne in the human imagination. . . .

WHAT IS LEFT BEHIND

Night is an account of a young boy's divorce from life, a drama of recognition whose scenes record the impotence of the familiar in the face of modern atrocity; at its heart lies the profoundest symbolic confrontation of our century, the meeting of man and Auschwitz—and this confrontation in turn confirms the defeat of man's tragic potentiality in our time, and the triumph of death in its most nihilistic guise. The book begins with the familiar, a devout Jewish family whose faith supports their human aspirations and who find their greatest solace—and assurance—in the opportunity of approaching, through diligent study, the divine intentions implicit in reality. The premises behind these aspirations are clarified for the boy narrator by Moché the Beadle, a humble, sagelike man-of-all-work in the Hasidic synagogue in the Transylvanian town where the boy grows up:

> "Man raises himself toward God by the questions he asks Him. . . . That is the true dialogue. Man questions God and God answers. But we don't understand his answers. We can't understand them. Because they come from the depths of the soul, and they stay there until death. You will find the true answers . . . only within yourself."

With this counsel, says the narrator, "my initiation began"; but the kind of questions one asks in his dialogue with God are determined by tradition and education and assumptions that have withstood the assault of adversity. Moché's wisdom is tested when he is deported, together with other foreign Jews from the small Hungarian town. One day (having escaped, miraculously, from his captors), he reappears with tales of Jews digging their own graves and being slaughtered, "without passion, without haste," and of babies who were thrown into the air while "the machine gunners used them as targets." The joy was extinguished from his eyes as he told these tales, but no one believed him—including the young narrator. . . .

The citizens of Sighet, the narrator's town, depend on the material "items" of their civilization, almost as if they were sacred talismans, for security. Their abandoned possessions, after their deportation, become symbols of a vanished people, a forgotten and now useless culture.

Throughout *Night,* Wiesel displays a remarkable talent for investing the "items" of reality, and of the fantastic "irreality" that replaces it, with an animistic quality, and then setting both on a pathway leading to an identical destination: death. For example, in this description of a landscape without figures, crowded with things but devoid of life . . . in this passage, presided over by an indifferent nature, symbols of an exhausted past turn into harbingers of a ghastly future:

> The street was like a market place that had suddenly been abandoned. Everything could be found there: suitcases, portfolios, briefcases, knives, plates, bank-notes, papers, faded portraits. All those things that people had thought of taking with them, and which in the end they had left behind. They had lost all value.
>
> Everywhere rooms lay open. Doors and windows gaped onto the emptiness. Everything was free for anyone, belonging to nobody. It was simply a matter of helping oneself. An open tomb.
>
> A hot summer sun.

. . . The fifteen-year-old narrator of *Night* is gradually deprived of the props which have sustained him in his youth; but his experience is such that self-knowledge . . . becomes more of a burden than a consolation, and "a more valid conception of reality" sounds like a piece of impious rhetoric.

TRANSITION FROM LIFE TO DEATH

The displacement of life by death as a measure of existence is metaphorically reinforced in *Night* ... by imagery that has become standard fare for much literature of atrocity, imagery facilitating the transition from one world to the other—the boxcars, for example, in which victims were transported:

> The doors were closed. We were caught in a trap, right up to our necks. The doors were nailed up; the way back was finally cut off. The world was a cattle wagon hermetically sealed.

"Liberation" from this hermetic world upon arrival in the camp, however, changes nothing; the "way back" ceases to have meaning, and man must turn his attention to absorbing the nature of the fearful "way ahead," and of finding methods to survive in spite of it, though the price he must pay for his survival is not calculable in figures inherited from the familiar past. He must somehow accommodate himself to an environment dominated by the macabre images of furnace and chimney, of flames in the night and smoke and reeking human flesh; and he must further acknowledge, against all his human impulses and religious training, the authenticity of this harsh, incredible fate:

> "Do you see that chimney over there? See it? Do you see those flames? (Yes, we did see the flames.) Over there—that's where you're going to be taken. That's your grave, over there. Haven't you realized it yet? You dumb bastards, don't you understand anything? You're going to be burned. Frizzled away. Turned into ashes."

The narrator's response introduces a tension that permeates the literature of atrocity: "Surely it was all a nightmare? An unimaginable nightmare?" With a desperate insistence he clings to a kind of emotional nostalgia, as if the stability of his being depends on an affirmative answer; but a subsequent experience shatters that stability permanently, and his efforts henceforth are devoted to making the reader relive the nightmare that continues to haunt him. His world crumbles ... over the suffering of little children: his first night in the camp he sees babies hurled into a huge ditch from which gigantic flames are leaping:

> I pinched my face. Was I still alive? Was I awake? I could not believe it. How could it be possible for them to burn people, children, and for the world to keep silent? No, none of this could be true. It was a nightmare. . . . Soon I should wake with a start, my heart pounding, and find myself back in the bedroom of my childhood, among my books. . . .

The waking dream, haunted by the omnipresence of death, filled with "truths" unacceptable to reason but vivid, nevertheless, in their unquestionable actuality, leads first to a disorientation—the new inmates of the camp begin reciting the Jewish prayer for the dead *for themselves*—then to an attempt, at least by the young narrator, to discover mental attitudes commensurate with what the mind initially finds incomprehensible. The ritual incantation which marks his inauguration into the concentration camp . . . it signifies not only a boy's despair, but the exhaustion of meaning in a world henceforth unlike anything men have ever encountered: . . .

> Never shall I forget that nocturnal silence which deprived me, for all eternity, of the desire to live. Never shall I forget those moments which murdered my God and my soul and turned my dreams to dust. Never shall I forget these things, even if I am condemned to live as long as God Himself. Never. . . .

When the first night ends, the narrator presumably has left normality behind, and death has infected his future: "The student of the Talmud, the child that I was, had been consumed in the flames. There remained only a shape that looked like me. A dark flame had entered into my soul and devoured it." The flame illuminates a vision of the self which under ordinary circumstances might be called self-knowledge, but here leads to a futility that negates tragedy and prefigures a complete exile . . . , a human condition that will have to create new terms for its existence, since Auschwitz has irrevocably breached any meaningful alliance between it and the past:

> Those absent no longer touched even the surface of our memories. We still spoke of them—"Who knows what may have become of them?"—but we had little concern for their fate. We were incapable of thinking of anything at all. Our senses were blunted; everything was blurred as in a fog. It was no longer possible to grasp anything. The instincts of self-preservation, of self-defense, of pride, had all deserted us. In one ultimate moment of lucidity it seemed to me that we were damned souls wandering in the half-world, souls condemned to wander through space till the generations of man came to an end, seeking their redemption, seeking oblivion—without hope of finding it. . . .

In the world of Wiesel's narrator, a diametrically opposite principle of negation prevails, whereby events silence the creative spirit, destroy the longings of youth, and cast over reality an all-embracing shadow of death.

FACING A NEW REALITY

One of the dramatic pinnacles of *Night* illustrates this with unmitigated horror: . . . three prisoners, two men and a young boy, have been "convicted" of sabotage within the camp and are sentenced to be hanged before thousands of inmates. One imagines the boy, a "sad-eyed angel" on the gallows in the middle, the older victims on either side of him, a grotesque and painful parody—though literally true—of the original redemptive sufferer; the sentence is executed, and the prisoners are forced to march by the dangling bodies, face to face with their own potential fate. . . .

More than one boy's life and another boy's faith is extinguished here, and more than soup loses its familiar taste—a rationale for being, a sense of identification with the human species (as well as a divine inheritance), all the feelings which somehow define our world as a "civilized" place of habitation, are sacrificed on this gallows-crucifix, until it is no longer possible to establish a connection between one's intelligence and its apprehension of surrounding reality. The ritual of death, the agonizing struggle between living and dying which always has one inevitable outcome, even if some fortunate few should literally survive—for a time—the ritual of death ungraced by the possibility of resurrection, becomes the focus of existence and shrouds reality in an atmosphere of irrational, impenetrable gloom—"Our senses were blunted," as Wiesel wrote earlier; "everything was blurred as in a fog."

Under such circumstances men learn to adopt toward totally irrational events attitudes that one would expect only from insane or otherwise bewildered human beings: the result is that the incredible assumes some of the vestments of ordinary reality, while normality appears slightly off-center, recognizable, one might say, "north-northwest." Neither total confusion nor absolute comprehension, neither a mad world in which men behave sanely, nor a reasonable one in which human conduct seems deranged— this is the schizophrenic effect Wiesel achieves in his autobiographical narrative. It is scarcely necessary to arrange literal episodes or invent new ones to create the nightmare atmosphere which imaginative works in the tradition will strive for—such is the unique nature of reality in the concentration camp. . . .

For the victims who seek sustenance in their faith are reduced to a more degrading role by the subsequent episode, a "selection"—which in plain language meant that some men, usually those physically weaker, were periodically designated for death in a ritual that resembled the weeding-out of defective parts in a machine-assembly plant. Men who know in advance that their life depends on the opinion of an SS "doctor" run past this official, hoping that their numbers will not be written down; most pass the "test," but a few are aware that they "fail," that in two or three days they will be taken to the "hospital" and never be seen again. After such knowledge, what humanity? What logic or reason or connection between what men do and what they suffer, can prevail in one's conception of the universe? In one's conception of one's self? For the narrator, existence is reduced to an elemental struggle between acquiescence to death— "Death wrapped itself around me till I was stifled. It stuck to me. I felt that I could touch it. The idea of dying, of no longer being, began to fascinate me."—and the need to live, in order to support his weakening father, broken in health and spirit by the rigorous discipline of the camp.

DEAD INSIDE

Ultimately, the contest between Death and the Father, the one representing the concentration camp with its insidious and macabre dissolution of reasonable longings, the other all those familiar inheritances which constitute the basis of civilized existence—ultimately, this contest assumes symbolic dimensions, as if normalcy in its dying gasp makes one final effort to assert its authority over the gruesome power seeking to dispossess it. But when death intrudes on the imagination to the point where memory and hope are excluded—as happens in *Night*—then this rivalry, with the accompanying gesture of resistance, proves futile; a kind of inner momentum has already determined the necessary triumph of death in a world disrupted beyond the capacity of man to alter it. The extent of the disruption, and the transformation in humanity wrought by it, is painfully illustrated by the cry of SS guards to the prisoners being transported westward in open cattle-cars from Auschwitz (because of the approaching Russian troops) to Buchenwald: "Throw out all the dead! All corpses outside!"—and by the response of those still surviving: "The living rejoiced. There would be more room."

Thus disinherited, bereft of any value that might permit him to confront the inevitable death of his father with at least the dignity of an illusion, and compelled in the depths of his heart to accept the desolate rule of the concentration camp—"Here there are no fathers, no brothers, no friends. Everyone lives and dies for himself alone."—the narrator helplessly watches his last living link with the familiar world of the past expire and learns that grief has expired with him. Not only have normal feelings lapsed—plunging us into a shadowy realm where men cease to respond to reality by following any predictable pattern—but they have been replaced by attitudes which a "normally" disposed reader, still bound by the moral premises of pre-Holocaust experience, would characterize as verging on the inhuman. But to the reader who has himself submitted imaginatively to the hallucination-become-fact of this experience, the narrator's reaction to his father's death can more accurately be described as one illustration of what happens when human character is pressed beyond the limits of the human: "in the recesses of my weakened conscience, could I have searched it, I might perhaps have found something like—free at last!" . . .

At this moment, . . . the son . . . is severed from his patrimony and thrust forth onto a stage which requires the drama of existence to continue, though without a script, *sans* director, the plot consisting of a single unanswerable question: How shall I enact my survival in a world I know to be darkened by the shadow of irrational death, before an audience anticipating a performance that will be illuminated by the light of reason and the glow of the future? Out of some such query as this, representing a paradox of private existence, is born a principle of schizophrenic art, the art of atrocity.

The final, haunting moment of *Night* occurs when the narrator, Wiesel himself, following his liberation, gazes at his own visage after lingering between life and death (a result of food poisoning):

> One day I was able to get up, after gathering all my strength. I wanted to see myself in the mirror hanging on the opposite wall. I had not seen myself since the ghetto.
> From the depths of the mirror, a corpse gazed back at me.

The look in his eyes, as they stared into mine, has never
left me.

An unrecognizable face from the past and a living death-
mask—variations on this confrontation, spanning two worlds
with a current linking regret to despair, characterizes the literature that grew out of the nightmare of history which
transformed a fifteen-year-old boy into a breathing corpse.

Night Is the Anti–"Coming of Age" Story

David L. Vanderwerken

Author David L. Vanderwerken contends that *Night* is the opposite of the traditional coming of age story. Instead of leaving the confusion of childhood for the understanding of adulthood, Eliezer travels in the opposite direction. His imprisonment forces his life to shrink and contract instead of growing and expanding. The adults that would normally be guiding his entrance into maturity are forced by their circumstances to abandon their roles, leaving Eliezer empty and fractured instead of complete.

One of our most familiar fictional forms is the story of a young person's initiation into adulthood. That the form remains rich, inexhaustible, and compelling can be confirmed by pointing to the success of John Irving's *The World According to Garp*, for one. Although specifically coined to describe a certain tradition of German novel deriving from Goethe's *Wilhelm Meister*, "*Bildungsroman*"—while untranslatable into English—has become our flexible label for hundreds of works that treat a youth's apprenticeship to life. . . .

Many *Bildungsromane*, especially modernist ones, gain power and point by parodying or even inverting the traditional formulae of the genre. . . . No better example of the *Bildungsroman* turned inside out and upside down exists than the story of Eliezer Wiesel in *Night*. In his chapter "The Dominion of Death" in *The Holocaust and the Literary Imagination*, Lawrence L. Langer posits that inversion, reversal, and negation are the overt strategies of much Holocaust memoir writing, skewed *Bildungsromane*, of which *Night* is the most powerful.

Traditionally, the story of maturation takes a youth through a series of educational experiences, some through

Excerpted from "Wiesel's *Night* as Anti-Bildungsroman," by David L. Vanderwerken, *Yiddish*, vol. 7, no. 4, 1990. Reprinted by permission of *Yiddish*.

books and classrooms, but most not, and exposes the youth
to a series of possible mentors and guides who become, as
Ralph Ellison puts it in *Invisible Man,* "trustee[s] of consciousness." Of course, Ellison's young man has trouble distinguishing the truth-telling mentors from the liars. Usually,
however, such life teachers shape the youth toward a cultural ideal of adulthood. The function of education, mythol-
ogist Joseph Campbell tells us in *Myths to Live By,* is to shift
the "response systems of adolescents from dependency to responsibility." . . . Often the initiation process is worked out
on a journey, some movement through space, which has the
effect of accelerating the rate of maturation. . . . And often
the journey implies a spiritual quest. The result is a story of
moral, emotional, intellectual, and spiritual growth. Normally, the initiate not only achieves self-definition, but also
social definition, ready to assume a role in a community. . . .
In *Night,* Elie Wiesel inverts and reverses, even shatters, the
elements of the traditional paradigm.

Turning Off the Light

The very title itself implies a reversal since the *Bildungsroman* usually opens out into day, illumination, awareness,
life. Instead, *Night* leads us into darkness and death. While
the traditional raw initiate grows out into a knowledge of the
richness, fullness, complexity, and multivariety of life—its
open-ended possibilities—*Night* starts out with a sense of
richness in heritage and culture that is violently and quickly
stripped away, denuded, impoverished. Instead of expanding
and ripening, young Eliezer's life narrows, withers, contracts, reduces to enclosure. Instead of finding a self and a
place in the world, Eliezer begins with a sense of self, located in a coherent, unified community, and ends up when
Buchenwald is liberated alone, isolated, and numb. Instead
of becoming aware of his own potential, in touch with resources he was hitherto oblivious of in himself, Eliezer
looks in the mirror on the last page and sees a corpse. The
pious young boy of Sighet has been incinerated. And the
corollary spiritual quest that usually leads to some satisfying
accommodation or resolution . . . leads in *Night* to the void.
Instead of climbing the mountain, Eliezer spirals into hell.
And at the bottom lurk only questions, no answers.

The opening chapter introduces us to this pious and spiritual adolescent who lives in the eternal world, who knows

more about what happened 5000 years ago than what is occurring in Hungary in 1943. The only son in a family of five, Eliezer has been groomed for a life of study, his future as a Talmudic scholar or rabbi tacitly understood. Now twelve, Eliezer feels impatient to delve into the mystical realm of Judaism, the Cabbala, if he can find a teacher. Although his father refuses Eliezer's request to study Cabbala on the grounds of his youth, precocious or no, Eliezer finds a master in Moche the Beadle, the synagogue handyman. In Moche, Wiesel offers an apparently traditional mentor character, the sage who will guide the initiate through the gates of truth: "It was with him that my initiation began." Moche is a Socratic sort of teacher, asking challenging and paradoxical questions that have no easy answers, if any at all. He tells Eliezer that the answers to all our ultimate questions are within ourselves. As a result of their studies, Eliezer says, "a conviction grew in me that Moche the Beadle would draw me with him into eternity." Suddenly Moche vanishes, deported in a cattle car with other foreign Jews, presumably to a work camp.

Just as suddenly, months later, Moche reappears in Sighet having escaped from the Gestapo, and he no longer talks of "God or the Cabbala, but only of what he had seen." Wiesel now reveals Moche's significance as Eliezer's mentor, neither as tutor of the verities of the ancient sacred texts, nor as agent of Eliezer's developing self-knowledge, but as witness and prophet of the reality of the Holocaust, a reality Sighet is not only oblivious of, but also refuses to believe. Consciousness simply reneges at Moche's preposterous tales of mass murder. The town dismisses him as mad; in Wiesel's withering refrain, "life returned to normal." Although Eliezer continues to pursue the truth of the eternal as Moche-I had taught him, it is the truth of temporal fact taught by the Lazarus-like Moche-II—his insights into the concentration camp, the kingdom of night—that will prove to be the most imperative, the most influential, perhaps the most authentic in Eliezer's near future.

WHERE HAVE ALL THE GOOD MENTORS GONE?

That, for Wiesel, only the mad could imagine the mad truth finds reinforcement in the figure of Madame Schächter on the train to Auschwitz. In chapter two, her hysterical shrieks of furnaces and flames are received like Moche's stories, an obvious consequence of madness. After all, she has been separated from her family. Finally, some of the people beat her into silence. Yet as the train nears its destination, she rouses to scream again, "'Jews, look! Look through the window! Flames! Look!'" Eliezer does look and realizes that Madame Schächter's cries all along have been premonitions, not psychotic hallucinations, for now he sees the chimneys of what he will learn are the crematoria. This woman of fifty becomes an indirect mentor who provides Eliezer with another insight into contemporary truth.

Of the other adults that Eliezer encounters in the camps, two stand out in offering contradictory advice on how to survive in hell. The first, the prisoner in charge of Eliezer's block upon arrival, makes a speech to the new arrivals that echoes the sentiments of innumerable, traditional moral sages:

> "Have faith in life. Above all else, have faith. Drive out despair, and you will keep death away from yourselves. Hell is not for eternity. And now, a prayer—or rather, a piece of advice: let there be comradeship among you. We are all brothers, and we are all suffering the same fate. The same smoke floats over all our heads. Help one another. It is the only way to survive."

Comforted by this plea for faith, community, interdependence, civilization, Eliezer thinks: "The first human words." Yet are they the "'teachings of our sages'?" For this condition? In Buchenwald two years later, after the death march evacuation of Buna, Eliezer hears another sort of advice from a block leader, at a time when Schlomo Wiesel is dying. This sage counsels Eliezer to look out for number one:

> "Here, there are no fathers, no brothers, no friends. Everyone lives and dies for himself alone. I'll give you a sound piece of advice—don't give your ration of bread and soup to your old father. There's nothing you can do for him. And you're killing yourself. Instead, you ought to be having his ration."

Of course, this is practical wisdom as Eliezer knows, but "I dared not admit it." Yet this is the ethical dictum of hell, into which Eliezer has been fully initiated. No ties are sacred.

Night's most powerful dramatization of an inverted mentor-initiate relationship is that of father and son. Schlomo Wiesel, respected community leader upon whom others rely for guidance and strength, represents the patriarchal Jewish father, a *mensch*, or as Bellow's Moses Herzog puts it, "a father, a sacred being, a king." Normally, the father helps the son make the transition in adolescence from dependence to independence. In the kingdom of night, however, the roles completely reverse; the son becomes the parent. In the end, the man whom others looked to has "become like a child, weak, timid, vulnerable." This reversal of the normal order is prefigured at Birkenau when the veteran prisoner urges father and son to declare their ages to be forty and eighteen, not their actual fifty and fifteen, the better to survive Dr. Mengele's selection. Indeed time itself does warp, becoming nightmare time, accelerating human changes. "How he had changed! His eyes had grown dim," comments Eliezer about his father the first night at Birkenau. As time unfolds, Eliezer takes the ascendancy in the father-son relationship, making decisions, taking charge of their common welfare, even feeling angry at his father for not knowing how to avoid the Kapo's wrath and getting beaten: "That is what concentration camp life had made of me." Although he never abandons his father the way Rabbi Eliahou's son had, Eliezer has his mental moments of filial disloyalty and betrayal. When they are temporarily separated during an air alert at Buchenwald, Eliezer thinks "'Don't let me find him! If only I could get rid of this dead weight'," but he immediately feels ashamed. However, when his father is carried away to the crematory in the night, perhaps still alive, Eliezer must face the terrible truth: "And, in the depths of my being, in the recesses of my weakened conscience, could I have searched it, I might perhaps have found something like—free at last." He sees himself, then, as finally no better than Rabbi Eliahou's son.

A SOUL EMPTIED

Just as Wiesel radically overturns the stock *Bildungsroman* pattern of master and apprentice, he alters the traditional process of the evolving self on its way to fulfillment. On the day of deportation, Eliezer looks back at his home where he had spent so many years "imagining what my life would be like." The ancient story of youth's departure from the nest, encountering the world and fleshing out the skeletal self, becomes for Eliezer a story of decomposing flesh, of becoming a skeleton. Literally overnight, Eliezer tells us, his sense of self evaporated: "The student of the Talmud, the child that I was, had been consumed in the flames. There remained only a shape that looked like me." Even the name for the "shape that looked like me" dissolves with the engraving of

A-7713 on his left arm. The identity nurtured for twelve years collapses in one day.

Eliezer's sense of self is identical with his spiritual life. The worst of *Night*'s outrages, movingly worded by François Mauriac in the Foreword, is the "death of God in the soul of a child who suddenly discovers absolute evil." Again, the flames of the first night, fueled by the truckload of babies, "consumed my faith forever," "murdered my God and my soul and turned my dreams to dust." The two most powerful dramatizations of the consequences of Eliezer's sundered faith—the faith that had given richness and depth to his living—are the hanging of the boy and the first High Holy Days spent in Buna. For Eliezer, God is "hanging here on this gallows." If God is not dead, then he deserves man's contempt, Eliezer feels. The bitterness pours forth during Rosh Hashanah and Yom Kippur with the mockery of the prisoners carrying out the forms, the absurdity of the starving debating whether to fast. While thousands pray, Eliezer offers up outraged accusations:

> "But these men here, whom You have betrayed, whom You have allowed to be tortured, butchered, gassed, burned, what do they do? They pray before You! They praise Your name!"

Like Huck Finn, Eliezer knows you can't pray a lie:

> My eyes were open and I was alone—terribly alone in a world without God and without man. Without love or mercy. I had ceased to be anything but ashes, yet I felt myself to be stronger than the Almighty, to whom my life had been tied for so long. I stood amid that praying congregation, observing it like a stranger.

Also in this scene of the praying ten thousand, one can see Wiesel's ironic presentation of the community that the prepared initiate is to take his place in upon completion of apprenticeship, the culmination of *Bildungsromane,* public and ceremonial like the ordination of clergy or the commissioning of officers. This is a congregation of the living dead, a community of corpses acting out a charade. This is as anti as a *Bildungsroman* can get.

CHAPTER 5

The Legacy of *Night*

Night Defines Holocaust Autobiography

Joseph Sungolowsky

As part of a collection of articles about the Holocaust in art and literature, Joseph Sungolowsky, professor of French literature and Jewish studies at Queen's College, focuses on *Night* as a defining work of Holocaust autobiography. He first discusses the elements that characterize a pure autobiography and then considers the difficulties and challenges that the writer encounters when the autobiography takes place during the Holocaust.

Autobiography is usually defined as a retrospective narrative written about one's life, in the first person and in prose. Such writing has appeared with increasing frequency in Western literature since the beginning of the nineteenth century. As a result of the events of World War II, it gained considerable significance. . . .

The history of the destruction of European Jewry by the Nazis has relied heavily upon the accounts written by survivors, which will probably remain a prime source of information concerning the magnitude of the catastrophe. Autobiography written as a result of experiences lived during the Holocaust is therefore an integral part of its literature. Since such literature cannot be linked to any of the norms of literary art, it has been termed a literature of "atrocity" or "decomposition." Holocaust autobiography inherits, therefore, the problematic aspect of both autobiography and the literature of the Holocaust. . . .

Autobiography is generally written in midlife by an author who has achieved fame thanks to previous works which have been recognized for their value, or by an individual who has played a significant role in public life. . . .

Writing autobiography at an earlier age or as a first book is considered an exception. Elie Wiesel's *Night* is such an exception. He recounts how fortuitous his career as a writer was in its beginnings, especially considering that he might not have survived the concentration camps at all. Upon his liberation, he vowed not to speak of his experience for at least ten years. It was the French novelist François Mauriac who persuaded him to tell his story, and Wiesel adds that at the time Mauriac was as well-known as he was obscure. Thus, at the age of 28, Wiesel published his autobiographical narrative concerning his experience in the concentration camps, first in Yiddish under the title *Un die velt hot geshvigen,* subsequently in French under the title *La Nuit.* In 1976, Wiesel stated that *Night* could have remained his one and only book; indeed, when he began to write fiction, the French critic René Lalou wondered how Wiesel could have undertaken to write anything else after *Night.* Clearly, at the time Wiesel published *Night,* he lacked the fame as an author of previous works usually expected of an autobiography. . . .

IDENTIFYING AUTOBIOGRAPHY

An autobiography is deemed authentic when there is identity between the name of the author appearing on the title page and the narrator of the story. In *Night,* Wiesel relates that during a rollcall in Auschwitz, he heard a man crying out: "Who among you is Wiesel from Sighet?" He turned out to be a relative that had been deported from Antwerp. Subsequently, Wiesel is called by his first name "Eliezer" by that relative, by Juliek, a fellow-inmate, and by his father. . . .

Autobiography is considered genuine when the author states, either in the text itself or in connection with it, that his intent has indeed been autobiographical. [Literary critic Philippe] Lejeune calls such a statement an "autobiographical pact"—an agreement between author and reader according to which the reader is assured that he is reading the truth. . . .

Wiesel's autobiographical pact was established twenty years after the publication of *Night,* when he told an interviewer: "*Night,* my first narrative, was an autobiographical story, a kind of testimony of one witness speaking of his own life, his own death."

Autobiography is written in order to come to terms with oneself. Recapturing the past is, therefore, the most common preoccupation of the autobiographer. . . .

Autobiography is written as a testimony, especially when the author has lived a particular moment of history that must not be forgotten. Such was Elie Wiesel's intent when he wrote *Night*. For him, "Auschwitz was a unique phenomenon, a unique event, like the revelation at Sinai." Had it not been for the war, he would not have become a storyteller but would have written on philosophy, the Bible, and the Talmud. He recalls that as he looked at himself in the mirror after his liberation, he realized how much he had changed and decided that someone had to write about that change. Although he had vowed to remain silent for ten years, he had absorbed "the obsession to tell the tale." He states: "I knew that anyone who remained alive had to become a storyteller, a messenger, had to speak up."

Autobiography may also be written to educate. The autobiographer wishes his reader to learn from his experience. . . .

RISING TO THE CHALLENGE

No matter how sincere or truthful the autobiographer intends to be, he must face the technical and literary problems related to the writing. Such problems are even more acute in the case of Holocaust autobiography. Before they write autobiography, authors will make sure that a reasonable amount of time has elapsed between the events they wish to relate and the actual writing. Such "distanciation" ensures orderliness to the narrative. In the case of Holocaust autobiography, the waiting period is not only technical but also emotional. Elie Wiesel states that he feared being unable to live up to the past, "of saying the wrong things, of saying too much or too little." He therefore decided to wait ten years before writing. . . .

With the best faith or memory in the world, it is impossible to re-create in writing a reality long gone by. In this respect, Holocaust autobiographers are even more frustrated. They constantly suspect that whatever the form and content of their narrative, they have not succeeded in conveying the past adequately. Wiesel feels that, while *Night* is the center of his work, "what happened during that night . . . will not be revealed.". . . However, since they represent an attempt to recapture whatever is retained of the past, such memories, as fragmented as they may be, remain invaluable. As put by book critic Leon Wieseltier, they are "all the more illuminating, because memory is the consciousness of things and events that have not yet disappeared completely into knowledge."

No matter how truthful the autobiographer tries to be, he cannot avoid having recourse to fictional or literary devices. Indeed, autobiography is necessarily linked to related literary genres such as the novel, the theater, the diary, or the chronicle. Thus, despite Theodore W. Adorno's contention that it is barbaric to write literature after Auschwitz, the Holocaust writer or autobiographer must engage in a "writing experience" if he wishes to express himself.

The terse language of Wiesel's *Night* is occasionally broken by harrowing scenes such as that of Madame Shachter gone mad in the cattle car or by dialogues such as those that take place between himself and his erstwhile master Moshe-the-Beadle or with his dying father. Fantasy is present when he depicts his native Sighet as "an open tomb" after its Jews have been rounded up. He uses irony when he recalls that a fellow inmate has faith in Hitler because he has kept all his promises to the Jewish people. Images express the author's feelings. Gallows set up in the assembly place in preparation of a hanging appear to him as "three black crows," and the violin of a fellow inmate who has died after playing a Beethoven concerto lies beside him like "a strange overwhelming little corpse." The grotesque best portrays his fellow inmates, "Poor mountebanks, wider than they were tall, more dead than alive; poor clowns, their ghostlike faces emerging from piles of prison clothes! Buffoons!". . .

KEEPING IT REAL

While autobiography may choose to embrace a greater or smaller part of one's life, Holocaust autobiography will essentially deal with the period marked by the events of the Nazi genocide. Just as any autobiography related to a troubled historical period acquires an added significance, so does Holocaust autobiography exert a unique fascination upon the reader because of its central motive. . . .

Evocations of childhood are all the more dramatic as they abruptly came to an end. . . . What follows . . . are scenes of departures. When Wiesel's family must join the roundup of Jews in Sighet, he sees his father weeping for the first time. Looking at his little sister, Tzipora, he notices that "the bundle on her back was too heavy for her.". . .

As painful as it may be to both author and reader, these autobiographical writings attempt to come to grips with the hard reality of the concentrationary universe. If *Night* has become a classic, it is because it remains one of the most concise and factual eyewitness accounts of the horrors. Wiesel goes into such details as the early disbelief of the victims ("The yellow star? Oh! well, what of it?" says his own father), the anguish of those who have been marked by death by Mengele in the course of a selection and Wiesel's own joy at having escaped it, the careless trampling of inmates by their own comrades in the course of the agonizing death marches. . . .

THE IMPORTANCE OF THE WORD "I"

In a conversation with his friend and fellow U.S. Holocaust Memorial Committee member Harry James Cargas, Wiesel explains that the word "I" takes on great importance in his autobiographical writing.

In every word that we pronounce or that we use or that we hear, we must find the ur-word, the original word, the primary word. I would try to find in that word the tone of Adam, when he used the word. When Adam said "I" and I say "I," what is the link between these two "I"s? And this is true of all the other words. If I could read, properly, a word, I could read the history of humankind. This is language, of course, if you trace it, on the highest level of communication and of memory. Language, after all, is a deed of memory. Every word therefore contains not only myself, having said it, but all the people who have said it before me.

Harry James Cargas, ed., *Telling the Tale: A Tribute to Elie Wiesel on the Occasion of His 65th Birthday*, Saint Louis, MO: Time Being Books, 1993, p. 104.

"Autobiography," writes [literary critic] Georges May, "is capable of absorbing the most diverse material, to assimilate it and to change it into autobiography." Inasmuch as Holocaust autobiography deals with the events of one of the greatest upheavals of the twentieth century and the most traumatic destruction of the Jewish people, it is natural that autobiographers reflect upon the impact of those events on their personality, on the destiny of the Jewish people and on the post-Holocaust world.

Confession is an essential ingredient of autobiography. Its degree of sincerity remains the sole prerogative of the autobiographer who can choose to shield himself behind his own writing. In Wiesel's *Night,* the frankness of his confession serves as a testimony to the extent of the dehumanization he has reached as a result of his concentration-camp life. While he has been separated forever from his mother and sister upon arrival in Auschwitz, he has managed to stay with his father. Both have miraculously escaped selection for death on several occasions. Yet, the survival instinct has overtaken him in the face of his dying father. When a guard tells him that in the camp "there are no fathers, no brothers, no friends," he thinks in his innermost heart that the guard is right but does not dare admit it. When he wakes up the next morning (less than four months before the Liberation) to find his father dead, he thinks "something like—free at last." Henceforth, Wiesel's life is devoid of meaning. *Night* concludes with the episode of the author looking at himself in the mirror. He writes: "a corpse gazed at me. The look in his eyes as they stared into mine has never left me." As indicated by Ellen Fine, the shift from the first to the third person in that sentence points to the "fragmented self," and, as indicated by Wiesel himself, that sight was to determine his career as a "writer-witness.". . .

SO OTHERS WILL UNDERSTAND

Meant as a stark narrative of the events and despite the ten-year period that preceded its writing, Wiesel's *Night* is devoid of reflections extraneous to his experiences in the concentration camps. He has stated that, except for *Night,* his other works are not autobiographical, although he occasionally brings into them "autobiographical data and moods." Yet, Wiesel has emphasized the importance of *Night as* the foundation of his subsequent works. He states: *"Night,* my first narrative, was an autobiographical story, a kind of testimony of one witness speaking of his own life, his own death. All kinds of options were available: suicide, madness, killing, political action, hate, friendship. I note all these options: faith, rejection of faith, blasphemy, atheism, denial, rejection of man, despair, and in each book I explore one aspect. In *Dawn,* I explore the political action; in *The Accident,* suicide; in *The Town Beyond the Wall,* madness; in *The Gates of the Forest,* faith and friendship; in *A Beggar in Jerusalem,* history, the return. All the stories are one story except that I build them in concentric circles. The center is the same and is in *Night.*" Such a position illustrates Philippe Lejeune's concept of "autobiographical space." Indeed, according to Lejeune, it is not always possible to derive the total image of a writer solely on the basis of a work explicitly declared to be autobiographical. Such an image is to be sought rather in the totality of his work which cannot fail to contain autobiographical data. Reflections on Jewish destiny and identity and on the post-Holocaust world are surely the very essence of Wiesel's writings whether they take the form of fiction, tales, plays, or essays.

Autobiography does not necessarily encompass a whole life. Many autobiographers choose to write about a part of it which they deem significant enough to reflect a profound if not crucial human experience. The Holocaust illustrates this aspect of autobiographical writing. . . . [Holocaust autobiographers] feel a compelling need at one point or another in their lives to tell of their experiences. Whether they write to settle the past, to testify or to educate, they mobilize a variety of devices and themes available to the autobiographer who seeks to share his experiences with the reader. As the Holocaust continues to be represented in an ever-growing multiplicity of forms, autobiography remains a fascinating means to express it. It is noteworthy, therefore, that the Holocaust autobiographer encounters consciously or not many of the problems faced by any autobiographer. However, in the case of the Holocaust autobiographer, such problems become even more crucial because of the nature of the material he is dealing with. Autobiography universalizes one's life. In the hands of Wiesel, Holocaust autobiography not only serves as an invaluable testimony of events that must never be forgotten, but also strengthens the feeling of all those who wish to identify with the victims of the greatest crime that ever took place amidst modern civilization.

Why People Resist the Truth

Ora Avni

Ora Avni, a professor of French at Yale University and the author of an upcoming book on post-Holocaust historical consciousness, addresses the disbelief people exhibit when presented with Holocaust testimony. Before and during the Holocaust there were many cases where warnings went unheeded. It seemed that no one—not the European Jews nor the world at large—could believe such atrocities against humanity were actually happening. Avni suggests that one reason for this is that people need a framework, a background to draw from, before they can process new ideas. And before the Holocaust, no one could conceive of such evil. They resist making the truth part of their reality. He demonstrates how Wiesel took this knowledge and framed *Night* so that readers would be able to shed their own disbelief.

[*Night's*] opening focuses not so much on the boy, however, as on a foreigner, Moshe the Beadle, a wretched yet good-natured and lovable dreamer, versed in Jewish mysticism. When the town's foreign Jews are deported by the Nazis to an unknown destination, he leaves with them; but he comes back. Having miraculously survived the murder of his convoy, he hurries back to warn the others. No longer singing, humming, or praying, he plods from door to door, desperately repeating the same stories of calm and dispassionate killings. But, despite his unrelenting efforts, "people refused not only to believe his stories, but even to listen to them."

Like Moshe the Beadle, the first survivors who told their stories either to other Jews or to the world were usually met with disbelief. When the first escapees from Ponar's killing grounds tried to warn the Vilna ghetto that they were not

Excerpted from "Beyond Psychoanalysis: Elie Wiesel's *Night* in Historical Perspective," by Ora Avni, in *Auschwitz and After*, edited by Lawrence D. Kritzman (New York: Routledge, 1995). Reprinted by permission of Ora Avni.

137

sent to work but to be murdered, not only did the Jews not believe them, but they accused the survivors of demoralizing the ghetto, and demanded that they stop spreading such stories. Similarly, when Jan Karski, the courier of the Polish government-in-exile who had smuggled himself into the Warsaw Ghetto so that he could report the Nazi's atrocities as an eyewitness, made his report to Justice Felix Frankfurter, the latter simply said, "I don't believe you." Asked to explain, he added, "I did not say that this young man is lying. I said I cannot believe him. There is a difference." How are we to understand this disbelief? What are its causes and effects, and above all, what lesson can we learn from it? . . .

FROM THE BEGINNING

We must also note that Moshe the Beadle's narrative does not only *open* the boy's narrative as it first appears, but frames it on both ends: once the reader is aware of the consequences of telling such a story, he or she extends this awareness to the story told by the boy. The opening episode thus invites the reader to read beyond the abrupt end of *Night,* all the way to the moment absent from *Night* proper, when the newly freed boy tells his own tale of survival: will this story, too, meet with hostility, disbelief, and denial? (And who better than the reader knows that the boy did eventually tell his story, and that this tale constitutes the very text he or she is reading?) The scene of narration of the opening episode thus prefigures the scene of reading of *Night.* . . . It warns the reader of the consequences of disbelief no less than it warns the town folks.

Shoah [another word for the Holocaust] narratives have given rise to a host of false problems. Faced with the horror of the *Shoah* and the suffering of its survivors, some have felt overwhelmed and, overcome with a sense of simple human decency, have questioned their right to examine an extreme experience in which they had no part. These scruples are, I think, misplaced: no one questions the right, or even the need of survivors to sort out their experience, or to bear witness. We readily concede survivors' wish and right to bear witness, to leave a historical account of their ordeal for posterity. But what about this posterity (ourselves), what about the recipients of those narratives? We—the latecomers to the experience of the *Shoah*—shall never be able to fully grasp the abysmal suffering and despair of the survivors.

And yet, not only do we share with them a scene of narration, but our participation in this scene of narration may have become the organizing principle of our lives and our own historical imperative. How, then, are we going to face up to this task? Like the town folks, we have gone through disbelief and denial. But today, two generations later, we have rediscovered the *Shoah,* as the numerous publications on the subject will attest (some even claim that we have trivialized the *Shoah* with excessive verbiage). How, then, are we to dispose of the knowledge conveyed by survivors' narratives? How can we integrate the lesson of their testimonies in our historical project—at least, if ours is a project in which there is no room for racial discrimination, genocide, acquiescence to evil, passive participation in mass murder; a project in which "get involved" has come to replace "look the other way"? . . .

Like Moshe, Wiesel came back; like Moshe, he told his story; and like Moshe, he told it again and again. It is therefore not merely a question of informing others (for information purposes, once the story is told, one need not tell it again). Like Moshe, Wiesel clearly does not set out to impart information only, but to *tell the tale,* that is, to share a scene of narration with a community of readers. This explains why, while the *Shoah* is in fact the subject of all his texts, Wiesel, wiser than Moshe, never recounted his actual experience in the death camps again. Like the opening episode of *Night,* his other works deal with "before" and "after": before, as a premonition of things to come; after, as a call for latecomers to see themselves accountable for living in a post-*Shoah* world. The opening episode thus encapsulates Wiesel's life project, in that it invites us to reflect not only on the nature of the *Shoah* itself, but first, on living historically (that is, on living in a world of which the *Shoah* is part), and second, on transmitting this history from one person and one generation to the other. . . .

To what, then, does this episode owe its exemplary value? Why has Moshe, the ultimate *Shoah* survivor-narrator, come back? Why does he feel compelled to endlessly repeat his story? Why does he no longer pray? On the other hand, why are his listeners so recalcitrant? Why do they not believe him? Why do they accuse him of madness or of ulterior motives? Why do they all but gag him? That this episode illustrates widespread attitudes towards all accounts of Nazi

TRIAL RUN FOR NUCLEAR WAR?

A. Alvarez, essayist and renowned literary critic, declares in Beyond All This Fiddle *that decades after it ended, the Holocaust still haunts us because of what it could indicate for our future.*

The atrocities [of the Holocaust] have in no way been diminished by the passage of time, but their meaning has changed slightly, and in changing it has become more, rather than less, urgent. In the beginning, the horror of the camps was heightened by a certain relief—'Thank God it wasn't me'—and this in turn provoked guilt. To judge from their writing, even former inmates seem to have felt obscurely guilty at having survived when friends and family had gone under—as though survival were almost a mark of cowardice, as though it certainly meant, for them, that they had had to compromise with the omnipresent and contagious corruption. For the rest of us, there was the far obscurer guilt of being Jews who had never been exposed to the camps at all. In these circumstances, the rhetoric of so much concentration-camp literature was comforting; it enabled us to feel engaged while in reality preserving our safe distance. Since then the situation has changed. The question of survival is less obvious, but more ubiquitous, more pervasive. I once suggested (in a piece for *The Atlantic Monthly*, December 1962) that one of the reasons why the camps continue to keep such a tight hold on our imaginations is that we see in them a small-scale trial run for a nuclear war.

atrocities and Jewish victimization is unquestionable. We shall therefore focus on the *self-positioning* of the subject (teller or listener, knowledgeable or uninformed) in the face of accounts of the *Shoah*, be it at the dinner table, in the classroom, on the psychoanalyst's couch, in academe, or in the morning paper. . . .

LISTEN TO ME

The *Shoah* has shaken our vision of man so profoundly that, half a century later, we are still grappling with its aftermath, with our urgent albeit terrifying need for a radical reevaluation of our concept of man-in-the-world. And, as the reluctance to believe the stories or even to listen to them shows, this reevaluation does not befall only those who were the subjects of the event or their children (victims, perpetrators, or even bystanders). It extends to an entire generation. As

Between 1940 and 1945, four-and-a-half-million people died in Auschwitz; the same number would die in minutes if a hydrogen bomb landed on London or New York. Then there are those other curious, upside-down similarities: the use of modern industrial processes for the mass production of corpses, with all the attendant paraphernalia of efficiency, meticulous paperwork and bureaucratic organization; the deliberate annihilation not merely of lives but of identities, as in some paranoid vision of a mass culture. And so on. It adds up to a perverted, lunatic parody of our own engulfing but otherwise comfortable technological societies. So the literature of the camps has become, insidiously and unanswerably, our own under-literature. Its connections with our lives, our despairs, our fantasies are subterranean but constant and powerful. When the façade of our bright, jazzy, careless affluence rifts, and our well-conditioned domestic psyches explode, what oozes out is the same sour destructiveness—passive or active, the need to destroy or be destroyed—as once, for some years, contaminated almost the whole of European morality. If our century has invented unprecedented ways of making life easier, it has also provided us with multitudinous, sophisticated, and equally unprecedented means of annihilation. The camps are a proof of that, and a working model. In them the language of our sickness was created.

A. Alvarez, "The Literature of the Holocaust" in *Beyond All This Fiddle*, New York: Penguin Press, 1968, pp. 23–24.

[writer] Terence des Pres rightly notes, "the self's sense of itself is different now, and what has made the difference, both as cause and continuing condition, is simply knowing that the Holocaust occurred.". . .

The exemplary value of *Night*'s opening episode hinges upon its containing the narrative of Eliezer, and by extension of any survivor, within the problems raised by this self-positioning.

Prior to his own encounter with Nazism, he asks Moshe: "Why are you so anxious that people should believe what you say? In your place, I shouldn't care whether they believe me or not. . .". Indeed, in comparison with the ordeal from which he has just escaped, there seems to be little reason for Moshe's present distress. What, then, hangs upon the credibility of his story? Why do the town people refuse to listen to the beadle? What effect does their reaction have on the *pro-*

ject that brought him back to town? Somehow tentatively, Moshe answers the boy's query:

> "You don't understand," he said in despair. "You can't understand. I have been saved miraculously. I managed to get back here. Where did I get the strength from? I wanted to come back to Sighet to tell you the story of my death. So that you could prepare yourselves while there was still time. To live? I don't attach any importance to my life any more. I'm alone. No, I wanted to come back, and to warn you. And see how it is, no one will listen to me. . . ."

Moshe's anguished insistence on being heard undoubtedly illustrates the well-known recourse to narrative in order to impose coherence on an incoherent experience (a commonplace of literary criticism), to work through a trauma (a commonplace of psychoanalysis), the laudable drive to testify to a crime (a commonplace of *Shoah* narratives), or even the heroics of saving others (a commonplace of resistance literature). Although such readings of *Night* are certainly not irrelevant, I do not think that they do justice to the gripping urgency of his unwelcome and redundant narrative, unless we read the text literally: Moshe came back "to tell you the story."

We must rule out simply imparting knowledge, since Moshe's undertaking clearly does not stop at communicating the story. A scenario in which the town folks gather around him to listen to his story, and then go on about their business would be absurd. In this case, to "believe" the story is to be affected by it. Moshe's story is therefore a speech act. Allow me an example to clarify this last point: Paul Revere tearing through the countryside and screaming "The British are coming!" His message was immediately understood. No one suspected him of either madness or excessive need of attention. Unlike Moshe and the town folks, and unlike *Shoah* survivors and ourselves, Paul Revere and his New Englanders lived in the same world, a world in which British might and probably would come; a world in which that would be a very bad thing indeed; and a world in which should they come, clear measures must be taken. If the story is to realize its illocutionary force, not only does it have to be integrated into its listeners' stock of "facts they know about their world," but it must also rely on a known formula (a convention) by which an individual reacts to such knowledge. For example, one has to know that if the British are coming, one is expected to arm oneself and prepare for resistance (a clean shave would be a highly inappropriate reaction to Paul Revere's message). Revere could therefore speedily spread his message while never dismounting his horse, and still secure its uptake. In short, to be a felicitous speech act, the story must affect its listeners in an expected, conventional manner (that is, following clear precedents). Until it does, its force is void.

TOO BIG A BURDEN

Speech act theorists unanimously agree on the conventional aspect of a speech act, that is, on its reliance on a preexisting convention shared by the community of its listeners. But sometimes, such a precise convention does not exist. It has to be inferred and activated out of the stock of beliefs and conventions that both utterer and listeners find workable, plausible, and altogether acceptable. In invoking their shared beliefs, the felicitous speech act thus becomes a *rallying point* for the utterer and the listeners. It binds them together. A community is therefore as much the *result* of its speech acts as it is the necessary condition for their success. In other words, if, as he claims, Moshe came back to town in order to tell his story, and if indeed he is determined to secure the felicitous uptake of his narrative's illocutionary force, then this determination reveals yet *another project,* one that is even more exacting in that it affects his (and his fellow villagers') being-in-the-world: his return to town is also an attempt to reaffirm his ties to his community (its conventions, its values), to reintegrate into the human community of his past—a community whose integrity was put into question by the absurd, incomprehensible, and unassimilable killings he had witnessed. Through his encounter with Nazism, Moshe has witnessed not only the slaughter of a human cargo, but the demise of his notion of humanity— a notion, however, still shared by the town folks. As long as they hold on to this notion of humanity to which he can no longer adhere, he is, *ipso facto,* a freak. Coming back to town to tell his story to a receptive audience is therefore Moshe's way back to normalcy, back to humanity. Only by having a community integrate his dehumanizing experience into the narratives of self-representation that it shares and infer a new code of behavior based on the information he is imparting, only by becoming part of this community's history, can Moshe hope to reclaim his lost humanity (the question remains, as we shall see, at what price to that community). It is therefore not a question of privately telling the story as of having others—a whole community—*claim* it, *appropriate* it, and *react* (properly) to it.

The closing scene of *Night* echoes this concern. Upon his liberation by American troops, the narrator first rushes to a mirror to look at himself. Is he still himself? Can the mirror show him unchanged since the last time he looked at himself in the mirror, before he was taken out of his village? Can he reintegrate into himself? Will the mirror allow him to bridge over pain and time, and reach the cathartic recognition that will bracket out the horror of the death camps and open the way for a "normal" life; or will it, on the contrary, irreparably clinch his alienation not only from the world but from the supposed intimacy of his self-knowledge? Like Moshe then, the boy leaves it to a third party (a willing community or a mirror) to mediate between his present and past selves, and cancel out the alienating effect of his brush with inhumanity. Just like the town folks, however, the mirror does not cooperate. Instead of the familiar face that would have reconciled him with his former self (and consequently, with a pre-*Shoah* world), his reflection seals his alienation: "From the depth of the mirror, a corpse gazed back at me. The look in his eyes, as they stared into mine, has never left me."

Night is the story of a repeated dying, at once the death of man and of the *idea* of man. The final recognition never obtains. Instead, the subject is propelled out of himself, out of humanity, out of the world as he knew it. It is a double failure: both Moshe and the boy fail to recover their selves' integrity and to reintegrate into the community of the living; both fail to assimilate the traces left by their experience (either in a narrative or in a physiognomy) into a coherent picture to be accepted by the other(s) they so wish to reach. But the story goes on: *Night* is a first-person narrative. Like Moshe, the boy will try again to reintegrate the human community, this time, by telling his story (and many others). Like all survivors' narratives, *Night* is thus yet another plodding from door to door to solicit listeners, so as to reclaim one's ties to the community of the living by inscribing oneself into its shared narratives. . . .

Moshe and the town folks occupy two opposite ends of a transaction. Moshe wants the community to assimilate his story, to take it in and learn its lesson, in the hope that it will allow him a way out of the unbearable solitude into which his experience has cast him, and bridge over the tear that his encounter with the dispassionate force of evil has introduced in his life. . . . The town folk, however, do not want to take up this horror, to make it theirs, to make this story the *rallying point* between themselves and the narrator, since if they did, his burden would become theirs. . . .

DEALING WITH THE *SHOAH*

It has often been said that *Night* is the gloomy story of a loss for which no solace, no solution is offered. Indeed, "Elie Wiesel has repeatedly stated that survivors of the Holocaust live in a nightmare world that can never be understood. . . ." But it should also be noted that, although *Night* is the only novel in which he dealt directly and explicitly with his experience of the *Shoah*, Wiesel's whole life has been dedicated to its ensuing moral and historical imperatives. Moshe the Beadle (Wiesel's spokesman) thus offers a critique of facile answers to post-*Shoah* difficulties—narrowly individualized answers that, despite their limited usefulness, nonetheless overlook the collective dimension and its impact on the individual's self-positioning. Excessive separateness of past and present is yet another form of repression, another defense mechanism. The historical imperative today is not to "sort out" but, on the contrary, to find a way of *taking in* the reality of industrialized killing, knowing fully that this reality contradicts every aspect of our historical project, everything we would like to believe about ourselves. To date, we have not resolved this incongruity. If we are to deal with the legacy of the *Shoah*, we must make room in our project for the disturbing truths of the *Shoah*. Our historical imperative is to go beyond this contradiction and to integrate the lesson of the *Shoah* into the coherence of the stories and histories by which we define our sociohistorical project (by "project" I mean the future we wish upon ourselves as a society, and according to which we shape our present perception and representations of ourselves). None of us, therefore, escapes the need to "deal" with the *Shoah*; but none of us can do it alone.

Wiesel Talks About *Night* and Life After the Holocaust

Elie Wiesel, interviewed by Bob Costas

In a rare interview with Bob Costas—best known for being an award-winning sportscaster—Wiesel fills in some of the gaps in *Night* and talks about what his life was like after being liberated from the camp. The interview appeared on the NBC show *Later . . . with Bob Costas* in 1992, and it was only the second time in his life that Wiesel had talked about life in the concentration camps. Since *Night* can only scratch the surface of Wiesel's true experience, this interview gives the reader an invaluable piece of the puzzle.

BC: When they first gathered you up and took you from your home, were you actually hopeful? Could you rationalize some possibility, some outcome here, other than death, other than this unthinkable outcome?

EW: We didn't think of death. It happened in March— March 19, 1944, the Germans came into Hungary. Two months or so before the Normandy invasion. The Russians were very near. And then the ghetto arrived. Two weeks later, we were all in the ghetto. At night we would see the artillery exchange between the Russians and the Germans. They were only twenty kilometers away. We could have escaped. There was nothing to prevent us from escaping because there were two Germans, Eichmann and someone else, some fifty Hungarian gendarmes, and there was no problem. We could have left the ghetto into the mountains. We had non-Jewish friends who wanted us to come and stay with them. But we didn't know. We thought the war would end soon, and the Russians would come in, and Hitler would be defeated, and everything would come back to normalcy.

BC: When they loaded you all up and took you out of

town, did you think then that this was the end of the line, or did you think that perhaps you would simply be detained for a while and, when the war ended, liberated?

EW: Well, the Germans had developed a psychology, a kind of mass psychology, how to fool, how to deceive the victims. And we were all victims. We didn't know. Until the very last moment, we believed that families would remain together, and we should be in some labor camp. Young people would work, and the parents would stay home and prepare food, meals. We didn't know until the very last minute, until it was too late.

THE DEHUMANIZING BEGINS

BC: I know that you'll never forget the words "Men to the left, women to the right." That's how they separated you from your mother and your sisters, you and your father.

EW: Well, of course, that was the real shock, the brutality of the words. The words were simple, "left" and "right," but what they meant, the meaning of those words, hit me much later. For three days or so I was in a haze. I thought I was dreaming. For three days I was dreaming. We were there in the shadow of the flames, and to me it wasn't real. I couldn't believe it. I write about it in *Night*. I couldn't believe it that in the twentieth century, in the middle of the twentieth century, people should do that, could do that, to other people. I somehow couldn't accept it, and to this day I cannot accept it. Something in me rejects that notion that would dehumanize a killer to such an extent. And the complicity, the indifference of the world—this, to this day, it moves me to anger.

BC: When they tattooed a number on your arm, was that the single most dehumanizing moment, or is it just one, in a litany of dehumanizing moments?

EW: Oh, that didn't mean a thing, but the first dehumanizing incident was the day when we arrived, really. (I mean the next day—we arrived at night.) And there was a Kapo, and my father went to him saying he would like to go to the toilet. And my father was a respectful man. And the Kapo hit him in his face, and my father fell to the ground. That was the beginning of the experience really, that I, his only son, couldn't come to his help. Usually I should have thrown myself at the tormentor and beat him up. But that was the first realization there that he and I were already in prison, and not only I, but my mind is in prison, my soul is in prison, my being is in prison, and I am no longer free to do what I want to do. . . .

BC: What were the most conspicuous examples of heroism, under the circumstances, that you saw, and were there examples of cowardice that you saw among the captive Jews?

EW: Cowardice is a word that we didn't apply because, logically, everyone should have been a coward—could have been and probably was because one SS man with a machine gun was stronger than a thousand poets. Heroism . . . I've seen heroism, a spectacular kind of heroism, which I described when three members of the underground were hanged, and the way they faced the execution was heroic. But then I've seen heroism in a simple way. Let's say a man who would come to us on the Sabbath—I don't even know his name—and would simply say, "Don't forget that today is *Shabbat.*" Don't forget that today is Sabbath. To us it meant nothing, because how could it? Same thing, Sabbath, Sunday, Monday. We were all destined to be killed. The fact that he said, "Don't forget that it is the Sabbath, a sacred day." Or somebody would come and say, "Don't forget your name. You are not only a number, you have a name." I've seen people giving their bread to their comrades whom they didn't know. I've seen a person who has offered himself to be beaten up instead of somebody else, whom he didn't know. In general, you know, the enemy, the killers, what they wanted to do there was to dehumanize the victim by depriving him of all moral values. Therefore the first lesson that they gave us was you are alone; don't count on anyone, don't think of anyone, only of yourself. You are alone, and only you should matter to yourself. And they were wrong. Because those who did care for somebody else—a father for his father, a son for his father, a friend for a friend—I think they lived longer because they felt committed, which means humanity became heroic in their own hearts.

A Son's Guilt

BC: As I said, you and your father were separated, as they broke the men and the women apart, from your mother and your sisters, and you would never see your younger sister or your mother again; they perished. The theme of *Night* (your first book) that runs through the whole thing is your father trying to support you, you trying to support your father, at all costs not becoming separated from each other. And then just one of the tragic facts of those years is that your father finally succumbed only months before the U.S. forces liberated the concentration camp.

EW: As long as my father was alive, I was alive. When he died, I was no longer alive. It wasn't life; it was something else. I existed, but I didn't live. And even when we were together we had a certain code. We didn't talk about my mother, my sisters. We didn't talk. We were afraid. There were certain things in those times and in those places that people cannot understand today. We didn't cry. People didn't cry inside that universe. Maybe because people were afraid if they were to start crying, they would never end. But people didn't cry. Even when there were selections and somebody left somebody else, there were no tears. It was something so harsh—the despair was so harsh—that it didn't dissolve itself in tears, or in prayers either.

BC: You saw the reverse, though, too. I mean, you detail situations where a son beat his father because that was the way he thought, at least temporarily, to get into the good graces of his captors; a situation where a younger, stronger son took a morsel of bread from his dying father.

EW: Yes, I've seen, but there were very few, really, in truth, there were few. It's normal. But what happened there, the killers managed to create a universe parallel to our own. The kind of creation, a parallel creation, and there they established their own society with its own rulers, with its own philosophers, its own psychologists, its own poets, with a new society outside God, outside humanity. And, naturally, some succumbed. I cannot even judge them. I cannot be angry at them. Imagine a child of twelve arriving in Auschwitz, and he knows that only violence could be a refuge. Either he becomes an author of violence or a victim of violence. So, a child of twelve overnight aged and became an old person. How can I judge such a child? He didn't do it. He was made to do it by—he was conditioned to do it—by the tormentor. If I am angry, I am angry at the tormentor, not at the victim.

BC: Toward the end of *Night*, you describe your father's death. And he did not go to the furnaces, except to burn his corpse. He died of dysentery and a combination of the hardships.

EW: The hunger. Hunger and exhaustion, fatigue.

BC: And the last night, he was calling out to you for water, but at the same time a guard was beating him. And your best judgment was that you couldn't help him. You were helpless; you didn't respond. And then you write, "There were no prayers at his grave. No candles were lit to his memory. His last word was my name. A summons to which I did not respond." You couldn't possibly feel guilt about that, if you are being hard on yourself.

EW: I do, I do. I do feel guilt. I know that logically I shouldn't, but I do feel guilty because we were terribly close. We became very close there. But, at the same time, the instinct prevented me from being killed. If I had moved, I would have been killed. Beaten up to death. I was as weak as he was. And who would have known that he would die that night? And we didn't know. But I do feel guilty.

BEARING WITNESS

BC: You saw a child, who you described as having the face of an angel—saw that child hanged. That's one of the most moving passages in the book. This is (obviously you have steeled yourself) your life's work, to tell of these things, so that's why I feel no reluctance to ask you to tell again, but how does somebody watch these things—these things unthinkable if we read them in fiction—unfold and then find some reason to keep on living?

EW: Well, first, you know, I don't speak about this often. I have written a few books, very few. I prefer, I think, books on the Talmud and the Bible. And through them, I transmit certain obsessions, certain fears, or certain memories. At that time it was my father who kept me alive. We saw it together. And I wanted him to live. I knew that if I die, he will die. And that was the reason I could eat after having seen that scene, the hanging, And I remember it well, I remember it now. I didn't forget a single instant, a single episode.

BC: Did you assume, as you and your father tried as best you could to survive, that your mother and your sister were dead?

EW: Oh, we knew, but we didn't talk about it. I knew. He knew. At one point only, the very first night, when we were walking toward the flames—we didn't know yet anything, but we were walking toward the flames—my father said, "Maybe you should have gone with your mother." Had I gone with my mother, I would have been killed that night too. But we never talked about this. There was a kind of rule: we don't talk about it, about those who are absent, because it hurts too much. We couldn't accept such pain.

BC: Everyone, except those deranged and hateful souls who try to propound this preposterous theory that the Holocaust didn't occur, knows it occurred, and, statistically, they understand the dimensions of it. But until one hears the stories of Holocaust survivors and just a tiny number of the hundreds of thousands of particulars, until you hear that, you can't begin to grasp the ghastly horror of it. There is just no way, if you stood on a mountaintop for five thousand years and screamed to the top of your lungs, to overstate it.

EW: We cannot *overstate* it. We must *understate* it. To make it understandable, we must understate it. That's why in this little book, *Night,* which has few pages actually, what I *don't* say is important, as important as the things that I *do* say. But even if you read all the books, all the documents, by all the survivors, you would still not know. Unfortunately, only those who were there know what it meant being there. And yet we try. One of my first goals, really, was to write for the survivors. I wanted them to write. In the beginning we didn't speak. Nobody spoke. We felt, who would understand? Who would believe? And why talk? And, really, the main reason for writing *Night* was not for the world or for history; it was for them. Look, it's important to bear witness. Important to tell your story. At the same time I know that even if all the stories were to be read by one person—the same person—you would still not know. You cannot imagine what it meant spending a night of death among death. . . .

HOW COULD THEY DO IT?

BC: Did you ever see any humanity in the actions or in the eyes of your captors, any humanity at all?

EW: I did not.

BC: How do you suppose it is possible to purge humanity from so many people?

EW: Bob, this is the question of my life. After the war, I had a series of shocks, and one of the shocks was when I discovered that the commanders of the so-called *Einsatzkommando,* that did firing in Eastern Europe, meaning in the Ukraine and Russia, had college degrees. Some of them had Ph.D.s, and that, to me, an educator—I am a professor, I teach, I write—I can't understand it. What happened? Culture is supposed to be a shield, a moral shield. What happened to the shield? I don't understand that to this day. . . .

BC: You came face to face with Dr. Joseph Mengele, who wore a monocle, carried a baton in his hand, an almost theatrical looking character. Can you describe him beyond that?

EW: He used to sing opera while he was doing what he was doing. He would sing melodies from opera. I heard it later on, really, from people who worked with him, inmates. He was an intelligent man, intellectual, polite. He even developed friendships with Jews, or with Gypsy children. There was a Gypsy camp, and he got fond of one of the Gypsy children, and his fondness then was translated in his own personal care of him: he took him to the gas chamber. The young Gypsy child whom he loved and caressed and embraced and kissed. I don't understand what happened to humanity, in the human being. I don't know. . . .

BC: A question which every kid with a high school education has heard, even one who's given scant thought to philosophy, is, if there is a God, how does God allow something like a Holocaust to happen?

EW: I don't know. If there is an answer, it is the wrong answer. But you see it's wrong, I think, to put everything on God's shoulders. That is something I understood later. Where was man? Where was humanity? Look, after all, we had faith in humanity—I had faith in humanity. To us, President Roosevelt was more important than Ben-Gurion. I had never heard of the name of Ben-Gurion in my little town. But I knew the name of Roosevelt. I remember we said prayers for him. He was the father of the Jewish people. He knew. Absolutely he knew. And yet he refused to bomb the railways going to Auschwitz. Why? Had he done that—at that time, during the Hungarian deportation, ten thousand Jews were killed every day in Auschwitz. Even if the Germans had tried to repair the rail . . .

BC: So even as the U.S. waged war against the Axis powers, you're saying they didn't do enough to hit the specific targets. They could have stopped that cold.

EW: They could have. Look . . . they . . . I admire the American soldiers who fought Hitler, and I think we should be eternally grateful to them, to their families, to their children, to their parents. Many died in the war. They were heroes. But somehow the war that Hitler had waged against the Jewish people was forgotten. In the process. And that was wrong. A few bombing operations would have at least shown Hitler that the world cared. Hitler was convinced to the end that the world didn't care about what he and his acolytes had done to the Jewish people. . . .

GETTING OUT

BC: Do you recall what you saw and what you felt the day the troops liberated Buchenwald in April of 1945?

EW: It was April 11, 1945, in the morning hours. We were the last remnants in Buchenwald, and I had been already at the gate almost every day. And, by accident, really, by chance, that the gate closed in front of me. So I came back to the camp. I remember when they came in. We were then already terribly hungry, more than usual because no food was given to us for six days, since April 5th. And I remember the first American soldiers. I remember black soldiers. I remember a black sergeant, huge. And then he saw us; he began sobbing and cursing. He was so moved by what he saw that he began sobbing—he sobbed like a child, and we couldn't console him. And we tried somehow to console him, and that made him sob even deeper, stronger, louder. So I remember those soldiers, and I have a weak—a soft spot—for the American soldier, really. I gave a lecture a few years ago at West Point, and it was amusing to me. I never had any military training or military affinity, and I came to give a lecture, and I told them what I felt about the American uniform, because that meant not only victory, it meant a triumph, the triumph of humanity. And to me, that black sergeant incarnates that triumph.

BC: Toward the end of *Night,* you write about looking into a mirror. Apparently, you didn't have any access to a mirror for two years. What did you see when you looked into that mirror?

EW: Well, when the Americans came in they threw us food, and it was the wrong thing to do because they should have used medical supervision, and they didn't. And I remember I picked up a can, some dessert, something with ham in it. Now during the camp, I would have eaten anything, but I was already free, and my body knew it even before I did, and I put it to my lips and passed out, literally; I got some blood poisoning. So, I woke up in a hospital, a former SS hospital which was taken over by the Americans for inmates. So, I almost died. I was, I think, closer to death after the liberation than before. And then one day, really, I saw myself in that mirror. And I saw a person who was ageless, nameless, faceless. A person who belonged to another world, the world of the dead.

BC: If you belonged to the world of the dead (especially after your father slipped away from you only several weeks before the liberation came, which—the sad irony—just adds to the heartache), if you were dead inside at that point, from where did you summon the strength to direct a life so purposeful in the ensuing forty-plus years?

EW: In the beginning it was again, I repeat, a passion for study. I studied. I came to France together with four hundred youngsters, children, orphans, invited by DeGaulle. And we were taken over by an organization in a children's home, an orphans' home. And the first thing I did, when I came there, I asked for pen and paper. I began writing my memoirs. And for quotations of the Talmud to study. It's later that I developed that since I am alive, I have to give meaning to my life. Oh, it may sound, you know, bombastic, but it is true. That is how I switched. That means that my life as it is, if it is only for myself, then it is wrong. I have to do something with it. I even have to do something with my memory of my death. . . .

THE AFTERLIFE

BC: Did you ever, subsequent to Auschwitz, come face to face with Gestapo officers?

EW: No.

BC: Former Nazis? Not once?

EW: No. I came face to face, and I wrote about it in one of my books, in Israel, during the Eichmann trial. I saw Eichmann at the trial, but he was in a glass cage. But later, I saw, in a bus, going from Tel Aviv to Jerusalem, a man that I—I recognized his neck. He was a kind of blockhouse, or barracks, head in Auschwitz. My barracks head. And I passed him, and all of a sudden I said, "Tell me, where were you during the war?" And he said, "Why?" And I said, "Aren't you a German Jew? Weren't you in Poland?" He said, "Yes." "Weren't you in Auschwitz?" "Yes." "In the barracks?" "Yes." I gave him the number, at which point he paled because had I said, "You were a head of a barracks," they would have beaten him up during the Eichmann trial, and for a few seconds, I became his judge. Literally, I had his fate in my hands. And then, I decided, I am not a judge; I am a witness. I let him go.

BC: You understand, of course, the passion that fuels the

work of so-called Nazi hunters. But your position has been different. Yours is to bear witness . . .

EW: Yes.

BC: . . . rather than to exact revenge or even pursue justice.

EW: Well, pursue justice, yes. But it's not my doing; I cannot do that. I admire those people who are doing it very well, and there are several of these young people, young people who dedicate their lives for the pursuit of justice, and all honor is due them. But my work is something else. I write. I teach. And I bear witness in my way. That doesn't mean I'm better, not at all, or worse. I don't think so. Except we all have our area of competence and activity. . . .

BC: Please, don't think for a moment that this question is intended to trivialize the most important aspects of your experience, but I think people who admire you would wonder about it. Are there moments of gaiety and spontaneous laughter in your life, or is the enormity of this experience such that it is always with you, that there is a certain solemnity about you at all times?

EW: Oh, no, no. Really not. I laugh, and I am happy, and I love good concerts, and I love my good friends, and we tell jokes to each other. And then I give lectures at the Y, for instance, or at Boston University. I try to introduce as much humor . . . no, I am not a person who believes in macabre or serious despairing moods. Nonsense. I don't have the right to impose that upon anybody else, the opposite: I like good cheer and good theatre and good comedies, and, in general, I think life is not only tears. Life also has happiness to offer and to receive.

BC: Do you worry that as Jewish culture becomes less distinct, at least here in America, and there are pockets of exceptions to that in the Hasidic community, or whatever, but as Jewish culture becomes less distinct and as generational memory blurs as we move further and further from the Holocaust, that the meaning of this will slip further into the ash heap of history, and as witnesses grow older and perish . . .

EW: I do worry. I am not afraid that the event will be forgotten. There were many years in my life that I was afraid that it will be, might be, forgotten. And, therefore, I try to work. I try to inspire and to convince many of my friends also to work. Now I know it won't be forgotten because there are enough documents and books and pictures and even masterworks that will prevent people from forgetting. Today, if I am afraid, and I am afraid, it is that the event will be trivialized, cheapened, reduced to commercial kitsch. That is a source of anguish.

YOU HAVE TO BE TAUGHT TO HATE

BC: At least once in this conversation, but I think only once, you used the word "hatred." No one could blame anybody who was even witness to this, let alone victim of it (and you were both) for hating everybody involved. But hate can consume a person as they move through their life. How have you subdued it or channeled it?

EW: At times I missed it, I wanted it. There were times when I even wrote; I said, we need some kind of hatred. It's normal, it's natural, to channel this hate out, to drive it out, but to *experience* it. Why I didn't—during the war I had other problems on my mind. My father. You know, I really didn't *see* the Germans. I saw the Germans as angels of death. I couldn't lift my eyes. It was forbidden to lift my eyes to see a German SS because he would kill you. After the war, I had my problems: how to readjust, how to readjust to death. It was more difficult to readjust to death than to life, to see in death an exception to the rule, not the normative phenomenon. It was difficult because we were used to death as a normative experience. We lived in death; we lived with death. And then to think about death as a scandal, as a tragedy—it took me some time. So we had to do so many things, really, after the war, to find myself again, and to find the language, to find a life, to find a destiny, to find a family, that I didn't think about that, about hatred. But I knew that it had to exist because it was on the other side. And that's why, since the Nobel Prize, really, I've devoted years to organize seminars all over the world called "Anatomy of Hate." I want to understand the power, the destructive power, of hate. The masks that hate can put on. The language of hate, the technique of hate, the structure of hate, the fabric of hate, the genesis of hate.

BC: Is there a single insight about that that you've come to, that you feel certain of?

EW: I learned from those who participated in a few of my seminars—psychiatrists—saying that a child, until the age of three, doesn't hate. Children can be taught to hate after they are three years old. That means something.

A Letter to Wiesel Questions *Night*'s Preface

Eva Fleischner

In the form of a letter directed to Elie Wiesel, Eva
Fleischner, professor of religion and philosophy at
Montclair State College in New Jersey, wonders
whether it is still necessary and valid to include
François Mauriac's preface to *Night* (from the original
publication in 1958) in new editions of the book today.
When the preface was originally written it may have
needed the introduction from this famous Catholic
writer, but now it can certainly stand on its own.

Dear Elie:

Whenever I use *Night* in my classes, I tell my students:
"Be sure to read Mauriac's Preface. Not all prefaces deserve
to be read, but this one does. It will give you a key to the
book." All these years *Night* has remained linked to Mauriac's name. This had always seemed quite normal to me,
even fitting. After all, it was Mauriac who, in your own
words, had launched you as a writer. I can imagine that it
had been an honor for you—at the time a young, unknown
Jewish journalist—to have the famous French writer and
member of the *Académie Française* introduce your first
book, and thus introduce you to the world.

But decades have gone by. You no longer need Mauriac to
introduce you to the world. The world knows you well. You
have written many other books, each new book eagerly
awaited. You have received the Nobel Peace Prize. Mauriac is
dead. And yet, you have kept his Preface as prelude to *Night*,
and thereby as prelude to your entire work. What may have
been grateful acceptance on your part decades ago has long
since become deliberate choice.

Could this choice have had its moments of difficulty for

Excerpted from "Mauriac's Preface to *Night:* Thirty Years Later," by Eva Fleischner,
America, November 19, 1988. Reprinted with permission from the author.

you? I wonder about this because of all that Mauriac represents, not only in literature (fame and success), but also in religion (Catholicism). Given the profoundly tragic history of the relationship between your faith and his (and mine), was it really so easy for you to accept the endorsement of your work by France's leading Catholic writer? All the more so because, as you make vividly clear in "An Interview Unlike Any Other," Mauriac's approach to Judaism was cast—at least initially, and quite understandably—in the mold common, prior to Vatican II, even to those Catholics who were sympathetic to Judaism. At best—as you mentioned in *A Jew Today*—they saw Judaism as no more than a prelude to Christianity, as the setting for Jesus: "Every reference led back to him. Jerusalem? The eternal city, where Jesus turned his disciples into apostles. The Bible? The Old Testament, which, thanks to Jesus of Nazareth, succeeded in enriching itself with a New Testament. Mendes-France? A Jew, both brave and hated, not unlike Jesus long ago." You leave no doubt in the reader's mind how deeply these words offended the Jew in you—to the point where, for the first time in your life, you "exhibited bad manners." So great was your anger that it overcame your shyness and you wounded the old man with your words, and he began to weep.

You allowed yourself to be angry, and he allowed himself to weep. Each of you had the courage to be in touch with who you truly were at that moment. And it was this that broke down the wall between you. There is no downplaying of the moment of harshness. Mauriac's humanity made him weep over his insensitivity to you as Jew. Your humanity caused you to be deeply troubled because you had hurt an upright and profoundly moral man.

Your humanity, Elie, has seemed to me to be the constant in your life. No matter how much has changed for you and in you these long years, you are no longer homeless and alone. You have a beloved wife and son; you are revered the world over. This has not changed. If, at times, your judgment of Christianity has seemed harsh to me, in your personal interactions, whether with me or with my students or with the many Christian friends who love you, there has never been anything but gentleness and graciousness.

And is it any wonder that you should judge Christianity harshly? That, even as a child, you would cross the street out of fear whenever you passed a church? No, it is no wonder;

it is, alas, all too understandable. For Christians have incurred much guilt toward your people. What is surprising, what is extraordinary, is that you have been able to distinguish between the tradition as a whole, and individual Christians. For this I have long been grateful to you.

Recently, since reading your new book *Twilight*, I am grateful in yet another way. For I sense in this book a change in your attitude. Not only is the hero, Raphael, saved by two

A CHRISTIAN WEEPS

When François Mauriac, one of France's best known Christian writers, met Wiesel in the 1950s, he encouraged him to tell his story. In Mauriac's Foreword (preface) to the resulting book, Night, *he explains how Wiesel's story allowed him to recognize the extent of the Jews' suffering at the hands of the Germans.*

The child who tells us his story here was one of God's elect. From the time when his conscience first awoke, he had lived only for God and had been reared on the Talmud, aspiring to initiation into the cabbala, dedicated to the Eternal. Have we ever thought about the consequence of a horror that, though less apparent, less striking than the other outrages, is yet the worst of all to those of us who have faith: the death of God in the soul of a child who suddenly discovers absolute evil? . . .

And I, who believe that God is love, what answer could I give my young questioner, whose dark eyes still held the reflection of that angelic sadness which had appeared one day upon the face of the hanged child? What did I say to him? Did I speak of that other Jew, his brother, who may have resembled him—the Crucified, whose Cross has conquered the world? Did I affirm that the stumbling block to his faith was the cornerstone of mine, and that the conformity between the Cross and the suffering of men was in my eyes the key to that impenetrable mystery whereon the faith of his childhood had perished? Zion, however, has risen up again from the crematories and the charnel houses. The Jewish nation has been resurrected from among its thousands [now known to be six million] of dead. It is through them that it lives again. We do not know the worth of one single drop of blood, one single tear. All is grace. If the Eternal is the Eternal, the last word for each one of us belongs to Him. This is what I should have told this Jewish child. But I could only embrace him, weeping.

François Mauriac, *Forward to* Night, New York: Hill and Wang, 1960, pp. viii–xi.

peasants "who are good Christians," but in describing the age-old pogroms that used to break out during Holy Week in Rovidok (as in so many other villages and towns of eastern Europe) you speak of the perpetrators as "Christians who were not necessarily followers of Christ."

Why do these few words move me so? Let me try to explain. For us Christians, the sense of guilt at our corporate history of persecution of Jews becomes, at times, almost too heavy to bear. The burden is lightened when we discover, or remember, that there have been through the centuries Christian women and men who did not run with the mob, even—also—during that darkest of times that will forever be known as the Holocaust.

Because of the weight your words carry for millions of people, non-Jews as well as Jews, the text I have quoted can, and I believe will, make a crucial contribution to the reconciliation between our two peoples. Thus, more than ever will you have become the messenger of peace the Nobel Peace Prize citation calls you.

And perhaps, also, your relationship with your old friend François Mauriac will have entered a new phase. Were you to talk once more face to face today yet another barrier between you would have fallen. Perhaps, indeed, the dialogue continues? After all, both Jews and Christians worship a "God who raises the dead."

Permit me to end these reflections with a wish. Won't you, please, as you promised in *A Jew Today*, publish your conversations with Mauriac, which continued over the years? Then we would know a little more of the relationship between you, of what enabled you both to transcend your religious and political disagreements. Only you can give us answers to this and, by so doing, shed further light on one of the most remarkable friendships of this century.

Happy birthday, and Shalom!

CHRONOLOGY

1928

Elie Wiesel is born on September 30, in Sighet, Transylvania (originally part of Romania, at the time of the World War II it was part of Hungary) to Shlomo and Sarah. Two daughters, Hilda and Bea precede him, and another, Tzipora, is born a few years later.

1930

The Nazi Party gains a stronghold in the German government.

1933

Adolf Hitler is elected chancellor of Germany and begins his war against the Jews. The SS and Gestapo are created. The first Nazi death camp is built in Dachau, Germany. All Jewish teachers and government workers are fired.

1934

Hitler becomes führer.

1934–1944

Wiesel studies the Torah, Talmud, and cabbala and enjoys a happy childhood in his tightly-knit Jewish community.

1935

The Nuremberg Laws limiting the freedom of Jews are decreed.

1937

Another concentration camp, Buchenwald, opens in Germany and begins exterminating Jews.

1938

Delegates from thirty-two countries meet in France to discuss saving the Jews from Hitler; no one offers to accept them. German Jews are forced into ghettos. In one night, called Kristallnacht (the Night of Broken Glass), nearly 7,500 Jewish-owned businesses and 267 synagogues are destroyed.

1940

Auschwitz is built near Warsaw in Poland and becomes the Nazi's largest concentration camp.

1944

The Nazis deport Wiesel's family to Auschwitz, where his mother and younger sister are killed. Wiesel is imprisoned in Auschwitz and Buna.

1945

Wiesel and his father join the death march to Buchenwald, where his father dies. Wiesel is freed by Russian soldiers on April 10. World War II ends in Europe in May and Wiesel goes to France.

1946

Wiesel studies French in Paris and is reunited with his two older sisters, who had presumed him dead. He teaches Bible, Yiddish, and Hebrew. The Nuremberg trials begin.

1947–1950

Wiesel studies philosophy, literature, and psychology at the Sorbonne, University of Paris.

1948

Israel becomes an independent Jewish state. Wiesel becomes a foreign correspondent for various Jewish news organizations.

1952

Anne Frank's *Diary of a Young Girl* is published in English.

1954

Wiesel interviews famous French writer François Mauriac who convinces him to tell the story of his experiences at the hands of the Nazis.

1956

Wiesel publishes an 862-page memoir, written in Yiddish, titled *Un di Velt Hot Geshvign* (*And the World Remained Silent*). During a trip to New York City to report on the United Nations he is struck by a taxi. While recovering, he applies for U.S. citizenship.

1958

A much shortened version of his Yiddish memoir is published in France under the title *La Nuit*.

1960

The English version of *La Nuit*, called *Night*, is published in America.

1961

Wiesel's first novel, *Dawn*, is published in America.

1962

The Accident is published.

1963

Wiesel receives U.S. citizenship.

1964

Wiesel visits Sighet, his hometown. *The Town Beyond the Wall* is published.

1966

Jews of Silence and *The Gates of the Forest* are published.

1968

A Beggar in Jerusalem is published in France, and wins the Prix Medicis, one of France's most distinguished literary awards.

1969

Wiesel marries Marion Rose, who becomes the translator of most of his books.

1970

One Generation After is published, marking twenty-five years since Wiesel was freed from Buchenwald.

1972

Wiesel's son, Shlomo Elisha, is born. Wiesel receives the Eleanor Roosevelt Memorial Award and the American Liberties Medallion, and is appointed distinguished professor of Jewish studies at the City College of New York. *Souls on Fire* is published.

1973

The Oath is published. Wiesel is awarded the Martin Luther King Medallion from the City College of New York and the Jewish Book Council Literary Award.

1974

Wiesel's play, *The Madness of God*, is performed in Washington, D.C.

1976

Wiesel is appointed Andrew Mellon Professor in the Humanities at Boston University. *Messengers of God* is published.

1979

President Jimmy Carter appoints Wiesel Chairman of the Presidential Commission on the Holocaust, later re-named the U.S. Holocaust Memorial Council.

1980

Wiesel is appointed Honorary Chairman of the World Gathering of Jewish Holocaust Survivors, Jerusalem. *The Testament* is published.

1983

Wiesel is awarded the Belgian International Peace Prize.

1985

Wiesel is awarded the Congressional Gold Medal of Achievement by President Ronald Reagan. *The Fifth Son* is published and wins the Grand Prize for literature from the city of Paris.

1986

Wiesel is awarded the Nobel Peace Prize for "his self-accepted mission as a messenger to mankind: his message is one of peace, atonement and human dignity." He establishes the Elie Wiesel Foundation for Humanity to "create forums for the discussion of urgent ethical and moral issues confronting mankind."

1992

President George Bush awards Wiesel the Presidential Medal of Freedom. *The Forgotten* is published.

1993

Wiesel speaks at the dedication of the U.S. Holocaust Memorial Museum in Washington, D.C.

1995

Wiesel publishes the first volume of his memoirs, *All Rivers Run to the Sea.*

2000

Wiesel publishes the second volume of his memoirs, *And the Sea Is Never Full.* By this time he has been awarded nearly eighty honorary degrees from some of the world's most prestigious universities.

FOR FURTHER RESEARCH

WORKS BY ELIE WIESEL

The Accident. Trans. Anne Borchardt. New York: Avon, 1962.

All Rivers Run to the Sea: Memoirs. New York: Knopf, 1995.

Ani Maamin. Trans. Marion Wiesel. New York: Random House, 1973.

A Beggar in Jerusalem. Trans. Lily Edelman and Elie Wiesel. New York: Random House, 1970.

Dawn. Trans. Frances Frenaye. New York: Hill & Wang, 1961.

Dimensions of the Holocaust. Evanston, IL: Northwestern University Press, 1977.

Evil and Exile. Trans. Jan Rothschild. Notre Dame, IN: University of Notre Dame Press, 1990.

The Fifth Son. Trans. Marion Wiesel. New York: Summit Books, 1985.

Five Biblical Portraits. Notre Dame, IN: University of Notre Dame Press, 1978.

The Forgotten. New York: Summit Books, 1992.

Four Hasidic Masters and Their Stuggle Against Melancholy. Notre Dame, IN: University of Notre Dame Press, 1978.

From the Kingdom of Memory: Reminiscences. New York: Summit Books, 1990.

The Gates of the Forest. Trans. Frances Frenaye. New York: Holt, Rinehart and Winston, 1966.

The Golem. New York: Summit Books, 1983.

The Jews of Silence. Trans. Neal Kozodoy. New York: Holt, Rinehart and Winston, 1966.

A Jew Today. Trans. Marion Wiesel. New York: Random House, 1978.

A Journey into Faith. New York: Donald I. Fine, 1990.

Legends of Our Time. New York: Avon, 1968.

Messengers of God. Trans. Marion Wiesel. New York: Random House, 1976.

Night. Trans. Stella Rodway. New York: Hill & Wang, 1960.

The Oath. New York: Avon, 1973.

One Generation After. New York: Pocket Books, 1970.

Sages and Dreamers. New York: Summit Books, 1991.

Somewhere a Master. Trans. Marion Wiesel. New York: Summit Books, 1982.

Souls on Fire. Trans. Marion Wiesel. New York: Random House, 1972.

The Testament. Trans. Marion Wiesel. New York: Summit Books, 1981.

The Town Beyond the Wall. Trans. Stephen Becker. New York: Avon, 1964.

The Trial of God. Trans. Marion Wiesel. New York: Random House, 1979. (Play)

Twilight. Trans. Marion Wiesel. New York: Summit Books, 1988.

ANALYSIS AND CRITICISM

Irving Abrahamson, ed., *Against Silence: The Voice and Vision of Elie Wiesel.* 3 vols. New York: Holocaust Library, 1985.

Michael Berenbaum, *The Vision of the Void: Theological Reflections on the Works of Elie Wiesel.* Middletown, CT: Wesleyan University Press, 1979.

Harry James Cargas, *Harry James Cargas in Conversation with Elie Wiesel.* New York: Paulist Press, 1976.

Ellen S. Fine, *Legacy of Night.* Albany: State University of New York Press, 1982.

Irving Greenberg and Alvin Rosenfeld, eds., *Confronting the Holocaust: The Impact of Elie Wiesel.* Bloomington: Indiana University Press, 1978.

Irving Halperin, *Messengers from the Dead: Literature of the Holocaust.* Philadelphia: Westminster Press, 1970.

Carol Rittner, ed., *Elie Wiesel: Between Memory and Hope.* New York: New York University Press, 1990.

Simon P. Sibelman, *Silence in the Novels of Elie Wiesel.* New York: St. Martin's Press, 1995.

BIOGRAPHIES

Ted L. Estess, *Elie Wiesel.* New York: Frederick Ungar, 1980.

Michael A. Schuman, *Elie Wiesel: Voice from the Holocaust.* Berkeley Heights, NJ: Enslow Publishers, 1994.

HISTORICAL INTEREST

David A. Adler, *We Do Remember the Holocaust.* New York: Henry Holt, 1989.

Anne Frank, *The Diary of a Young Girl.* New York: Doubleday, 1952.

Daniel Jonah Goldhagen, *Hitler's Willing Executioners: Ordinary Germans and the Holocaust.* New York:Knopf, 1996.

Lawrence D. Kritzman, ed., *Auschwitz and After.* New York: Routledge, 1995.

Primo Levi, *Survival in Auschwitz.* New York: Collier, 1959.

Lois Lowry, *Number the Stars.* Boston: Houghton Mifflin, 1989.

Han Nolan, *If I Should Die Before I Wake.* San Diego: Harcourt Brace, 1994.

Hana Volavkova, ed., *I Never Saw Another Butterfly.* New York: Schocken, 1978.

David W. Zisenwine, *Anti-Semitism in Europe: Sources of the Holocaust.* New York: Behrman House, 1976.

INDEX